CRITICAL LIVES

The Life and Work of

Thomas Jefferson

Alan Axelrod, Ph.D.

ALPHA

A Pearson Education Company

Copyright © 2001 by Alan Axelrod, Ph.D.

International Standard Book Number: 0-02-864142-6
Library of Congress Catalog Card Number: Available upon request.

03   02   01   8   7   6   5   4   3   2   1

Interpretation of the printing code: The rightmost number of the first series of numbers is the year of the book's printing; the rightmost number of the second series of numbers is the number of the book's printing. For example, a printing code of 01-1 shows that the first printing occurred in 2001.

Printed in the United States of America

Publisher: Marie Butler-Knight
Product Manager: Phil Kitchel
Managing Editor: Jennifer Chisholm
Senior Acquisitions Editor: Randy Ladenheim-Gil
Senior Production Editor: Christy Wagner
Copy Editor: Krista Hansing
Cover Designer: Ann Jones
Book Designer: Sandra Schroeder
Production: Mary Hunt, Lizbeth Patterson

CRITICAL LIVES

Thomas Jefferson

Nickel Portrait

Thomas Jefferson is buried in a hillside family plot at Monticello, the home he designed and built in the Blue Ridge foothills as a brick-and-mortar expression of the best that Old World civilization might give to the New World. An obelisk (also originally designed by Jefferson) bears the inscription Jefferson composed for it:

Here was buried
Thomas Jefferson
Author of the Declaration of American Independence
of the Statute of Virginia for religious freedom
and Father of the University of Virginia

This simple epitaph is a catalogue of remarkable achievement. But at least equally remarkable is what Jefferson left out of it. He was, after all, much more.

Trained in the law—and a brilliant lawyer—Jefferson began his political career as a member of Virginia's House of Burgesses, the most venerable legislative body in colonial America. He then became a creator of the revolutionary movement that would lead to American independence. In 1774, at age thirty-nine, he wrote and published *A Summary View of the Rights of British America,* a scathing indictment of the British crown and a key statement of the motives for the Revolution. Two years later, Jefferson's colleagues in the Continental Congress asked him to draft the Declaration of Independence. In this same year, he served in Virginia's House of Delegates and single-handedly tackled the monumental task of revising Virginia's crusty body of British law into a set of sleek statutes suited to a new republic of reason.

After drafting the *Virginia Statute for Religious Freedom* in 1777, he went on the next year to write a *Bill for the More General Diffusion of Knowledge,* in the belief that education would be the firmest foundation of enduring liberty. From 1779–81, Jefferson served as the first governor of revolutionary Virginia; in 1783, he was a delegate to Congress; and from 1784–89, he was the United States minister plenipotentiary (in effect, ambassador) to France. While in France, he secretly helped lay the foundation for *that* nation's revolution.

Also while in Europe, Jefferson completed *Notes on the State of Virginia,* an extraordinary natural history of what was then the nation's largest state and a book that earned Jefferson worldwide acclaim; since its first U.S. publication in 1788, it has never been out of print. *Notes* reveals yet another side of Thomas Jefferson not reflected in his epitaph. Like Benjamin Franklin, Jefferson was a "natural philosopher," what we would call today a scientist. His fascination with the natural world certainly equaled and sometimes surpassed his interest in the political world. From 1797–1815, he would serve as president of the American Philosophical Society— the most prestigious scientific association in the young republic. From 1790–93, Jefferson served in George Washington's Cabinet as the nation's first secretary of state, and from 1797–1801, under John Adams, he was the nation's second vice president. When he arrived in Philadelphia, capital of the United States in 1797, Vice President-Elect Thomas Jefferson carried in his baggage the bones of a prehistoric animal to add to the collection of the American Philosophical Society.

The greatest monument that Jefferson left to science was the Lewis and Clark Expedition, which, as president, he commissioned in 1803 to explore the vast Louisiana Territory that he was in the process of acquiring from France.

Beyond politics and science, Jefferson loved literature, theater, and, most of all, music. He purchased and treasured a fine Italian violin—it was quite possibly a Stradivarius—and he played it with great skill. His curiosity was insatiable and seemingly boundless.

An inveterate tinkerer, Jefferson produced a series of ingenious inventions, including a new streamlined plow; a "wheel cipher," a mechanical device for encrypting and decrypting confidential diplomatic communications; an innovative sundial; and an even more innovative "great clock." The sundial and the clock he designed expressly for Monticello, and he even devised a special folding ladder for the purpose of maintaining and repairing the clock. Always looking for ways to improve the process of writing and correspondence, Jefferson developed an improvement to the portable copying press originally invented by James Watt, and he perfected Englishman John Hawkins's "polygraph"—not a lie detector, but a machine to make simultaneous copies of written documents. Jefferson devised a unique folding desk for travel; a revolving bookstand, to facilitate research reference to multiple volumes; a dumb waiter system in Monticello; and what might be described as semiautomatic sliding doors for his home. Monticello also featured unique hideaway beds in the mansion alcoves and comfortable revolving chairs, incorporating leg rests and writing arms, innovations entirely novel in Jefferson's day.

Monticello itself, of course, is a singular architectural masterpiece, certainly one of the most beautiful homes in America. Designing and building it was for Jefferson a lifelong labor of love, but it was not his only architectural work. In 1806, he designed and built Poplar Forest, an octagonal house at the center of his 4,800-acre tobacco farm near Lynchburg, Virginia. At the end of his life, Jefferson designed the campus (he called it an "academical village") of the University of Virginia; known as "the Lawn," it remains the heart of the university. Beyond designing the university, the eighty-year-old Jefferson outlined its curriculum and articulated its academic philosophy. He then directed recruitment of the institution's first faculty and served as its rector, with responsibility for drawing up class schedules, reading lists, student rules, and faculty bylaws. He had aimed at an educational scheme even more ambitious than the university; Jefferson laid out an entire system of state-supported education, from elementary schools, to secondary institutions, and up to the university, but a shortsighted Virginia legislature, in the end, funded only the university.

Whatever else he did, Jefferson always considered himself a farmer. Monticello was the heart of a working plantation, and, for most of his life, Jefferson believed that the future of the United States, as a democracy built on personal integrity and collective virtue, would be an agrarian one. Accordingly, he worked tirelessly to improve his farm and to gather the best agricultural knowledge from farms abroad. During his European years, he incessantly studied agricultural methods, looking not only for new ways of cultivating and harvesting crops, but also for new crops—especially grapes for wine, olives that grew even in poor soils, and rice varieties that could be cultivated in climates and with methods suited to yeoman farmers rather than the slaveholding owners of large Tidewater plantations. The latter prospect seemed so important to Jefferson that he smuggled rice specimens out of the Italian Piedmont, despite a law forbidding exportation of its unique crop under penalty of death. Jefferson was always looking for ways his countrymen could earn their living and more productively create a viable economy for the new nation.

With all of this, the most striking omission from Jefferson's headstone epitaph is, of course, any mention of his two terms as president of the United States. During his administration, from 1801–09, Jefferson greatly liberalized the office, defining the president truly as a chief executive who worked with a powerful Cabinet rather than as a solo ruler in the manner of some republican monarch. He sought to purge the fledgling government of what he deemed its autocratic, even "monarchal" Federalism and to replace it with the more truly democratic philosophy of the Democratic-Republican Party that he and James Madison had virtually built from scratch.

President Jefferson saw to the final dismantling of the outrageous Alien and Sedition Acts, which, as vice president, he had fought against at substantial risk to himself. No longer would newcomers have to wait fourteen years to apply for citizenship; five years of residence would secure this privilege. No longer did resident aliens have to fear instant deportation at the whim of the president. And no longer would it be a federal crime for persons to assemble "with intent to oppose any measure of government" or to print, utter, or publish anything "false, scandalous and malicious" against the government.

As president, Jefferson successfully prosecuted a war with the so-called Barbary States, North African countries whose state-sponsored piracy preyed on United States and European shipping. Most spectacularly, Jefferson more than doubled the extent of the new nation by acquiring the great Louisiana Territory from France. More than either Washington or Adams before him, Jefferson turned the United States toward the future, a future tied to Western expansion.

To describe a life and career so varied, words such as *architect* or *designer*, applied to all aspects of Jefferson's activity, are probably more appropriate than *revolutionary*, *politician*, or *statesman*. For as Jefferson in life resisted tyranny of any kind, his legacy resists easy classification. The term "Founding Father," for example, is certainly justified to describe a figure so seminal in our history, yet it seems strangely inappropriate. We see Washington as heroic beyond the level of mere mortals. Jefferson, in contrast, appears noble but accessible, a genial genius and a most uncommon common man. In this, perhaps, he seems the most *American* of the nation's founding personalities, embodying the open-minded, open-hearted, frank, and richly contradictory qualities that many of us like to think of as the best and most representative traits of the American character.

Franklin, Washington, Adams, Madison, Monroe—all of these men had important, profound ideas, but it is the ideas of Thomas Jefferson that most people still talk about, admire, and debate. Politicians do not speak about reforming current government along the lines of Washington or Adams or Lincoln, but about "returning to the ideals of Jefferson." And those ideals have been appropriated by the likes of Franklin Delano Roosevelt to justify expanding the federal government into the colossus of the New Deal, as well as by the likes of Ronald Reagan to amplify a call to tear down the "monstrous" federal bureaucracy.

That people of all political stripes have adopted Jefferson as their "private" icon and "personal" example suggests that, for all his public eloquence and intellectual openness, Jefferson was a complex, often enigmatic figure. Certainly, in his own time he was controversial, and many of the controversies persist. Today's politicians elbow one another aside in their eagerness to embrace his "legacy." Few, however, would embrace *him* if he were alive and active today. His political philosophy, circa 1776 and 1800, is far too radical for the candidates of our twenty-first century, whose politics and policies are so homogenized that the presidential election of 2000 was a dead heat settled by a tortured Supreme Court decision impenetrable to voters who, in significant number, couldn't even trouble themselves to decipher the ballots that they had cast. Few politicians today, even the most partisan Democrats and Republicans, would approve of Jefferson's willingness to define his Democratic-Republican Party so absolutely, totally, and vehemently in opposition to the Federalist Party. In the name of creating "a more perfect union," Jefferson was willing to be ruthlessly divisive.

The freight of controversy that Jefferson bore and continues to bear would crush any modern politician. On the international scene, he shamelessly played favorites, courting the radical French even as he shunned and antagonized the more powerful British. In matters of religion, he espoused a deist philosophy that, as many saw it, frequently crossed the line into atheism. Separation of church and state notwithstanding, this alone would disqualify any political candidate running today.

And then there is the matter of slavery. Jefferson perpetually antagonized his fellow Virginians and others by proposing legislation to end the institution (his condemnation of slavery in the Declaration of Independence was blue-penciled out by the Continental Congress), but he owned slaves all his life. Moreover, if a combination of rumor, historical evidence, and DNA testing is believed, he even fathered one or more children by one of his slaves, Sally Hemings.

Bold, eloquent, and an advocate of the common man, Jefferson is nevertheless elusive, an oracle who invites and, indeed, requires interpretation and reinterpretation. His profile appears on the U.S.

nickel, in an earlier economy the quintessential coin of the common man. (Liberals point out that he faces left!) A Jefferson portrait also appears on the two-dollar bill, currency so rarely used that most Americans either are unaware of its existence or erroneously believe that it's no longer in circulation. Not too many years ago, when people commonly carried a rabbit's foot or other good-luck charms, those who happened to get a two-dollar bill often held on to it, as if keeping the image of one who declared the pursuit of happiness an inalienable right would ensure happiness itself. Jefferson, who in the final letter of his life (written on June 24, 1826) decried "monkish ignorance and superstition," would have scorned such a use of his image. He believed neither in luck nor in the cult of personality. But even those of us who admire Jefferson most for his dedication to reason and rationality in human affairs feel an affinity with him that transcends reason. We carry him close to us.

In later years, Jefferson explained what he had aimed at in writing the Declaration of Independence. He said that he had wanted to compose an "expression of the American mind." Add to the end of this phrase the words *heart* and *soul,* and you have a description not just of the Declaration project, but of the project that was the life and work of Thomas Jefferson. Whatever identity we carry with us as Americans we owe, in some unmistakably significant measure, to the Sage of Monticello.

Mount Rushmore National Monument, Keystone, South Dakota. Between 1927–41, Gutzon Borglum and four hundred workers sculpted the sixty-foot busts of Presidents George Washington, Thomas Jefferson, Theodore Roosevelt, and Abraham Lincoln to represent the first one hundred fifty years of American history.

(Collection of the author)

Part One

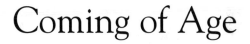

Coming of Age

Chapter 1

The Albemarle Boy

Flip the nickel from the bust of Thomas Jefferson to the portrait of his home, Monticello, and you see a striking image of the Enlightenment values that we associate with the man. Monticello embodies the grace and beauty of an Age of Reason. It is Mozart in brick and mortar, conjuring a world of heightened intellect and imagination—and also a world of wealth and privilege, the world of the great plantation. It is, we have come to believe, the world of Thomas Jefferson.

But it is not really the world into which he was born on April 13, 1743. Jefferson was the son of a gentleman farmer who was, by the standards of the neighborhood, prosperous. That neighborhood, however, was not the cosmopolitan and long-established Virginia Tidewater, but Albemarle County, in the Virginia Piedmont, much closer to the looming peaks of the Blue Ridge Mountains—the wilderness frontier—than to the Atlantic surf.

Peter Jefferson, about thirty-five years old when his son Thomas was born, already held a place among the Albemarle elite. He had been named justice of the peace in 1734, sheriff in 1737, and county surveyor in 1740. In 1739, he had married Jane Randolph, for him an excellent match because her family was significantly more prominent in Virginia society than his. Yet, within the grand halls and drawing rooms of Williamsburg, Peter Jefferson's offices and honors, his social standing, would have impressed no one. The planters of the Tidewater would have regarded him as a frontier farmer and his son a son of the wilderness.

Peter Jefferson's house was a far cry from what Monticello would be. Grandiosely dubbed Shadwell, after the London parish where his wife had been born, it was simply a one-and-a-half-story frame farmhouse set in the middle of a semicircle of outbuildings in a patch of land cleared from pine and dogwood. No other houses were in sight; what the Jeffersons saw instead was the lovely Rivanna River, the Southwest Mountains, and, through a gap in them, the Blue Ridge Mountains, which, at the time, represented the farthest frontier of white Virginia settlement.

Peter Jefferson was a farmer, a justice of the peace, and a sheriff, but in later years his son would speak most proudly of his father's role as a surveyor of the wilderness. In the 1740s, Peter was a member of an expedition that traveled throughout the vast extent of Virginia to make the first useful map of the country. Surveying, measuring, mapping the wilderness—these had a profound meaning for the younger Jefferson. He saw his father as a uniquely American hero: a man who imposed civilization—in the form of rational measurement—upon the wilderness. Years later, as president of the United States, Thomas Jefferson would acquire for his nation the vast wilderness beyond the Blue Ridge, and he would design a great expedition under Lewis and Clark to explore it and take its measure.

If Jefferson saw himself as his father's son, an American living on the fertile frontier between wilderness and civilization, he also grew up well aware of a more ancient pedigree. "The tradition in my father's family," Jefferson wrote in an autobiography unpublished during his lifetime, "was that their ancestor came to this country from Wales, and from near the mountains of Snowdon." A recent biographer has traced Jefferson's descent on his father's side to Welsh kings. His mother's family, Jefferson himself wrote, "trace their pedigree far back in England and Scotland" in fact, to a lord chief justice of England, to one of the barons who signed the Magna Carta in 1215, and back even further to King David I of Scotland; to Hugh Magnus, who led the First Crusade; to Alfred the Great; and to Charlemagne. But all that had been long ago. Since 1619, Jeffersons had lived in Virginia.

At age two, Tom moved with his family to Tuckahoe, the estate of William Randolph, nephew of his maternal grandfather, Isham Randolph. Five years younger than Peter Jefferson, William Randolph died suddenly, having named Peter Jefferson his executor. For seven years, the Jeffersons would live at Tuckahoe, as Peter honored the memory of his in-law and close friend by caring for Randolph's estate and two children while he left his own Shadwell in the hands of an overseer. In contrast to Shadwell, Tuckahoe was a genuine mansion, and in its graceful rooms and halls young Tom first learned to love architecture and the harmony it represented among reason, imagination, utility, and society.

With the two Randolph children and his own two older sisters, Jane and Mary, as well as assorted cousins, five-year-old Thomas was tutored in a one-room schoolhouse built on the grounds of Tuckahoe. Outside the classroom, he must have begun to learn another lesson on the great plantation: that there were white people and black people, and that white people commanded and black people obeyed. Simultaneously (as one of Jefferson's many modern biographers, Willard Sterne Randall, observes), Tom heard Peter Jefferson's fatherly advice: "It is the strong in body who are both the strong and free in mind" and "Never ask another to do for you what you can do for yourself."

Thomas Jefferson was born into a slaveholding culture; his father owned slaves, and he himself would own slaves all his life. He was a product of his time and place, a time and place that included not only the institution of slavery, but also the liberal spirit of his father's counsel concerning freedom and self-reliance. Thus, young Jefferson must have learned early the lesson of conflict between the ideal and the actual, between pristine moral aspiration and the compromised reality of the real world. For even as Jefferson continued to own slaves, to profit from their work, and to use their bodies, he struggled from the beginning of his political career to bring about the end of slavery.

At age nine, after the Jeffersons had returned to Shadwell, Tom began five years of schooling with Rev. William Douglas, who taught him, among other things, the rudiments of Latin, Greek, and French. By his early teens, Tom had also become an enthusiastic, accomplished, and wholly self-taught fiddler who delighted in accompanying his sister Jane as she sang. He also became a great walker who loved to wander the dense woods surrounding Shadwell, studying with precocious intensity the flora and fauna of his home place. His fascination with the natural world would only increase as he grew into adulthood. And if Tom Jefferson enjoyed walking in the woods, he took even greater delight in riding through them. Early on, he learned to love and admire fine horses, and he became a strong and graceful rider. Into adulthood and old age, he insisted on setting aside at least four hours every day for recreational walking, riding, or both.

> *Later in life, Jefferson recalled candidly that his "father's education had been quite neglected," but that did not stop him from ensuring that his son was thoroughly educated. "Being of a strong mind, sound judgment, and eager after information, [my father] read much and improved himself .... He placed me at the English school at five years of age and at the Latin at nine, where I continued until his death."*

The world of Jefferson's childhood and youth, with all its pleasures, wonders, and painful contradictions, changed suddenly in 1757. Peter Jefferson, planter, county official, and intrepid surveyor-explorer, died of an unspecified illness at age forty-nine. As important as his father had been to him, Tom had seen rather little of him. Peter died when the boy was fourteen, having spent a total of at least seven of those years away from home, on expeditions to explore and survey wilderness lands.

Peter Jefferson left his family—eight children and a thirty-seven-year-old widow—well off. Tom inherited half his father's 7,500-acre holdings, one of two plantations, and a body servant. At twenty-one, he would come into the rest of his inheritance: an additional twenty-five slaves and whatever portion of the estate remained at that time; Peter had willed to his widow the lifetime use of one third of his estate, including the house and home farm, to be forfeited only if she remarried. In tradition-bound Virginia, this was a highly liberal arrangement. Most fathers adhered to the feudal tradition of primogeniture, by which the oldest son inherited everything. Peter Jefferson saw to it instead that his *entire* family would continue to be provided for.

This, the last lesson his father taught him, was not lost on Tom. From 1779–81, as governor of Virginia, Jefferson would craft and then champion democratic legislation to expunge from the state's inheritance statutes the institution of primogeniture as well as entail, a law of feudal origin requiring that large estates be passed to descendants whole and intact, thereby ensuring the perpetuation of a small, elite ruling class of landed gentry.

There were a few more items Peter Jefferson left to his son: a library of forty books (large by the standards of Albemarle County) that Tom treasured and devoured; a fine writing desk; a set of surveyor's instruments; and, family members later reported, a deathbed wish that Tom continue to pursue his education.

The young man had no difficulty honoring that last request. In February 1758, about to turn fifteen and accompanied by a body servant named Sawney, he traveled fourteen frontier miles to a classical academy run by Rev. James Maury. A demanding taskmaster, Maury was nevertheless an intellectually able man with a true love of learning and an undeniable gift for teaching. In addition to continuing Jefferson's study of Latin, Greek, and French, Maury taught the future author of the Declaration of Independence English composition, with an emphasis on style as well as on how to convey precise meaning through the use of precise and persuasive language. A formidable man of letters, Maury was no closet scholar. He led Tom and his other students on frequent field trips through the wooded neighborhood of his academy, imparting lessons in what was then called "natural philosophy" and which today would encompass, zoology, botany, geology, physics, and chemistry. Young Jefferson's mind and imagination took fire on these expeditions.

Bereft of his father, Tom clearly adopted Rev. Maury as a surrogate. He respected and admired him, drank in his lessons eagerly, reveled in his four-hundred-book library, and took special note of the three qualities Maury told him were indispensable to a learned leader: caution, self-discipline, and patience. In old age, Jefferson reflected on the two years he spent under Maury's tutelage: "Reviewing the course of a long and sufficiently successful life, I find no portion of it happier moments than these were."

Tom studied hard, and he developed a lifelong habit of maintaining a "Commonplace Book," a kind of intellectual scrapbook into which he copied summaries as well as key extracts of books he read and admired, as if to make their ideas his own. However hard he studied, he always found time for violin practice—typically three hours a day—and he also made time to develop close and lively friendships. During this period he met Dabney Carr, a youth of much promise who became Jefferson's best friend and also the husband of his youngest sister, Martha. Tom was also delighted by an exuberant boy from Hanover County, Patrick Henry, destined one day to electrify the House of Burgesses, the colony of Virginia, and all of revolutionary America with the ringing declaration of his desire to be given nothing less than "liberty or death."

After completing his studies with Rev. Maury at age sixteen, Jefferson was better educated than most young men of his social and economic rank. He returned to Shadwell to live with his mother and sisters and to manage the plantation, perhaps planning to become a surveyor some day and take on a county office or two. But, as he declared to his uncle John Harvie in a letter of 1760—one of some twenty-eight thousand Jefferson letters that exist— "By going to the College, I shall get a more universal acquaintance which may hereafter be serviceable to me."

"The College" was the College of William and Mary, then, as now, located in Williamsburg, Virginia. Today, Williamsburg is part quiet college town and part outdoor museum—"Colonial Williamsburg." In March 1760, when Tom Jefferson arrived—red-haired, freckle-faced, lanky, a bit rawboned, perhaps, and, at six foot two, uncommonly tall for the era—Williamsburg was the bustling capital city of Virginia. No place in America was more sophisticated or cosmopolitan. Located on the coast, one hundred fifty miles from Albemarle County's Shadwell, it was truly a world apart from the home Jefferson had known. Replete with carnal temptation—some dubbed it "Devilsburg"—it was also the seat of the biggest and economically most important colony in British

America. It was a portal between the Old World across the Atlantic, freighted with millennia of accumulated civilization, and the New World, largely unexplored and charged with dreams, prospects, and possibility beyond the mountains and rivers of the vast American continent. About to enter this portal, Thomas Jefferson was one month shy of seventeen.

Chapter 2

Williamsburg Enlightenment

Between Albemarle County and the capital of colonial Virginia was a one hundred fifty-mile road through virgin forest punctuated by fields cleared for farming. The road led to the mile-long central thoroughfare of Williamsburg, Duke of Gloucester Street, anchored on the east by the Capitol and on the west by the College of William and Mary, already more than sixty years old, having been chartered in 1693 by King William III and Queen Mary II. This was the second institution of higher learning in British North America, after New England's Harvard, which had been founded in 1636.

Jefferson officially enrolled at William and Mary on May 25, 1760. For the next two years and one month, the college and the town were his home. He was no callow backwoodsman: He was far better read and educated than most youths of his age and station. Yet to a boy raised in the forested foothills of the Blue Ridge, seeing the town's handsome Capitol, the House of Burgesses, and the college, a building modeled after Sir Christopher Wren's magnificent Chelsea Hospital in London, must have been a heady experience. Add to this the sedate but sumptuous Governor's Palace and the Georgian town houses of the well-to-do, and it is easy to see why Virginia's Tidewater aristocracy thought of Williamsburg as the center of the universe, little considering those who lived, like Jefferson, in Virginia's Piedmont. A sophisticated Londoner had remarked that Williamsburg reminded him of a "good Country Town in England," but the men and women of the capital dressed like proper London lords and ladies, lavishing small fortunes on the latest fashions and indulging themselves in a London-scaled array of vices, especially gambling, drinking, and sexual recreation. Not for nothing was Williamsburg nicknamed Devilsburg.

Governor's Palace, Williamsburg, Virginia. The photograph was taken shortly after the building was reconstructed in the 1930s.

(Collection: Library of Congress)

Beyond the cosmopolitan institution and the town it occupied, a ferocious struggle was raging. The French and Indian War, which began in 1754, was the North American theater of the Seven Years' War, a conflict that encompassed Europe, India, Cuba, and the Philippines as well as North America. Jefferson's fellow Virginian George Washington, a colonel of militia, had fought the very first battle of the war, which had gone badly for the British during its early years but by 1760 was well on its way to being won. Nevertheless, it would not be over until 1763, after nine years of combat, much of it between French-allied Indians and the beleaguered British-American settlers of the frontier. It was a fire in the wilderness, which the British crown and the Tidewater aristocracy, for the most part, let burn. At least, that's the way the people of the frontier saw it. They received scant military aid from the commanders of the regular British forces and, even more galling, little support from Tidewater-based colonial politicians and militia leaders. The result was a widening gulf of resentment not only between the frontier and the mother country, but between the frontier and the Tidewater as well.

Rooted in that frontier, Jefferson was now a sojourner in the Tidewater, destined to mediate between these worlds. He understood the concerns of the frontier; all his life, his views would harmonize with those of westerners, and he would always see the future of the nation not in the East, but in the West. At the same time, he imbibed the best the East had to offer: the thought of the great progressive philosophers, John Locke of England, and the whole roster of the French enlightenment: Montesquieu, Voltaire, Rousseau, and Diderot. He looked as well to the ancients, especially to the Romans (Cicero paramount among them) for examples of ethical government and the rational regulation of life.

Even before he entered the College of William and Mary, Jefferson was steeped in Greek and Roman mythology, and he would certainly have known of Janus, the Roman gatekeeper deity with one face looking backward and the other forward. If colonial places like Williamsburg were portals of passage from the Old World to the New, young Americans like Jefferson were Januses, looking back to the civilization of Europe present and past, while looking forward to a wilderness of peril, possibility, risk, and reward, a vast region on which a new civilization, for better *or* worse, would be created.

These days, Jefferson was paying little attention to the French and Indian War. "I was a hard student," he wrote in later life, reflecting on his college days. He studied voraciously and untiringly. Unfortunately, the college was in general decline when Jefferson enrolled, but he did manage to fall under the tutelage of the best professor on the faculty. William Small was the only faculty member who was not an Anglican clergyman. Trained in philosophy at the Scottish college at Aberdeen, Small was personally acquainted with the likes of James Watt, inventor of the first practical steam engine; Erasmus Darwin, poet, physician, naturalist, botanist, and inventor, destined to be the grandfather of Charles Darwin; and Joseph Priestley, the scientist who discovered oxygen, among many other things, and who earned notoriety as a political and religious radical. Small opened for Jefferson the world of mathematics (in which Jefferson would delight lifelong) and brought him to the cutting edge of science as well as moral and political philosophy. Chiefly through Small, Jefferson became acquainted with the French *philosophes* and the other architects of the Age of Reason. With Small's approval, Jefferson also continued to nurture his aesthetic inclinations, devouring volumes of early English verse, reveling in Chaucer, Shakespeare, Spenser, and Milton as well as the more modern English writers such as Dryden, Thomson, Gray, Pope, Congreve, Addison, and Steele. He enjoyed the evolving literary form that would come to be called the novel, and eagerly read Tobias Smollett and Samuel Richardson, but reserved his greatest affection for Laurence Sterne's *Tristram Shandy*. This work appeared serially from 1759–67 and is a wry, often enigmatic satire of the very Age of Reason to which Jefferson was so deeply committed. From an early age, Thomas Jefferson was earnest and brilliant, passionate in the cause of rational liberty, yet he was also curiously detached, with an uncanny ability to regard all around him, including himself, with keen irony.

> "The College of William and Mary is the only public seminary of learn-
> ing in this state …. The buildings are of brick, sufficient for an indiffer-
> ent accommodation of perhaps an hundred students. By its charter it was
> to be under the government of twenty visitors, who were to be its legisla-
> tors, and to have a president and six professors, who were incorporated.
> It was allowed a representative in the general assembly. Under this char-
> ter, a professorship of the Greek and Latin languages, a professorship of
> mathematics, one of moral philosophy, and two of divinity, were estab-
> lished. To these were annexed, for a sixth professorship, a considerable
> donation by [the English scientist Robert Boyle], for the instruction of the
> Indians, and their conversion to Christianity."
>
> —Thomas Jefferson, Notes on the State of Virginia, *1781 and 1787*

Not all of Jefferson's William and Mary education came from
Professor Small and his books. He maintained close friendships
with fellow students Dabney Carr, John Page, and Jack Walker—
all prominent names from Albemarle County—and John Tyler,
with whom he often played violin duets. Tyler was well-connected
in Williamsburg society and introduced Jefferson into the Tidewater inner circle. More important, however, like Jefferson, he was
a skeptic, a rebel, and a devotee of French Enlightenment thought.
Jefferson and his friends held discussions—philosophical and otherwise—in the Apollo Room of the Raleigh Tavern, convening
meetings of their "secret" society, the Flat Hat Club, in which the
use of what Jefferson called "hog Latin" was frequent and hilarious.

At William and Mary, Jefferson dedicated fifteen out of every
twenty-four hours to study. What was he studying for? He was not
sure. It was fairly common, though certainly not the inevitable custom, for gentlemen planters to get a sound classical education and
then return to the plantation to pursue the eighteenth-century
equivalent of agribusiness for the rest of his life. But this prospect
seemed dreary and wasteful to Jefferson. Fortunately, there was a
practical and fulfilling alternative: the law.

As Jefferson saw it, training for a legal career served a variety of
purposes. It would be difficult to make a living in backwoods
Albemarle working exclusively as a lawyer, but a law practice could
be as a profitable adjunct to a main income derived from farming.

And bringing to Albemarle the benefit of a competent lawyer would be a great service to planters and farmers of all economic strata, who frequently disputed issues involving land and other property. But most important of all was Jefferson's rapidly evolving view of the nature and significance of the law. He saw it not merely as a way to manipulate statutes, judges, and juries to the benefit of one's clients, but as the very science of civilized existence. Civilized society was driven by law, Jefferson reasoned, and the man who commanded a thorough, systematic, and scientific knowledge of the law had his hands on the reins of society. The law was an opportunity to make a difference in the world—the world of Albemarle County and the larger, more challenging world to which the College of William and Mary had opened the door.

Chapter 3

The Law

When Thomas Jefferson told Professor William Small that he had decided to study law, his college mentor introduced him to George Wythe. Anyone who even casually studies the period of the founding of the United States must be struck by one remarkable fact: Colonial America was blessed with an abundant supply of extraordinarily intelligent, wise, idealistic, practical, passionate, and courageous men. We think foremost of Washington, Franklin, the two Adamses (Samuel and John), Madison, Jay, Marshall, and, of course, Jefferson. But if we investigate beyond the most famous names, we find a host of less well-known figures who are almost equally accomplished. George Wythe was one of these.

Wythe was born in 1726 in what is now Hampton, Virginia, and was educated primarily by his mother, who was thoroughly conversant in the classics. Because Wythe was not the eldest son in his family, he knew that he would not inherit his father's plantation, so he committed himself to training for a profession—law. He apprenticed with an attorney and then traveled the circuit for two years, finally moving to Williamsburg, where he served as attorney general and also in the House of Burgesses. Wythe earned a reputation for thorough knowledge of the law and for an eminently logical approach to legal questions based on careful research and analysis. Indeed, he regarded the proper practice of law as a stringent scientific endeavor, something that particularly appealed to young Jefferson. Later in his life, Wythe would be active in the American Revolution and, with Governor Thomas Jefferson and others, would be responsible for the creation of a new legal code for revolutionary Virginia. Perhaps even more significant is that Wythe would become the very first professor of law in the United States, joining the faculty of William and Mary in 1779 and serving until 1790.

But when Jefferson went to study with him, beginning in 1761, Wythe was not a professor, he was a practicing lawyer who took on a few fortunate students. In those days, there were no law schools in America; professional legal training consisted of serving an unpaid apprenticeship with an attorney from as little as a few months to five years. Law students who wanted to do no more than practice before county courts apprenticed only briefly and then took written and oral exams before the state bar. Those with loftier ambitions of pleading cases before the Virginia General Court, the highest court in the colony, had to apprentice with a lawyer who practiced before the high court, a distinguished lawyer like Wythe, and had to serve with him as an unpaid legal clerk for five full years. If the aspirant survived this far more demanding apprenticeship, he went on to take bar exams and typically was then allowed to argue cases before the county courts. If he did well in these venues, he was welcomed as one of legal Virginia's inner circle: a lawyer who practiced in the General Court.

Like Small, Wythe became Jefferson's mentor as well as something of a surrogate father. Mr. and Mrs. Wythe, who had no children of their own, virtually adopted the young man. "My ancient master," Jefferson would in his later years call Wythe, "my earliest and best friend."

If Jefferson was welcomed into the Wythe family, he also became a member of the great legal family of Wythe's other students, who included John Marshall, the fourth and perhaps greatest chief justice of the United States Supreme Court; James Monroe, fifth president of the United States; and Henry Clay, the "Great Compromiser," secretary of state under John Quincy Adams and one of the most popular political figures in American history.

From 1761–66, whenever the General Court was in session, Jefferson strode early in the morning from his rented rooms to

Wythe's town house on Williamsburg's Palace Green. Wythe had set aside a back room as the clerks' study, and there, with Wythe's other acolytes, Jefferson pored over law books from the master's library. He also monitored each of Wythe's ongoing cases, studying them step-by-step. Recognizing Jefferson's aptitude, Wythe assigned him the most important tasks of research and preparation. Increasingly, he became Wythe's companion, very nearly a legal partner, remaining by his side in the General Court and accompanying him on excursions to the county courts. From his earliest youth, Jefferson was an aggressive reader, earnestly taking notes and even copying out entire passages of what he read. Now he created extensive legal "commonplace books," notebooks in which he analyzed key cases, distilling them to their essence so that relevant legal precedents could be readily extracted from them.

But Jefferson did not limit his studies to the law. With Wythe he discussed the classics, the great works of the Greeks and Romans, and also Shakespeare, Milton, and more contemporary authors. Discussion of law readily overlapped discussion of literature and philosophy; as Wythe viewed it, the subject of law dealt with matters at the very heart of literature and philosophy: the conduct of life.

Among the constellation of Williamsburg luminaries to which Wythe introduced his law clerk was Francis Fauquier, the royal governor of Virginia. Like Wythe and Jefferson, Fauquier was a student of the classics, and, like Jefferson, he had an abiding interest in music and science. Unlike the ever-earnest Jefferson, Fauquier was locally celebrated as a gambler of mythic proportions. It was rumored that he had lost his entire inheritance to Lord George Anson in a game of cards but that this Royal Navy admiral magnanimously compensated Fauquier by obtaining for him the Virginia governorship. (Technically, Fauquier was lieutenant governor; colonial governors typically remained in England, while lieutenant governors occupied the office on site and were locally addressed as governor.) Within a short time, Jefferson became a frequent guest at the Governor's Palace. Not only did Fauquier delight in the young man's erudite conversation, but he also enjoyed his virtuosity on the violin. Jefferson was often a featured player in the governor's weekly musicales.

> *As a boy, Jefferson taught himself to play the violin, then studied under Williamsburg music teacher Francis Alberti. Jefferson paid Williamsburg druggist Dr. William Pasteur £5 for a violin in 1768. Just before he left Williamsburg on the eve of the Revolution, John Randolph, attorney general of the colony, sold Jefferson his fine violin for £13. It may well have been a Stradivarius or of similar quality. During the Revolution, Governor Jefferson invited the well-known Venetian violinist Francis Alberti to Monticello to give him lessons and sought the foremost instructors for his children.*

Intellectually, Jefferson now found himself part of a quartet, which included his brilliant William and Mary tutor, Dr. William Small; his legal mentor, George Wythe; and Governor Fauquier. Not only did this company bring Jefferson great joy, it advanced his education in ways that no mere college stint or legal apprenticeship could. It admitted him into the precincts of wisdom as well as power, certainly to a degree unusual for a young man just leaving his teens and also quite remarkable for a backwoods "immigrant" from the Piedmont. Thus Jefferson was admitted to the Tidewater aristocracy, the center of colonial power, yet he would never forsake his Piedmont roots. He was learning to look eastward, but his most earnest gaze would continue toward the West.

Under Wythe, Jefferson navigated the notoriously muddy waters of the great English jurists, paramountly Sir William Blackstone and Edward Coke. Characteristically, Jefferson was able to penetrate to the heart of both writers. From Coke, who wrote in the sixteenth and seventeenth centuries, he mined a tortured but profound defense of individual liberties against the royal prerogative of the seventeenth-century Stuart kings. In Blackstone, very much alive and active in Jefferson's day, he found dangerous tendencies to subordinate, by legal means, individual rights to the power of the Crown. As Jefferson saw it, law was a profession with which to supplement his plantation earnings; but it was never *merely* that. From the beginning of his legal studies, Jefferson regarded law as nothing less than a vital means of securing and defending individual liberty.

And as hard as he studied law books—typically devoting to them the hours between 8 A.M. and noon—he integrated this reading into a much more ambitious ongoing program of study. Jefferson rose at 5 A.M. to read ethics, religion, and "natural law" until 8 A.M. He believed that the early morning saw the dawn of the day as well as the dawn of the intellect and imagination. The early hours, Jefferson held, were the period of the mind's greatest acuity, and to those hours he assigned his most intellectually demanding tasks. After completing his three hours of philosophical reading, he turned to law. Afterward, he would break for lunch, then resume his reading with political works, including those of John Locke, whose ideas of government formed a cornerstone on which Jefferson would raise the Declaration of Independence.

In the later afternoon, Jefferson visited with friends, but he also found time to read histories, including those of the ancients in the original Greek and Latin. At night, he read literature as well as "criticism, rhetoric and oratory." In part, this was recreational reading, a way to unwind, but Jefferson also read literary and oratorical works with an eye toward developing his own eloquence and power of expression. His classical education had taught him to believe, with the Greeks and Romans, that persuasive expression—rhetoric—was more than elegant speech. Effective rhetoric welded thought to expression. To reason effectively, one had to express oneself effectively, and, conversely, effective expression depended on effective reasoning.

Well before Jefferson had completed his legal apprenticeship, Wythe allowed him to argue certain cases on his own. He was rapidly maturing into a fine lawyer. A *great* lawyer? Perhaps, but perhaps not. One of Jefferson's recent biographers, Willard Sterne Randall, quotes *Essay on the Revolutionary History of Virginia,* by Jefferson's distant cousin Edmund Randolph. Randolph praises Jefferson as a young lawyer, calling him "indefatigable and methodical," with a style of courtroom presentation characterized by "perspicuity and elegance." He goes on to contrast Jefferson's approach to law with that of Patrick Henry: "Mr. Jefferson drew copiously from the depths of the law, Mr. Henry from the recesses of the human heart."

Randolph's analysis is acute for what it suggests about Jefferson's public presentation of himself. All through his life, friends and admirers—as well as critics—remarked on a certain distance, a removed or remote quality, in Jefferson. To everything he set his hand, he gave his all—yet it was not always apparent that he gave his heart. Whether he was making a case in the General Court of Virginia for the rights of one property owner over those of another or, as he did in the Declaration of 1776, making a case for the independence of the United States, Jefferson relied first and foremost on the law and a vigorously reasoned appeal to it. True, he could rise to heights of passionate eloquence, but reason always took precedence over passion. Revolutionary orators like Patrick Henry, in contrast, appealed first to the heart—often letting reason and the law fall where they may.

The legal profession in Virginia was much the better for having a young lawyer of Jefferson's caliber, but his placing of reason and law before the passions of the heart probably meant that he would never become a truly great courtroom attorney. Similarly, Jefferson would be a key architect of the Revolution and, afterward, of the government of the new American republic. Yet that Revolution and that republic also required the likes of Samuel Adams and Patrick Henry, who never felt themselves above making a naked appeal to the heart.

None of this is to say that Jefferson lacked a heart. His devotion to study seems to have kept him a bachelor beyond the age when most young men took their brides—in eighteenth-century America, unmarried nineteen-year-olds were truly deemed bachelors—but, at nineteen, in 1762, Jefferson was able to tear himself away from his books long enough to become smitten with sixteen-year-old Rebecca Burwell.

She was the sister of one of Jefferson's college classmates, an orphan of a prominent planter/lawyer, and now under the guardianship of an uncle who was a distinguished judge. By all accounts Rebecca was a beautiful and accomplished girl, and her place in colonial society made her an eminently desirable catch.

Jefferson, too shy to speak up, regarded her from afar for more than a year. At last, when the court session had ended and shortly before he left on the one hundred fifty-mile trip to visit his family at Shadwell, he worked up sufficient courage to ask Rebecca to cut a silhouette of herself so that he might carry it inside the back of his pocket watch while he was away. In the days before photography, the wealthy or extravagant might commission a miniaturist to paint a cameo-size ivory portrait of a loved one; more casually, one might simply ask for a paper silhouette. Either way, it was an act of some intimacy, and Rebecca was responsive. She furnished the silhouette, and Jefferson carried it home—but then suffered disaster. A leaky Shadwell roof resulted in water penetrating his watch case one night as it lay on Jefferson's nightstand. Jefferson attempted to take the silhouette out of the case to dry it, but, as he wrote in a letter to his friend John Page, "Good God! My cursed fingers gave [it] such a rent I fear I never shall get over." He continued: "And now, although the picture be defaced, there is so lively an image of her imprinted in my mind that I shall think of her too often, I fear, for my peace of mind and too often I am sure to get through Old Coke [Jefferson's law books] this winter …."

He had met Rebecca Burwell early in 1762, but not until October 7, 1763, at the Apollo Room of Williamsburg's Raleigh Tavern, did Jefferson work up sufficient courage to dance with her. To Page he wrote how diligently he had prepared for the encounter: "I had dressed up in my own mind such thoughts as occurred to me, in as moving language as I knew how, and expected to have performed in a tolerably creditable manner." But like so many shy lovers before and since, "When I had an opportunity of venting [my carefully prepared thoughts], a few broken sentences, uttered in great disorder and interrupted with pauses of uncommon length were the too visible marks of my strange confusion!"

Alas, Rebecca *was* a good catch, and while Tom Jefferson continued to pine and procrastinate, she married, in 1764, a man with the curiously feminine name of Jacqueline Ambler. Jefferson's immediate reaction to the news of her wedding was an attack of migraine, a lifelong disorder that recurred in moments of crisis and stress. Yet Jefferson seems hardly to have been heartbroken. Indeed, he felt a certain relief in Rebecca's marriage to another because this meant that he could continue to devote himself to study uninterrupted.

Even while trying his first cases—land patent disputes—Jefferson crammed for his bar exams. Since Virginia was a colony of England, he was responsible for mastering not only Virginia statutes, but the laws of the mother country as well. He passed his exams in October 1765.

Jefferson would argue a wide variety of cases, exclusively in the General Court rather than the lowly county courts, during an active legal career that spanned 1765–74. The field on which he concentrated most intensely was land law. This was no accident. Colonial Virginia was vast, its western boundary utterly undefined. As some interpreted the colony's original charter, Virginia stretched as far west as the Pacific. Land was the great natural resource of the colony, and by the mid-1760s, issues revolving around colonial land were more intense, urgent, and numerous than ever.

Consider what was happening in the world of this novice specialist in land law. First and foremost was the ineptitude of the British monarch. George III was twenty-two years old when he succeeded his grandfather, George II, to the British throne on October 25, 1760. His father, Frederick Louis, had died nine years earlier, not of disease or wounds sustained in gallant battle, but because he had been struck in the throat by an errant tennis ball. George III was hardly promising royal material. He was eleven years old before he learned to read his first word, and he has been variously described by historians and contemporaries alike as lethargic, apathetic, and childish. The distinguished British historian J. H. Plumb characterized him as "a clod of a boy whom no one could teach." Throughout his childhood, George's exasperated mother was heard repeatedly to admonish her son: "George, be a king!"

Of course, the lineage of George III was hardly more promising than the boy himself. George I had been no Englishman, but rather a German nobleman, the elector of Hanover, deemed heir to the

British crown as the grandson of King James I. He ascended the throne in 1714 and reigned for thirteen years, never bothering to learn English nor really to govern the nation, occupying his time instead with a succession of mistresses. His son, George II, did learn English, which he spoke with a heavy German accent, but he never developed affection for the country he ruled: "No English cook could dress a dinner," he complained, "no English confectioner set out a dessert, no English player could act, no English coachman drive, no English jockey ride, nor were any English horses fit to be ridden or driven. No Englishman could enter a room and no English woman dress herself." As for his hapless son, Frederick Louis, George II was hardly the proud papa. He called the young Prince of Wales "the greatest beast in the whole world" and then added, "and I most heartily wish he were out of it." Frederick Louis married a German, Princess Augusta of Saxe-Gotha, who bore him George III, among seven other equally dull-witted offspring.

Perhaps it was George III's desire to prove himself—to obey his mother's admonition to *be a king*—that moved him to endorse the series of repressive tax, commerce, and land laws that ultimately drove his American colonies to revolution.

Among the first of George's kingly decisions was to enforce a series of Navigation Acts, the first of which had been on the books since the mid-seventeenth century. These acts restricted some colonial trade to dealing exclusively with the mother country and, in all other cases, ensured that the mother country would be cut in for a disproportionately fat share of the profits. The Navigation Acts regulated imports as well as exports, specifying that most goods had to be purchased from Great Britain alone and that many items produced in America (so-called "enumerated articles") could be exported only to Great Britain or other British colonies. On paper, the Navigation Acts were oppressive, but, fortunately for colonial traders, they were rarely enforced—until 1760, when George III suddenly began to enforce them. He used a law that had been enacted (but little used) by George II in 1755, authorizing royal customs officers to issue writs of assistance to local provincial officers, compelling their cooperation and aid in identifying contraband and in arresting those who sought to evade the Navigation Acts. Worse, the writs also gave royal officials the authority to search not only warehouses but also private homes without a warrant.

As long as the colonies were struggling through the closing years of the French and Indian War, they had little choice other than to accept enforcement of the Navigation Acts. From King George's perspective, enforcement was absolutely necessary to the British economy. The war in North America, together with the concurrent Seven Years' War in Europe and other parts of the far-flung British empire, was a severe drain on the English coffers. British victory in the war humiliated France and effectively neutralized Spain as a New World power in 1763, but it also left England groaning under massive debt. George reasoned that the colonies existed solely to enrich the mother country. Besides, as George saw it, the colonies *owed* the mother country compensation for war-related expenses and ongoing defense. It was a just debt, and the squeeze, therefore, was on.

That squeeze became all the tighter when new violence erupted after the signing of the Treaty of Paris ended the French and Indian War in 1763. Pontiac, war chief of the Ottawa Indians, called a grand council of Ottawa and other tribes, including the Delaware, the Seneca (and elements of other Iroquois tribes), and the Shawnee. The chief persuaded the assembled war leaders to mount an attack on the frontier settlement of Detroit and many of the other western outposts that the French had just surrendered to the English. The violence of Pontiac's Rebellion was even more brutal than that of the just-concluded French and Indian War. Fortunately, it was also brief. Quickly exhausted, Pontiac and the other war leaders came to the peace table and found that George III had something to offer them.

On October 7, 1763, to the satisfaction of Pontiac and other Indians, the British king issued a proclamation limiting the extent of colonial western settlement to the Appalachian Mountains. No white settler was to be permitted to move west of the mountains. The Proclamation of 1763 brought Pontiac's Rebellion to an immediate end.

If it pacified the Indians, however, the Proclamation Line enraged the settlers, especially Virginians. Refusing to recognize a limit to westward expansion, they freely violated the decreed line. When the settlers trekked across the proscribed mountains, the Indians understandably felt betrayed and let loose their fury all along the trans-Appalachian frontier. This elicited settlers' pleas for military aid from the Crown, but royal authorities were not eager to assist settlers who had defied the king. The Proclamation Line had alienated the frontier. The royal refusal of aid now inflamed it.

More than ever, major landowners needed the services of top-notch lawyers. Even before the Proclamation, as early as 1761, the royal government had taken Indian land affairs out of the hands of governors and other local officials. This meant that applications for western land grants now had to go to officials in London. The Proclamation of 1763 complicated legal matters even further.

For the foreseeable future, Jefferson's specialty in land law would be in great demand. However, his involvement in land issues quickly moved beyond legal advocacy of individual clients. George Wythe was one of eight members of the House of Burgesses to be appointed to a Committee of Correspondence charged with direct-ing the activities of an agent hired to represent the Virginia colony in London before the Board of Trade and other Crown agencies. Although he was already practicing law on his own, Jefferson still served as Wythe's clerk. With Wythe's service on the Committee of Correspondence, Jefferson suddenly found himself involved in colonial and trans-Atlantic politics at the highest levels, and in the very thick of the deepening—and intensely exciting—crisis between Virginia and the mother country.

Part Two

The Revolutionary

Chapter 4

This New Man

Thomas Jefferson's entry into revolutionary politics as the law clerk of a burgess who was a member of Virginia's Committee of Correspondence and other key committees came on the eve of a bombshell: the infamous Stamp Act of 1765. Even those of us today for whom the American Revolution is a dim memory of grade-school history recall that it was the Stamp Act that made revolutionaries out of many hitherto loyal colonists.

The Stamp Act was the handiwork of Britain's conservative premier, Lord Richard Grenville. Coming into force on March 22, 1765, it taxed all kinds of printed matter, including newspapers, legal documents, and even dice and playing cards. On all such items a government tax stamp had to be purchased and affixed. The purpose of the Stamp Act, as well as other duty and tax measures enacted by the government of King George III, was to help defray the costs of the just-concluded French and Indian War as well as the cost of maintaining British soldiers in the colonies. But colonists had had their fill of British soldiery in the French and Indian War, and they resented the tax. More aggravating still was that fact that any infringement of the new tax was to be tried in the vice admiralty courts rather than by local magistrates; the Stamp Act effectively took the administration of local justice out of the hands of the colonies, denying colonists the hallowed right to a trial by a jury of one's peers.

Response to the Stamp Act was swift. In the British Parliament, Isaac Barré was among a handful of members who opposed passage of the act. In a speech, he referred to the colonists as "these sons of liberty." The phrase appealed to Sam Adams, a Boston brewer, bankrupt businessman, and brilliant political agitator who organized one of the first secret societies that would soon sprout throughout the colonies. Adams's group, like the others, called itself the Sons of Liberty, and members made it their business to harass and intimidate the royal stamp agents. They were most effective. All of the agents the Sons "approached" resigned—and promptly.

In Virginia, passage of the Stamp Act motivated Jefferson's friend Patrick Henry, a fiery and eloquent member of the House of Burgesses, to introduce seven resolutions that he hurriedly composed on the flyleaf of an old law book, the Stamp Act Resolves of 1765. The seventh of these resolves was key: It asserted that Virginia enjoyed complete legislative autonomy. More than a decade before Jefferson's great document of July 4, 1776, here was a declaration of independence (and we shall return to it shortly). But let us take note here that, while the Stamp Act is perhaps the best-known cause around which the colonies rallied, it was not the first of the mother country's new laws that worked to galvanize revolution.

Back in 1761, the distinguished Boston lawyer James Otis resigned from a lucrative position as the king's advocate general of the vice admiralty court at Boston because his conscience would not allow him to argue on behalf of the writs of assistance, the authority of royal officials to require local enforcement of trade and taxation laws and to make searches and seizures without warrants. On February 24, 1761, Otis spoke against the writs. John Adams, who heard the speech, took notes and recalled fully sixty years later that "Otis was a flame of fire! ... He burned everything before him. American independence was then and there born." Adams remembered most vividly one ringing phrase from the speech: "Taxation without representation is tyranny." Little wonder that it should remain lodged in his mind, for the phrase would echo and amplify throughout the colonies as the battle cry of revolution. As mentioned in Chapter 3, "The Law," those writs of assistance called for enforcement of taxation acts that had gone for many years without enforcement. In addition to the Navigation Acts of 1645, 1649, and 1651, and various additional Navigation Acts passed between 1660 and 1696, there were the Acts of Trade, all of which amounted to costly imposition of tariffs and stringent restrictions on colonial imports and exports.

The sudden decision to enforce a welter of trade restrictions and taxes was bad enough, but then Lord Grenville added insult to injury by creating a brand-new tax, officially called the American Revenue Act, but more familiarly known as the Sugar Act of 1764. Building on one of the old Acts of Trade, the Molasses Act of 1733, the Sugar Act actually reduced the duty on foreign molasses but simultaneously hiked the duties on foreign refined sugar and greatly increased duties on a long list of products imported from countries other than Britain. Associated with the Sugar Act was Grenville's Currency Act, which created a new vice admiralty court. This ensured that officials from the mother country—not local people—would have jurisdiction over all matters of taxation and customs.

The first colonial protest in response to the Grenville Acts was voted in Boston on May 24, 1764. A Non-Importation Agreement was put into place, whereby Massachusetts resolved to boycott a wide variety of English goods. By the end of the year, a number of colonies, including Virginia, had joined the boycott.

This was the prelude to rebellion that was swiftly and surely transforming Tom Jefferson, aspiring young lawyer, into Thomas Jefferson, leader of the American Revolution. Yet what most immediately propelled him into the revolutionary maelstrom was not Grenville's earth-shaking series of acts, but a local issue, unremembered today except perhaps by scholars who specialize in the history of Virginia.

The issue was known as the Parson's Cause. Anglican Protestantism, the state religion of Britain, was also the state religion of colonial Virginia. Traditionally, the Virginia government paid Anglican clergymen a stipend of sixteen thousand pounds of tobacco per year. With the onset of the French and Indian War, tobacco fetched a very high price in England, so in 1758 the House of Burgesses passed the Two-Penny Act, which called for payment to the clergymen in cash instead of the now much more valuable tobacco, at the rate of two pennies for each pound of tobacco wages due. Later, when cash became scarce and tobacco more plentiful, the Burgesses reinstated the traditional payment in tobacco.

At this point, Rev. James Maury, Jefferson's own early tutor, drafted a petition on behalf of the Virginia clergy addressed to the king's Privy Council in London. The petition asked the Privy Council to overrule the House of Burgesses and nullify the Two-Penny Act, and that is precisely what happened. Maury and the other clergymen then sued for three years' back pay. One of the cases was brought before the Hanover County court, where the defendant—namely, the taxpayers of the county—was represented by none other than young Patrick Henry. The great orator began not by addressing the merits of Maury's suit, but by attacking the government of King George III. He declared that the Two-Penny Act was a good law, enacted in conformity with the "original compact between King and people .... A King, by disallowing Acts of this salutary nature, [far] from being the father of his people, degenerates into a tyrant, and forfeits all rights to his subjects' obedience."

Thus Patrick Henry had elevated a local county-court lawsuit into what may have been the first public statement of what Jefferson already well knew was John Locke's "social compact" concept of government. A monarch, Locke held, derived his authority not from any divine right, but from a social compact, an implied contract between himself and his people. To the degree that the monarch fulfilled his part of the compact, his subjects were morally bound to fulfill theirs and to render the king allegiance and obedience. But to the degree that the king failed to hold up his part of the bargain, his subjects were under no obligation to maintain their allegiance to him.

If Jefferson was drawn to the logic as well as the passion of Patrick Henry's argument in the Parson's Cause, he was instantly electrified by Henry's role in Virginia's response to the Stamp Act. On May 28, 1765, Henry presented before the House of Burgesses his Stamp Act Resolves, asserting the proposition that only Virginia had the right to tax Virginians. "Caesar had his Brutus,"

Henry concluded his oration in support of the Stamp Act Resolves, "Charles the first, his Cromwell, and George III"— Henry paused dramatically, then dropped his voice—"may profit by their example." As the more conservative burgesses cried out, "*Treason! Treason!*" Henry closed grandly: "If *this* be treason, make the most of it."

John Locke (1632–1704) was the most influential liberal political theorist of his day. His Two Treatises of Government provided Jefferson with a blueprint for revolution by demolishing the doctrine of rule by divine right and replacing it with the concept of the social compact. Locke argued that if God had bestowed the right of divine rule on any human being, it was Adam, yet no one on earth could prove direct lineage to Adam; therefore, divine right had no force in the modern world. The right to govern can only be bestowed by the governed. Moreover, Locke argued, the role of the ruler is to protect the rights to life, liberty, and property. When a ruler fails, the people have the right to remove him.

Patrick Henry presents his Stamp Act Resolves of 1765 to the Virginia House of Burgesses. The engraving is attributed to H. B. Hall, after Alonzo Chappel.

(Collection: National Archives and Records Administration)

To Jefferson, present in the hallway just outside the House chamber, the speech was sufficiently stunning for him to recollect it a half-century later: "I remember the cry of treason, the pause of Mr. Henry at the name of George III and the presence of mind with which he closed the sentence and baffled the charge vociferated." Although the first five Stamp Act Resolves were passed on May 30, 1765, the fifth was subsequently retracted, and the governor dissolved the assembly before it could act on the other two. It didn't matter: The text of the complete Stamp Act Resolves made the round of the other colonies before the end of summer, and nine of thirteen American colonies enacted some form of the Resolves.

One effect of the Stamp Act Resolves was a general boycott of the courts, not only in Virginia, but in most of the colonies as well. If the king required tax stamps to be affixed to all legal documents, colonial lawyers were determined that there would be no legal documents to stamp, which meant that there would be no legal proceedings to generate paperwork. During this enforced hiatus in his budding legal career, Jefferson returned to Shadwell, where he used his time chiefly to study works of political philosophy. Fiery men like Patrick Henry in Virginia and Sam Adams in Massachusetts fanned the flames of revolution with bold oratory. It was up to more reflective men like Jefferson to provide the intellectual foundation on which a revolution might not only be built, but also justified to the world.

But it is misleading to label Jefferson a mere student. In April 1764, he turned twenty-one and therefore came into the balance of his father's estate. He took over all plantation operations, even paying his mother rent on her widow's portion of Shadwell, four hundred acres and five slaves, so that he could assume direct operational responsibility for these properties. He sought to run the plantation profitably and efficiently, and one of the key areas he identified as requiring improvement was the means of getting his produce to market. He had heard that the lower Rivanna River, a branch of the James, was navigable by canoe. Acting on his scientific curiosity, Jefferson confirmed this firsthand by exploring the river in his own canoe. But a canoe, of course, is no way to transport huge hogsheads of tobacco. Hitherto, the produce of Shadwell and neighboring plantations had to be carried over land all the way to the James River—an expensive and time-consuming operation. Jefferson observed that the Rivanna could be made passable for larger, cargo-carrying boats if the river were cleared of loose rocks.

What happened next was early vintage Jefferson. He lobbied his neighbors throughout Albemarle County, organizing a subscription drive to pay for the necessary dredging. Then he took the project a step farther, to the House of Burgesses, which voted up a bill to clear the river. Jefferson presided over the direction of what became an ambitious five-year public works project to clear the entire course of the Rivanna so that all plantations along the river would have free access to the James. The project was of inestimable benefit to Jefferson's part of the Piedmont. Many years later, after he had been elected president, Jefferson challenged himself with the question of whether the United States was any better off for all his political efforts. By way of answer, he jotted down a list of what he had achieved. No. 1 was the Rivanna River project. No. 2? The Declaration of Independence ...

In July 1765, Jefferson passed his bar exams, pursued his study of political philosophy, modernized operations at Shadwell, and initiated the Rivanna River project. His professional life was exciting and fulfilling. Jefferson was also personally delighted by the marriage of his sister Martha to his closest friend, Dabney Carr. But then, on October 1, 1765, his favorite sister Jane died, presumably of smallpox, at the age of twenty-five. Jefferson was devastated by the loss. "Jane Jefferson," he wrote in his *Account Book* ...

> *Ah, Jane, best of girls!*
> *Flower snatched away in its bloom!*
> *May the earth weigh lightly upon you!*
> *Farewell for a long, long time.*

On March 18, 1766, thanks to the pressure exerted by the united colonies, the Stamp Act was repealed. Colonial celebration temporarily drowned out protest over another piece of legislation enacted on the very day of the repeal. The Declaratory Act asserted Parliament's authority to make laws binding on the American colonies "in all cases whatsoever." Parliament had acknowledged colonial rights while simultaneously denying them.

Nevertheless, with the repeal of the Stamp Act, the boycott of the courts ended, and Jefferson embarked in earnest on an instantly thriving law practice. He had begun the study of law as a gentlemanly sideline to supplement his plantation income. Now, however, it became the primary focus of his professional life; he handled as many as five hundred cases each year.

Because Jefferson's specialty was land cases, and because he presented himself as the only General Court attorney available to the people of the western counties, his practice took him throughout most of present-day Virginia. Born and raised in Albemarle County, he was already more familiar with the colony's interior than were most other Williamsburg-trained lawyers and politicians. Now he saw even more of frontier Virginia. Under George Wythe, his training in the law had dramatically segued into a political education. Working among the people of Virginia's interior counties, Jefferson's sphere expanded even further beyond law books, beyond treatises on political philosophy, and even beyond the realm of heated political debate and oratory. He met the people and heard from them directly their concerns and their dreams.

In 1782, a French sojourner in America, J. Hector St. John de Crevecoeur, wrote a highly influential book about the freshly minted nation, *Letters from an American Farmer*. The book asked and answered a question that penetrated to the heart of the new republic: "What then is the American, this new man?"

This new man is precisely what Jefferson encountered in his Virginia law travels—not the colonial facsimiles of the London dandy who peopled so much of Williamsburg, but the men and women who had turned their faces away from the Old World and squarely toward the New—the "western pilgrims," Crevecoeur would call them, "a new race of man, whose labors and posterity will one day cause great changes in the world."

While representing his province in the assembly and his clients in court, Jefferson set about systematizing and rationalizing the impenetrable jungle that was colonial Virginia law. In 1768, he began assiduously collecting manuscript reports of hundreds of Virginia law cases. Today, an attorney can refer to the rows of books that line the walls of even the humblest practice, or punch a few keys and tap into law libraries on the Internet. In the Virginia of 1768, however, law books were the scarcest among scarce books. Just thirty-three were published before 1776, and the statutes of Virginia were not even available in printed form; they were compiled in a unique set of bound manuscripts stored in Williamsburg. Between 1768–74, Jefferson compiled a massive manuscript collection of Virginia law reports, an analytical compendium of the colony's case law, the legal precedents on which cases are tried and decided. The great work would be published posthumously, in 1829, as *Reports of Cases Determined in the General Court of Virginia from 1730 to 1740 and from 1768 to 1772.*

Jefferson believed that law and politics were one, that the former was the foundation of the latter and that the latter was the reason for the former. For the present, his legal work was a great service to his fellow Virginians and, for the future, a necessary prelude to the growing cause of democracy. Had Jefferson remained only a lawyer, he would be no more than a footnote in pre-Revolutionary history. His law practice broadcast the Jefferson reputation throughout the province, though, and in December 1768, he was elected to the seat that had once been his father's in the Virginia House of Burgesses. Jefferson's entry into the political arena was now official.

As a lawyer, as a budding political philosopher, and now, as a freshman burgess, Jefferson's point of view was shaped by a vision that students of American civilization have called agrarian romanticism. In his *Notes on the State of Virginia,* first privately printed in 1785, Jefferson wrote that "those who labor in the earth are the chosen people of God" and are "his peculiar deposit for substantial and genuine virtue." Having lived and worked in the worlds of Albemarle as well as Williamsburg, Jefferson was learning to see the future of America not in its coast-clinging villages, towns, and cities, places that took their measure by the villages, towns, and cities of Europe. Instead, he looked to the agrarian West, the vast land of farms, enlightened farmers, and plantations—self-sufficient, yet bound together in sacred political union and entirely independent of any "mother country" across the sea.

If Jefferson, the agrarian romantic, had begun to imagine independence from the mother country, he was also taking steps to formalize his independence from his own mother, Jane Randolph Jefferson, and the rest of his family still living at Shadwell. In 1768, atop a hill two miles from the parental home, he broke ground for what he planned as a small house of his own. It would be modest, even spartan, containing only the essentials for bachelor life, plus one guest room.

These early plans, of course, would change. The house would take root as much in Jefferson's mind, heart, and imagination as it did in the soil of the Virginia Piedmont. The plan would grow, maturing into majestic Monticello. Like the founding of the United States, the planning, construction, and perfection of Monticello would become a life's work for Thomas Jefferson. One thing, though, would remain unchanged from the beginning: The front door of that hilltop house always opened to the West.

Chapter 5

Pursuing Happiness

Among colonial assemblies in the years just before the American Revolution, Virginia's House of Burgesses, which first met in 1619, was both the most venerable and most formidable. Virginia was divided into fifty-seven counties, each of which sent two burgesses to Williamsburg (three separate boroughs and the College of William and Mary each sent one burgess), making the assembly one of the largest in the colonies. It was a big pond, and, in it, Jefferson may well have felt like a small fish. Unlike the bold and impulsive Patrick Henry, Jefferson, the new burgess from Albemarle County, rarely spoke in debate and almost never delivered a formal oration, even after he had matured as a legislator.

His first legislative session afforded Jefferson little opportunity to speak, in any case; it lasted a mere nine days. Jefferson rode into Williamsburg on April 6, 1769, accompanied by his favorite slave, Jupiter, and was sworn in on May 8. On May 16, the burgesses passed the Virginia Resolves. Not to be confused with Patrick Henry's Stamp Act Resolves of 1765 (which, unfortunately, are sometimes *also* called the Virginia Resolves), the Resolves of 1769 had been drafted by George Mason and were presented before the House of Burgesses by Mason's Potomac River neighbor, George Washington, a representative from Fairfax County. The 1769 Virginia Resolves restated the exclusive right of the governor and the legislature to tax the colony, the right to trial by jury, the right to communicate with other colonial legislatures, and the right to petition the king. Patrick Henry and Richard Henry Lee drafted a letter embodying the Resolves, which they transmitted to King George III.

On the very day the Resolves were enacted, Virginia's governor, Baron Botetourt, successor to Francis Fauquier, who had died in the spring of 1768, responded to what he deemed rogue legislation by summarily dissolving the assembly. Jefferson then joined his evicted fellow burgesses as they crowded into the Apollo Room of the Raleigh Tavern and promptly (and illegally) approved the Virginia Association, a boycott agreement banning importation of dutied British goods, slaves, and many luxury items from continental Europe. Ninety-four of 115 burgesses signed the Association, including twenty-six-year-old Jefferson, whose signature, number sixteen, was near the very top. By the end of 1769, every colonial legislature except New Hampshire's joined the boycott, which delivered a sharp blow to the British economy, reducing that nation's exports to the colonies by almost 40 percent.

While governor and burgesses were at odds and while colony protested to Crown, Virginia was swept by smallpox, one of the great scourges of the eighteenth century. Jefferson traveled all the way to Philadelphia to secure an inoculation, which was outlawed locally. Inoculation was, in fact, a frightening prospect. In 1796, the English country doctor Edward Jenner would introduce *vaccination*, a procedure by which a healthy person was purposely infected with cowpox, a disease of milk cows that is relatively harmless to human beings but which usually conferred immunity against smallpox. In 1769, however, *inoculation* meant deliberate infection with matter from the pustule of a person actually suffering from a mild case of smallpox. The idea was that the inoculated person would also develop a mild case of smallpox and thereby gain lifelong immunity. Usually it worked, but sometimes it was fatal. Understandably, the neighbors of the inoculated person commonly objected to having even a mildly infected individual in their midst.

As Jefferson saw it, the risks of inoculation, both to the individual and to his neighbors, were far outweighed by the benefits. When two Yorktown, Virginia, physicians, Archibald Campbell and John Dalgleish, became the targets of threats and even mob violence when they offered inoculation in Norfolk County,

Jefferson represented them in the General Court. He soon found himself pursuing civil suits on their behalf while defending civil suits as well as criminal actions brought against them. That Jefferson would depart from land law to take the physicians' cases speaks volumes about his view of public service. Inoculation was a controversial subject, fraught with grave risks, but Jefferson believed that it was in the public interest to promote and defend the practice, despite the risk not only of fatal infection but of the violence of the mob.

As it happened, in an age when legal proceedings moved even more slowly than they do today, the Revolution closed the courts before any of the issues involving Jefferson's clients were resolved. More immediately, Jefferson's law practice and political life were interrupted by another calamity. On February 1, 1770, while Jefferson was absent on business, fire destroyed Shadwell. A slave brought Jefferson the news, noting that no one had been hurt.

But had his books been saved? Jefferson asked.

"No, Master," came the answer, "all lost, but we save your fiddle."

Jefferson wrote to his friend John Page that he had lost "every paper I had in the world"—his copious legal records, the lifeblood of his law practice—"and almost every book." He estimated the cost of the books at £200 ($20,000 in modern money) and then concluded: "Would to God it had been the money; then had it never cost me a sigh!"

But sigh he did—and then, with characteristic resolve, set about painstakingly reconstructing his law notes. Furniture and other goods he hardly bothered to replace, but he began buying law books and other books at a breakneck pace.

The inoculation cases were hardly the only legal proceedings the Shadwell fire disrupted, and they were not the only cases of his to involve much more than an individual client's interests. Thomas Jefferson had been raised an Anglican Protestant and had served as a church vestryman, but his youthful reading among the works of the Enlightenment philosophers turned him increasingly away from traditional Christianity. Throughout his life, he would continue to attend church, at least irregularly, but the influence of rationalism, pervasive in advanced eighteenth-century thought, persuaded him that the traditional Christian images of God made little sense. Where Anglican priests and other clergymen preached the providential omnipresence of God in everyone, everything, and every action, Jefferson espoused deism. That is, he believed in God the Creator, but not in God the Puppeteer. Jefferson's deist God was like a watchmaker who creates the timepiece, endows it with life by winding it, and then allows it to keep time without any further intervention by him. For Jefferson, there was a God, but the deeds of humankind were the deeds of humankind, products of free will. Part of no providential, preordained universal plan, the deeds of men and women were answerable not in some world beyond this one, but in this one exclusively.

Deism was in vogue among the liberal intelligentsia of Jefferson's day. Founded on the rational philosophy of John Locke and the cosmology of Isaac Newton, deism held that the universe was "natural." Jefferson and other revolutionaries did not see this as incompatible with Christianity, provided one interpreted the "law of God" as the "law of nature" and penetrated to the uncorrupted core of Jesus's teachings. Jefferson's brand of deism, like John Adams's, was fairly mild, interested in persuading his fellow Americans that kings were not divine rulers, that God was not a judgmental being, and that human beings were free to modify the world around them to create a better existence for all.

"To the corruptions of Christianity," Jefferson wrote in an 1803 letter to the Philadelphia physician, philosopher, and revolutionary activist Dr. Benjamin Rush, "I am indeed opposed, but not to the genuine precepts of Jesus himself." Unfortunately, it was very difficult to separate the "genuine precepts" from their "corruptions." Jesus, Jefferson continued in his letter to Rush, "wrote nothing himself" and, in any case, was executed "at about thirty-three years of age, his reason having not yet attained the maximum of its energy, nor the course of his preaching, which was but of three years at most, presented occasions for developing a complete system of morals." Crucified before he had attained his full intellectual maturity and having written nothing himself, Jesus produced doctrines "defective as a whole," which was bad enough, but what "fragments he did deliver have come to us, mutilated, mis-stated and often unintelligible ... still more disfigured by the cor-ruptions of schismatizing followers, who have found an interest in sophisticating and perverting the simple doctrines he taught ...."

In short, Jefferson believed in God the Creator and in the teachings of Jesus, but he did not accept the traditional Christian religion, which put God before humanity and which twisted, tor-tured, and perverted the straightforward precepts of Christ. Little wonder, then, after the Shadwell fire, that he rushed to reconstruct not only the inoculation briefs, but the lost brief for another case as well, that of *Godwin v. Lunan*. If traditional religion was a man-ifest evil, Jefferson believed, how much worse was religion when it was made part and parcel of the state? The law of England, he held, was cursed by its connection with a state religion. Jefferson became increasingly determined to separate church and state in the laws of Virginia, and he saw *Godwin v. Lunan* as the wedge he might begin to drive between the two.

With his mentor, George Wythe, Jefferson appeared in General Court in October 1771 to represent the Anglican vestrymen and churchwardens (the parishioners who managed the day-to-day affairs of their church) of Nansemond County in their bid to remove a curate (or parish pastor) named Patrick Lunan. Lunan was a drunken adulterer who used profanity, publicly disavowed his faith, generally neglected his parish, and—to cap the list of his misdeeds—had indecently exposed himself to his congregation. The reasons for his removal, therefore, were many and quite clear, but he was nevertheless protected by the legal status of the Church of England. Neither Virginia clerics nor Virginia courts could remove him. Seeking to remedy this situation, Jefferson presented an argument by which a Virginia legal decision could take prece-dence over that of an English court. The argument Jefferson devel-oped, based on meticulous research into English ecclesiastical and common law, was intricate and subtle. At first glance, it may have also appeared narrow in its application—but, in the hindsight of history, it emerges as part of the legal foundation on which the American Revolution was raised.

Jefferson argued that the Crown itself had given parish vestries in colonies that lacked a bishop (as American colonies did) the right to nominate their own clergy without consulting the bishop of London. Because neither that bishop nor the king visited colonial parishes, the General Court, acting in its capacity as the king's chancellor, had the duty and the right to exercise the prerogative of the king.

In its immediate application to *Godwin v. Lunan*, this meant that the vestrymen could appeal to the General Court to remove Lunan and that the General Court had the requisite authority to remove him. And this was precisely what the General Court decided; Jefferson, Wythe, and their clients won the day. But the implications of the decision went far beyond removal of a single obnoxious cleric. For the first time in colonial history, a colonial court had upheld its own jurisdiction above that of the state-sanctioned Church of England. This represented both a movement toward the separation of church and state and, equally important, a movement toward colonial independence.

The defense of inoculation had been a step toward securing for the people of Virginia the benefits of Enlightenment science. The victory in *Godwin v. Lunan* was a step toward securing for them freedom of religion as well as political liberty. Together, these were strides taken in what Jefferson, in his great Declaration of 1776, would call the "pursuit of happiness."

That phrase, as many historians and political philosophers since 1776 have pointed out, is significant, curious, perhaps even ambiguous. Jefferson numbered the pursuit of happiness among humanity's three "inalienable rights." The first two, life and liberty, were borrowed from one of Jefferson's favorite philosophers, John Locke. But whereas Locke identified the third inalienable right as "property," Jefferson substituted "pursuit of happiness." Some historians have argued that, in Jefferson's day, *happiness* connoted little more than material prosperity, a concept not very different from Locke's "property." But the fact is that the word also held its modern meaning: not just material prosperity, but general contentment, satisfaction, well-being, fulfillment. Jefferson argued legal cases directed in part toward achieving the goal of happiness in this sense—collective, social happiness—but he had also begun to think about his own personal happiness. The Shadwell fire had spurred him to speed the building of Monticello, which he envisioned as a site and a place most decidedly conducive to his happiness.

Monticello, Italian for "little mountain," was the name Jefferson himself gave to the summit of the hill that he cleared and leveled in 1768 to make way for his home. The name would be extended to the mansion, which, in late 1770, was as yet nothing more than a one-room brick cottage that Jefferson occupied while the rest of the structure was built. By the time the Revolution came, Monticello looked pretty much as it does now, a graceful, neoclassical, two-story pavilion flanked by wings, even though the process of fashioning its every detail would happily occupy Jefferson throughout his life.

For Jefferson, Monticello was the center of an ideal universe, a place where he could raise a family and live by the quiet cultivation of the earth. Embodying in brick and mortar the sweet reason of Enlightenment ideals, it graced rather than defiled the natural world in which it was set. The seat of an agrarian lifestyle, it embodied a constructive, respectful, even loving stewardship of the earth. What could be more perfect?

If Jefferson asked himself this question, he did not have to look far to begin to answer it. For, as an idyll of happiness, Monticello, in all its magnificence, was fatally flawed. Like practically everything else in Virginia, it was in large part the work of slaves. Jefferson had thought about forgoing slave labor in the construction of his house, but, in the end, he made use of it. Once Monticello became the center of a working plantation, Jefferson also ran that all-too-rarely profitable agricultural operation with more than one hundred slaves. Yet, like a few of his Virginia contemporaries and in sharp contrast to more of them, he was never complacently comfortable with slavery.

This photograph of the Jefferson statue in the U.S. Capitol was made during the Civil War by Mathew Brady or an assistant.

(Collection: National Archives and Records Administration)

To be sure, by modern standards, Thomas Jefferson was a racist. He believed that blacks were inferior to whites in everything except their natural "musical superiority." He wrote that blacks were "as far inferior to the rest of mankind as the mule is to the horse, and as made to carry burthens." He presented this not as a moral argument for slavery, but as what he believed was a statement of scientific fact. An avid student of "natural philosophy," Jefferson had read descriptions of a newly discovered species of simian, the orangutan, and, in a twisted anticipation of Darwin's evolutionary theory, he conjectured that blacks might be more closely related to the orangutan than to the white race.

Like many other Southerners, Jefferson feared that the combination of the slaves' vast numbers and the inevitable discontent created by involuntary servitude created the ever-present danger of uprising and revolt. "We have the wolf by the ears," he wrote, "and we can neither hold him, nor safely let him go." Beyond this fear, however, and despite his racism as well as the fact that he owned slaves himself, Jefferson believed slavery to be a moral and social evil. It was fundamentally wrong to hold another in bondage. If slavery was inherently cruel to the slave, it was also debilitating to the slave owner, fostering a culture of cruelty, brutality, tyranny, and sloth. Jefferson believed—certainly he hoped—that slavery would gradually diminish, fade, and disappear of its own accord. When? Someday.

Even if Jefferson had wanted to emancipate his slaves immediately, Virginia law would not have let him do so, at least not easily. If a Virginia slave owner wanted to free a slave, he had to prove in court a basis of "meritorious service" on the part of the slave. Early in his career as a Virginia burgess, Jefferson drew up a bill to give Virginians the same right enjoyed by Georgians and North Carolinians: to free a slave at will. Because he was a junior member of the House of Burgesses, Jefferson gave the bill to a more senior legislator, his kinsman Richard Bland, to present. Bland did so, Jefferson seconded it, and the burgesses, as a body, responded by raucously shouting the pair down. As Jefferson later recalled, poor Bland "was denounced as an enemy of his country."

Having failed in the House of Burgesses to make a dent in slavery, Jefferson soon after took on a *pro bono* legal case on behalf of a slave suing to gain his freedom. His client was Samuel Howell, whose great-grandmother had been a white indentured servant who had had a daughter by a black slave. Howell was the grandson of this woman of mixed race. The case came to trial in April 1770, and it pitted Jefferson against his revered mentor, George Wythe.

Arguing before the court, Jefferson attempted to circumvent a 1705 Virginia law holding that "if any woman servant shall have a bastard child by a negro or mulatto, or if a free Christian white woman shall have such bastard child by a negro or mulatto ... the churchwardens shall bind the said child to be a servant until it shall be of thirty-one years of age." Jefferson argued to the court that a 1723 revision of the 1705 law did not apply to the grandchild of a female mulatto slave—a dubious argument at best, which he sought to bolster on high moral grounds:

> *Under the law of nature, all men are born free. Everyone comes into the world with a right to his own person, which includes the liberty of moving and using it at his own will. This is what is called personal liberty .... The reducing of the mother to servitude was a violation of the law of nature. Surely then the same law cannot prescribe a continuance of the violation to her issue, and that too without end ....*

Jefferson then attempted to tie up the loose ends of his argument: "The act of 1705 makes servants of the first mulatto; that of 1723, extends it to her children, but that it remains for some future legislature, if any shall be found wicked enough, to extend it to the grandchildren and other issue more remote ...."

At this juncture, Lord Botetourt, presiding over the General Court, gaveled the young attorney into silence. He then swiftly handed down his finding for the defendant, Wythe's client, the slaveholder, and against Howell. The slave would remain a slave.

Jefferson had lost, but he had spoken. Publicly and in open court, he had uttered the words that would soon enough echo in the Declaration of Independence: "Under the law of nature, all men are born free."

Issues of liberty and the pursuit of happiness increasingly occupied Thomas Jefferson during the years between the Stamp Act and the Revolution. But, settled now in his one-room Monticello, the twenty-six-year-old must have begun to realize that independence and the pursuit of happiness were not necessarily one hundred percent compatible—at least, not in one's personal life.

Back in his William and Mary days, Jefferson had been acquainted with a fellow student, Bathurst Skelton. While Jefferson left college to pursue the life of a bachelor law apprentice, Skelton married the beautiful and accomplished Martha Wayles. Tallish and slight—"exquisitely formed," according to one contemporary—she was possessed of large hazel eyes and a luxurious abundance of auburn hair. An avid reader, a skilled harpsichordist, and a sweet singer, she also loved to dance and ride. The daughter of a wealthy landowner, she made a fine bride, wife, and mother. But early in 1770, she found herself a widow; Skelton had died young.

Jefferson was smitten by the twenty-three-year-old widow. Through his friends, Robert Skipwith and his wife Tibby, who was Martha's sister, he arranged for Martha to visit Monticello. Knowing that she loved books, he showed her his library, newly and abundantly stocked after the Shadwell fire, and he playfully referred to his mountaintop home as the "new Olympus." Knowing, too, that she loved to walk and to ride, he walked and rode with her.

Over the next two years, Jefferson was a frequent visitor to The Forest, the estate of Martha's father, John Wayles. No different from most fathers of marriageable daughters, Wayles found fault in Jefferson—namely, that he lacked sufficient wealth—so he apparently encouraged the attention of other suitors for his daughter's hand. Jefferson, who had once been too shy to talk with a girl, now resolutely conceded nothing. Biographer Willard Sterne Randall relates a piece of Wayles family lore, which tells of the simultaneous arrival at The Forest, on an autumn day in 1771, of two other suitors for Martha's hand. The pair were shown into an antechamber to await Martha. As they waited, they listened to the music drifting in from the parlor. "They had no question who was playing the harpsichord, and they quickly guessed who was playing the violin. And when they heard Jefferson and his Martha singing together, stanza after stanza, they saw no point in staying."

Thomas Jefferson and Martha Wayles Skelton were married on New Year's Day 1772. If John Wayles still harbored any doubts about his son-in-law, they were decidedly not in evidence during the days of feasting and merrymaking that followed the ceremony

51

at The Forest. The newlyweds did not leave for Monticello until January 18. After stopping for a time at Tuckahoe, the Randolph plantation where Jefferson had spent seven years of his boyhood, they made their way through a blinding blizzard, first to Blenheim, a plantation belonging to the Carter family, and then on to Monticello.

It was night when they reached the one-room house atop what was now a windswept, snow-whipped mountain. Martha had temporarily left her three-year-old son with her parents. Since youth, Jefferson had made it a habit to jot a note of each expenditure in a little account book he carried in his pocket. For the next nineteen days, he made not a single mark in that book.

Chapter 6

The Hand of Force

Ensconced in a one-room cottage atop a little mountain, in the arms of his bride, Thomas Jefferson had found happiness. Holding on to it was another matter. In the Declaration of Independence, Jefferson would enumerate not a right to happiness, but to the *pursuit* of happiness, as if to acknowledge that no government could guarantee happiness in this life and that happiness, in any case, is always fleeting. Though an agent of revolution, Jefferson frequently wrote of his longing to huddle peacefully on his mountaintop, away from the turbulent stream of events swirling about him. But even if he had been able to remove himself from history, the newlywed husband would have discovered that happiness may be beautiful as a butterfly's wing, but also as fragile.

On September 27, 1772, a daughter was born to Thomas and Martha. She was a month premature. Doubtless with a mixture of anxiety, hope, and love in his heart, Jefferson insisted on naming her after her mother. Little Martha—whom the Jeffersons took to calling Patsy—clung to life through six months of illness and then stunned and delighted everyone by not only surviving but thriving. Her mother, the Martha familiarly called Patty, was not so fortunate. A glowing, lively young woman when Jefferson married her, she barely survived the pregnancy and remained ill for so long after Patsy's birth that Jefferson decided to forgo both the spring 1772 term of the General Court and the session of the House of Burgesses to remain by her side as a worried, faithful, and tireless nurse.

With his wife's illness heavy on his mind, Jefferson sought to divert himself by attending to the ongoing construction of Monticello and by running his plantation. But there was little solace in these activities. The costs of Monticello mounted, and the heavy snow that had ushered him and his bride across his home's threshold turned out to be part of a winter of unusually heavy snows. With spring, floods came, washing away Jefferson's mill alongside the Rivanna. Without a mill, he could not do his own grinding, and he had to shell out for transportation to another plantation owner's mill. This was an unexpected drain on his cash, and, on the eve of the Revolution, cash was in short supply everywhere. According to his account books, Jefferson should have been making a handsome living from his legal practice, but, in a cash-poor economy, he was able to collect only a fraction of the fees due him.

Like many other cash-strapped Americans, Jefferson was learning to resent the economic stranglehold in which the mother country held its colonies. With increased autonomy and local financial regulation of the local economy, Jefferson—and many others—believed, the American lot in life would be far easier and far more prosperous.

Jefferson had a strongly developed ability to see beyond the personal boundaries of whatever problems confronted him. He saw his growing financial crisis less as his individual burden than as a function of an unjust government. Likewise, when he took on a new and very interesting law case, he saw his client's problem in the context of his nation's current situation. For a newlywed, perhaps, it was an odd case to take on, but it involved a good friend of Jefferson's and the friend's brother. It was a case of divorce.

Jefferson took the case on November 25, 1772. In the spring of the year before, Dr. James Blair, a prominent Virginian who had twice served as acting governor of the colony, married Kitty Eustace. The union lasted a matter of months. Kitty moved with her mother just down the street from Dr. Blair and promptly sued for separate maintenance, in essence asking for half his estate. The suspicion was strong—and certainly Blair claimed that it was true—that Kitty Eustace was nothing more than a gold digger.

But how could he defend himself against her? She was asking for separate maintenance, not divorce, which was not even an option in Virginia; the colony was compelled to follow English divorce law, and the law of England permitted divorce only by special act of Parliament. If Blair *could* obtain a divorce somehow, he could probably do so on grounds that would keep his estate intact.

Grounds were not difficult to find. In the first place, it seemed that an obscure illness—"a violent nervous disorder that affects … every part of his body"—had rendered Blair impotent. He had never consummated the marriage. Second, it was widely rumored that Kitty Eustace had had an adulterous affair with none other than the Earl of Dunmore, the new royal governor of Virginia. Dr. Blair wrote a letter to Dunmore, accusing him of the liaison, to which Dunmore responded by confronting Dr. Blair's brother, John Blair, Jefferson's friend from William and Mary days. John Blair served as clerk of the Governor's Council, and Dunmore put it to him this way: Either get his brother to retract the charge of adultery or resign from the clerkship. In the interests of his brother's career, Dr. Blair withdrew the charge.

But grounds, ample or not, meant nothing in the absence of an independent divorce law for the colony of Virginia. Jefferson's answer to his client's need was to research the subject of divorce law for a full month. His immediate object was to craft a bill to be introduced before the House of Burgesses, specifically to obtain a legislative divorce for his client. This immediate object, however, had far-reaching implications. After all, *any* divorce bill, even one ostensibly legislated for an individual case, would be colonial law not only independent of English law, but, in fact, contrary to it. Thus Jefferson's research went into the very nature of the relationship between the laws of the mother country and those of its colonies. In looking for a solution to the marital dilemma of Dr. James Blair, Jefferson would have to lay a legal foundation for self-rule in Virginia—the very stuff of revolution.

Jefferson wanted to base his argument not in a moral appeal to right, but in a strictly legal appeal to the law. Jefferson's research revealed that, in the century and a half since its founding, Virginia had never granted a divorce. Even more surprisingly, it revealed that the first time Parliament had granted an absolute divorce by special legislative act was as recently as 1669. Jefferson argued that English laws enacted in England *after* America was colonized could not be applied to the colonies. As he saw it, the cutoff was 1607, the year in which Jamestown, the first permanent English colony in America, was founded. Laws enacted before 1607 applied to the mother country and colonies alike, but after that date, colonial law had to be regarded as separate from English law. Clearly, Parliamentary legislation enacted in 1669 missed the cutoff year; therefore, Jefferson concluded, Parliament had no authority over Virginia divorce. Without Parliamentary authority, however, Jefferson did not propose a radical new Virginia law of divorce. He took what seemed a more moderate course, proposing that the House of Burgesses follow Parliament's example in granting this particular divorce by special act. But the point was less in the fact of emulation than in the assertion of Virginia's legal independence from England.

In later years, Jefferson ranked the Blair divorce case as one of the most important of his legal career. This was because of its ramifications for colonial independence, not for its impact on the fortunes of James Blair. The good doctor died on December 26, 1772, before any bill was introduced in the House of Burgesses. After Blair's death, Kitty Eustace sued the Blair family for what she deemed her share of the estate. Thanks to the efforts of *her* lawyer, none other than Patrick Henry, she prevailed. Jefferson noted that Henry's victory had been due to his eloquence, an ability to say "the strongest things in the finest language," not to the logic of his argument, which, as Jefferson saw it, was totally absent.

Whatever Jefferson thought of Patrick Henry's skills and deficiencies as an attorney, it was with Henry and other radicals that he cast his political lot. Like Henry, he was increasingly concerned that Virginians were becoming complacent, losing their revolutionary edge. To overcome this, Jefferson and the other radical burgesses decided to introduce a set of resolutions protesting all Parliamentary actions that deprived Virginians "of their ancient legal and constitutional rights." Even more important, they resolved to create a "committee of correspondence and inquiry" to keep tabs on Parliament and to communicate with the other colonies. Jefferson composed the resolutions, and his friend and brother-in-law Dabney Carr presented them on March 12, 1773. They passed unanimously, right under the nose of Governor Dunmore.

Thus Jefferson spearheaded the legal creation of the first colony-wide revolutionary body in America. Furthermore, he had forged the first strong links of intercolonial cooperation. This was a significant step in transforming disparate colonies into one nation. Almost immediately, eleven of the other twelve colonies—with the exception of Pennsylvania—set up committees of correspondence on the Virginia model. Not only had the seeds of nationhood been planted, but a key condition for a successful revolution was established. This would become instantly apparent on April 19, 1775, when armed rebellion broke out in the battles of Lexington and Concord. Swift communication via the committees of correspondence transformed a local altercation into a truly national revolution, amplifying the musket fire in Massachusetts into what Emerson would later call "the shot heard 'round the world."

Jefferson returned to Monticello, pleased with what he had helped to start and even more delighted to be home again with Patty and Patsy and to be working in his garden, always a great personal pleasure. It was spring, and he was happy—until a thunderbolt struck on a May day in 1773: Dabney Carr, friend of his youth, husband of his sister Martha, had died at twenty-nine from a sudden and unspecified illness. Jefferson buried his friend at Monticello, beneath a headstone for which he composed the inscription:

> To his virtue, good sense, learning and friendship this
> stone is dedicated by Thomas Jefferson who, of all men
> living, loved him most.

Jefferson also provided for the widow and her children, bringing them to live at Monticello, now grown into a partly finished mansion of respectable dimensions. Jefferson virtually adopted Carr's seven-year-old son, Peter, resolving to provide for the boy's education.

Two weeks after Carr died, Jefferson found himself with yet another responsibility. Patty's father, John Wayles, died at age fifty-eight. Cash-poor, like most Virginians, he was nevertheless land-rich, and left his daughter eleven hundred acres of The Forest, together with many of The Forest's 405 slaves. Thomas Jefferson, who had unsuccessfully introduced legislation to bring about the beginning of an end to slavery, was now responsible for managing one of the largest slave-worked agricultural enterprises in Virginia.

Among the 135 slaves who came to Monticello was the family of Betty Hemings, which included, among others, Martin, who became the Jeffersons' butler, and James, who became Jefferson's body servant. In 1775, Betty herself came to Monticello, where Jefferson gave her her own cabin. She brought with her a beautiful toddler named Sally. Like James, Sally was probably the child of John Wayles, who frequently lay with Betty. This is not a certainty, though; according to Madison Hemings, one of Betty Hemings's grandchildren, she had seven children by white men and seven by black men. Certainly, not all historians agree that Sally Hemings was the half-sister of Thomas Jefferson's wife, but it *is* possible. It is also true that, for many years, most historians declined to believe that Jefferson had fathered at least one child by Sally Hemings, who grew into a beautiful young woman. However, as we will see in Chapter 14, "The Lover," DNA studies in 1998 forced a majority of scholars to change their minds.

Jefferson's attitudes about slavery were complex, and whatever moral qualms his wife's inheritance may have caused him, he was now a wealthy man—at least, wealthy in the paradoxical way of most large Virginia landowners. In slaves and land, he was enviably rich. In cash, his want was considerable and could even be heart-breaking.

One of Jefferson's sisters, Elizabeth, was mentally retarded. When she turned twenty-one, Jefferson assumed the care of her, but he could hardly watch her every minute. On February 21 and 22, 1774, a number of freak earthquakes shook Monticello and its outbuildings. Terrified, Elizabeth ran outdoors and, apparently confused, wandered off into the frigid mountain winter. She was not found until two days later, and she died soon afterward, presumably from the effects of exposure. Lacking the ready cash for a funeral, Jefferson sold two bookcases to raise the reverend's honorarium.

Three weeks after his sister's funeral, a second daughter was born to the Jeffersons. They called her Jane, after Jefferson's mother. Seventeen months later, with the United States recently embarked on revolution, the Jeffersons buried the infant.

The tide of revolution took no heed of Jefferson's personal pains and personal losses. Most Virginians, however, did not rush headlong into that revolutionary tide. One of Jefferson's fellow radicals, Richard Henry Lee, attempted to push the House of Burgesses closer to rebellion when, in May 1774, he chaired a committee that recommended not renewing the "fee bill," the legislation necessary to fund the activities of Virginia's royal officials. Refusing to renew the bill was partly a gesture of protest, but it was also intended to have the practical and immediate consequence of closing the courts, thereby preventing British creditors from collecting debts and foreclosing on collateral properties. This would bring welcome relief to strapped colonists and pressure the Crown to yield to certain colonial demands. On May 11, however, the House of Burgesses at large overruled Lee and his committee, directing that the fee bill be duly drafted.

Once again, the Virginia assembly had failed to follow through on a decisive step toward revolutionary protest. But something happened to shake even the dullest burgesses from their lethargy. The Sons of Liberty had just tossed a cargo of 342 chests of British tea into Boston Harbor.

Although by 1773 the Crown had yielded to colonial protest by repealing most of the odious taxes on import commodities, George III stubbornly retained a tax on tea because, he declared, "there must always be one tax" to preserve Parliament's right to tax the colonies. In principle, this was vexing enough to the colonies, but, in practice, the tax was easily evaded. Colonial consumers simply bought smuggled tea from Dutch rather than English sources. If anything, then, the tea tax was harder on the financially ailing British East India Company than on the colonials. Indeed, if the company didn't soon ship to America some of the seventeen million pounds of Indian tea lying in its London warehouses, the whole lot would go rotten at a great loss to the firm.

How could the colonists be compelled to buy East India Company tea instead of the smuggled Dutch stuff? The company appealed to the prime minister, and Lord North proposed a swift expedient. The East India Company paid two taxes, one when it landed tea in Britain, whether for sale or shipment elsewhere, and another when it landed a shipment in America. By means of the Tea Act (May 10, 1773), Lord North forgave the first tax and retained the lesser three-penny-a-pound duty due on landing in America. This allowed the East India Company to price its tea below the price of the smuggled tea. Revolutionary principle was one thing, Lord North believed, but the cash-hungry colonists would surely sacrifice principle for all the cheap tea they could drink.

But Lord North had miscalculated. Instead of enticing American consumers, the Tea Act actually drove hitherto moderate American merchants into the radical camp. The Tea Act had set up a cozy arrangement whereby East India Company tea would be wholesaled not to colonial merchants, but exclusively to royally designated consignees in the ports of New York, Charleston, Philadelphia, and Boston. That is, the American merchants were entirely cut out of the profit loop, and they were not about to stand still for it. They supported colonial activists, who intimidated into resignation the royal consignees in Philadelphia, New York, and Charleston. American captains and harbor pilots refused to handle the East India Company cargo, and the tea ships were turned back to London from Philadelphia and New York. A ship was permitted to land in Charleston, but the tea was impounded in a warehouse, where it lay unsold until the Revolutionary government auctioned it off in 1776.

In Boston, three tea ships landed and were prevented by the Sons of Liberty from being unloaded. Because the Massachusetts royal governor, Thomas Hutchinson, refused to issue permits to allow the ships to leave the harbor and return to London, a standoff developed. The tea could not be unloaded, but the ships could not return to London. At a December 16, 1773, meeting of the Sons of Liberty, Sam Adams and other leaders sent Captain Francis

Rotch to appeal to Hutchinson to grant the permit. While waiting for Rotch to return with the governor's reply, a crowd of some seven thousand gathered at Boston's Old South Church. At 6:00, Rotch returned with the news that the ships would not be permitted to leave unless the tea was unloaded.

"This meeting can do nothing more to save the country," Adams declared from the Old South's pulpit.

With that, an ungodly imitation of a Mohawk war cry was raised outside, and three troops of colonists, fifty men to a troop, with their faces painted Mohawk fashion, raced to Griffin's Wharf. They climbed into boats, rowed out to the three tea ships, boarded them, and quickly jettisoned ninety thousand dollars' worth of tea into the harbor.

The Boston Tea Party electrified the colonies, but the Crown's response to the event did the most to galvanize them into unified action. Despite the protests and counsel of a number of liberal voices in Parliament, a series of Coercive Acts—dubbed the Intolerable Acts by colonial activists—was immediately passed. These closed the port of Boston and greatly curtailed Massachusetts colonial government, such that most local officials would now be appointed by the royal governor. Additionally, town meetings, the heart of representative self-government, were restricted to a single meeting annually; the jurisdiction of Massachusetts courts was greatly abridged, and the Quartering Act, passed earlier, was extended, authorizing the permanent quartering of British troops in Boston.

In April 1774, the king dispatched to Boston a hardliner, Gen. Thomas Gage, to serve as royal governor of Massachusetts and commander in chief of all British forces in America. The Americans, he had told the king, "will be lions while we are lambs, but if we take the resolute part they will undoubtedly be very meek." On his arrival in Boston on May 17, Gage was greeted by the sound of church bells incessantly tolling as if for the dead.

On May 19, 1774, the *Virginia Gazette* printed "An Epitome [Summary] of the Boston Bill," which prompted the radical burgesses, Jefferson among them, to meet in secret on May 23. They agreed to draft a resolution—Jefferson was almost certainly its author—calling for a "Day of fasting, humiliation and prayer" on June 1, the day Thomas Gage would implement the Port Act, shutting down Boston not only to overseas traffic but to seaborne shipments from other colonies as well. The language of the resolution was calculated to inflame. It spoke of a "hostile invasion" of Boston, calling Massachusetts "our sister colony" and appealing to all colonists everywhere to act with "one heart and one mind firmly to oppose, by all just and proper means, every injury to American rights."

Sister colony? *American* rights? These were radical concepts. Traditionally, Britain's North American colonists thought of themselves as New Yorkers, South Carolinians, Virginians, and so on, but certainly not as Americans. If anything, the colonies were ruthless competitors for territory as well as trade. In contrast, the present resolution identified them as constituents of a nation, and this disturbing definition was not lost on Governor Dunmore. He responded to the resolution, which was passed over a single dissenting vote, by dissolving the assembly.

On May 24, about one hundred burgesses met in the Raleigh Tavern's Apollo Room (the Capitol was closed to them), where, after vigorous and even violent debate, they decided to call on the other colonies to form a "continental congress," not just to confer on the crisis created by the Port Act, but as a permanent body of colonial government.

In the meantime, Governor Dunmore himself fanned the kindling flame of revolution. He provoked warfare with the Shawnee over expansion of Virginia's western settlement, and he illegally called up the militia to fight the Indians in what was soon dubbed Lord Dunmore's War. This added local insult to the royal injury that had been inflicted up north on Massachusetts. Even moderate burgesses now joined the radicals in forming Committees of Safety—revolutionary militias—and in enforcing a boycott on British trade as well as a boycott to keep the courts closed. They also voted to send a Virginia delegation to the Continental Congress, which would convene on September 5, 1774, at Carpenter's Hall, Philadelphia, with fifty-six delegates representing twelve of the thirteen colonies.

In July, Jefferson was called upon to draft instructions for the Virginia delegation. At breakneck speed, he produced *A Summary View of the Rights of British America, Set Forth in Some Resolutions Intended for the Inspection of the Present Delegates of the People of Virginia*. Although it was explicitly directed to the Virginia delegates, Jefferson hoped and expected that it would be read by members of the British government, including King George III, and that it might appeal to the more rational and liberal members of Parliament. The manuscript was printed as a pamphlet in Williamsburg, reprinted in Philadelphia, and, from there, distributed all over the colonies. This was not only the first widely read justification of united American opposition to British rule, but it also defined that opposition firmly and specifically as a stand against arbitrary government. In this respect, *A Summary View* was a dramatic prelude to the even more momentous Declaration of Independence.

In prose driven by passion and energized by the rush of events, Jefferson asserted the "natural rights" of the colonies over the prerogatives arbitrarily "usurped" by the British state. Inasmuch as the cause of American liberty was the cause of "natural rights," it was intrinsically just ("self-evident," Jefferson would later write in the Declaration) and, therefore, morally stronger than any right or authority asserted by the mother country. Jefferson looked back toward the early history of England for justification of the present struggle. He argued—eloquently, if dubiously—that the colonials' true ancestors were the Saxons, who had been oppressed since the eleventh century by the tyranny of the Norman invaders. In the Declaration of Independence, Jefferson would far more convincingly put the American struggle for freedom in an international context both historical and timeless; in the present document, he argued less solidly that America's grievances did not begin with the Stamp Act of 1765 but were as old and as universal as the opposition of liberty and tyranny. The present crisis was a trans-Atlantic reincarnation of a struggle fought (and lost) in England back in 1066.

King George III, in a 1778 mezzotint after the painting by
Benjamin West.

Jefferson was on firmer ground in arguing that the past and continuing settlement of North America was and remained an
American rather than a British enterprise: "For themselves
[the colonists] conquered, and for themselves alone they have the
right to hold." To the argument that the mother country financed
this settlement and, therefore, could justly claim rights of sovereignty, Jefferson responded that the support had been rendered as

a business investment, in expectation of reaping profit from America's natural resources and from America's commercial potential. At various times, England had invested similarly in other nations, "states [that] never supposed that, by calling in her aid, they thereby submitted themselves to her sovereignty."

Jefferson offered specific economic justification for greater colonial autonomy, arguing that royal limitations on colonial trade retarded and crippled the colonial economy, and that Britain's refusal to allow the colonies to industrialize doomed them to remain economic and cultural backwaters, perpetual victims of subjugation. Such restrictions violated the *natural* rights of the colonies: "The God who gave us life gave us liberty at the same time; the hand of force may destroy, but cannot disjoin them." But while Jefferson thus provided a rationale for independence, he stopped short of calling for an outright break with the British Empire. The thrust of *A Summary View* is, after all, the "rights of *British* America." At this point, Jefferson, like all but the most radical colonists, hoped that King George himself could be induced to mediate between the liberty-starved colonies—desiring only their ancient rights as Englishmen—and a Parliament apparently bent on tyranny.

"Sire," Jefferson addressed the king directly, "this is our last, our determined resolution ... that you will be pleased to interpose ... to procure redress of these our great grievances ... [and] to establish fraternal love and harmony thro' the whole empire ...." Yet Jefferson also warned that Americans were "willing ... to sacrifice every thing which reason can ask to the restoration of that tranquility for which all must wish." That is, he concluded, if the king failed to demonstrate goodwill, and if Parliament refused to yield peacefully, the road to American "tranquility" would surely lead to the violence of an American revolution.

Chapter 7

Declaration

Having completed *A Summary View of the Rights of British America* to instruct Virginia's delegates to the First Continental Congress, Thomas Jefferson was seized with severe intestinal trouble and was too sick to serve as a delegate himself. Instrumental in creating revolution, he nevertheless fared poorly in times of stress. Digestive problems and migraine headaches dogged him throughout his life. Perhaps these lapses in health served in crises to make him even more introspective than usual.

Yet, even without Jefferson's presence in Philadelphia, his *Summary View* helped to propel the Continental Congress to make some bold decisions. Congress endorsed the *Suffolk Resolves*, a radical document adopted by a convention held in Suffolk County, Massachusetts, and rushed to Philadelphia by Paul Revere. The *Suffolk Resolves* condemned the Intolerable Acts as unconstitutional, urged Massachusetts to form an independent government and to withhold taxes from the Crown until the acts were repealed, advised citizens to arm themselves, and recommended a general boycott of English goods. In addition to endorsing the *Resolves*, the Congress declared thirteen acts of Parliament passed since 1763 to be unconstitutional. Each delegate pledged his colony's support of economic sanctions against Britain until all the acts were repealed. Finally, in a set of ten resolutions of its own, the Congress enumerated the rights of colonists, prepared addresses of protest to the king, and then concluded the session by creating the Continental Association, a prelude to a formal, permanent union. By a single vote, the delegates defeated "Galloway's Plan of Union," which proposed that the colonies remain loyal to the Crown, provided that they were granted dominion status.

> In "Galloway's Plan of Union," Philadelphia lawyer Joseph Galloway called for governance of all the colonies by a royally appointed president-general, who would enjoy veto power over acts of a Grand Council elected by the colonies. Colonial government would have broad authority in civil, commercial, and criminal affairs and would have veto power over Parliamentary legislation affecting the colonies. Had the delegates adopted this plan—and had Crown and Parliament approved it (which was doubtful)—revolution would have been avoided, or at least postponed.

Far from the tumult in Philadelphia, Jefferson recovered his health while he pushed forward construction of Monticello. In consultation with a new neighbor and friend, a Tuscan immigrant named Philip Mazzei, he began to plan what would become the first large-scale vineyard in North America.

For all his radical boldness, Jefferson, like the delegates to the Continental Congress, was shocked and chagrined by the continuous stream of belligerent denial and resistance issuing from the king and Parliament. A man of reason, he found it difficult to believe that George III and the British legislators refused to heed reason. With the colonies clearly moving toward revolution and farther from reconciliation, Jefferson set off for Richmond, where, on March 20, 1775, he served as one of 125 delegates to the Second Virginia Convention.

The moderates and radicals were more polarized than ever. Moderates urged what they called "nonresistance"—really, nonviolent resistance—to British measures, primarily through the continuation of boycotts. Radicals endorsed a Maryland proposal immediately to raise a "well regulated militia" for colonial "defense" against British incursions. The moderates—as well as the likes of George Washington, who leaned toward the radical view—pointed out that merely labeling the creation of a colony-wide militia a defensive measure would not disguise the fact that it was a highly provocative move toward armed insurrection. As usual,

Patrick Henry raised the temperature of the meeting with oratory both brilliant and bellicose. He reduced the question facing the delegates to a stark choice between the path of continued slavery and the path of liberty:

> There is no retreat but in submission and slavery. Our chains are forged. Their clanking may be heard on the plains of Boston. The war is inevitable. And let it come! I repeat it, sir, let it come!
>
> It is in vain, sir, to extenuate the matter. Gentlemen may cry, peace, peace—but there is no peace. The war is actually begun! The next gale that sweeps from the north will bring to our ears the clash of resounding arms! Our brethren are already in the field! Why stand we idle here? Is life so dear, or peace so sweet, as to be purchased at the price of chains and slavery? Forbid it, Almighty God!

Now Henry pantomimed the tearing asunder of imaginary manacles and continued: "I know not what course others may take"—he brandished an imaginary dagger—"but as for me, give me liberty or give me death!" And with that, he thrust the air-drawn dagger into his chest.

Henry's speech instantly radicalized a majority of the convention. It was a speech that Jefferson could not and would not have made—for he distrusted such melodramatic oratory as unreasoned demagoguery—but he endorsed its message, urging the convention to call for armed preparedness. The radical majority was slim, voting sixty-five to sixty to create a militia. While Henry was put in overall charge of defense, Jefferson, a most unmilitary man, found himself a key member of a twelve-man committee charged with actually planning the details of the colony's defense.

More congenial to Jefferson's talents was a simultaneous assignment to draft a response to the latest British outrage, the royal governor's proclamation ordering the immediate cash sale at auction of all vacant lands as well as lands with "imperfect patents" (lands claimed but as yet unoccupied or unimproved by the claimants). Put into force, this proclamation would have cut off the western expansion of most of the great cash-poor landholders of Virginia—Jefferson and Washington among them. Such issues on the eve of revolution demonstrate that, for the leaders of the rebellion, revolt was not just about upholding the noble principles of liberty and independence. It was also very much about preserving personal prosperity. The founding fathers were willing to take great personal risks and make great personal sacrifices to serve a noble and lofty cause, but at least some of their motives were selfish or, at least, frankly self-interested. In the present case, Jefferson advised a universal boycott on purchasing lands or accepting further land grants.

With his work at the Second Virginia Convention finished, Jefferson returned to Monticello to plant a crop of peas and to attend to a horse-breeding operation that he had just begun. During this period, the news reached Virginia that British troops had marched out of their Boston barracks to seize a cache of arms and ammunition stored at Concord, Massachusetts. A force of colonial militia—citizen soldiers calling themselves "minutemen" because they pledged instant preparedness to fight—battled the British at Lexington and then at Concord on April 19. Seventy-three redcoats were confirmed dead as a result of the battles, twenty-six went missing and were presumed dead, and 174 had been wounded. Among the minutemen, forty-nine had died, five were reported missing, and forty-one lay wounded. Patrick Henry had been right: The war was actually begun.

Jefferson's most anxious desire was, doubtless, to enjoy the pleasures of Monticello, to plant his peas, to raise his horses, and to plot out his vineyards. The violence at Lexington and Concord was abhorrent to him, but he now had no doubt who was to blame for it. The murderer was King George III. Accustomed to arguing arcane points of law, precedent, and principle, Jefferson now suddenly and sharply shifted his focus onto personality. Neither the laws of England nor the actions of Parliament had killed the redcoats and patriots in Massachusetts; as he wrote in a letter to his early mentor William Small, the king was to blame because, "instead of leading to a reconciliation of his divided people," he had chosen to "pursue the incendiary purpose of still blowing up the flames [with his] every speech and public declaration." For Jefferson, the lines of battle were becoming increasingly clear, personal, and emotional.

Virginia's royal governor, Lord Dunmore, issued orders forbidding Virginia to send delegates to the Second Continental Congress. The burgesses ignored the governor and sent their delegates. From London, Prime Minister North sent to the colonies a proposal for reconciliation, which arrived in Boston the day after the battles at Lexington and Concord. The plan made significant concessions concerning Parliament's authority to tax the colonies, but it also refused to allow Parliament to deal with any *union* of colonies; only individual colonies would be recognized. Dunmore ordered the burgesses to consider North's "generous" proposal. They did—and they promptly rejected it, as they also rejected Dunmore's demand that they authorize payment to those who had fought in Lord Dunmore's War and his further demand that the boycott of the civil courts be ended. It was Jefferson who, on June 5, 1775, composed the stinging reply to Governor Dunmore, accusing him of misrepresenting the colony to London, of impeding justice, and of crippling colonial trade.

A few days later, at the urging of the radicals who now narrowly controlled the House of Burgesses, Jefferson composed a frankly revolutionary address in even more direct response to Lord North's proposal. "For us," he wrote, "not for them, has government been instituted here .... We ... alone are the judges of the condition, circumstances and situation of our people, as Parliament are of theirs." The address concluded by expressing the intention of Virginia's legislators to "share one general fate with our Sister Colonies" and to agree to no action "distinct and apart from them."

Having delivered the address, Jefferson immediately set off for Philadelphia to serve as a delegate to the Second Continental Congress. This one was bigger than the first, with 342 delegates from twelve colonies (again, Georgia sent no one), including such prominent figures as John Hancock, Benjamin Franklin, and John Adams. The major piece of business was the creation of a Continental army. The already active Boston militia would be its core, but ultimately the force would be drawn from all the colonies, a truly national force and the strongest expression possible of union among the colonies. It was John Adams who proposed

George Washington, veteran officer of the French and Indian War, as commander in chief of the new national army.

The Congress well knew what Washington and his army were up against: the mightiest war machine in the world. Congress authorized a Continental army of 27,500. In 1775, Parliament authorized a British army of fifty-five hundred and a navy of twenty-eight hundred men. In 1775, the United States had a single warship; the Royal Navy numbered 270 vessels. Even more important was the fact that, if Britain had at least five times the military resources of the colonies, it had a *thousand* times the financial resources. The British government had access to a "sinking fund," ready cash, of two to three million pounds per year; in contrast, the total revenue that the colonies could generate annually amounted to about £75,000.

Against these long odds, the Second Continental Congress staked its belief that the Americans did enjoy a few critical advantages over the British. They were fighting on their own ground, in defense of their own homes, and for a cause they believed in—or, at least, could be *made* to believe in. Yet even as the Battle of Bunker Hill raged in Charlestown, just outside of Boston, on June 17, 1775, the colonies were by no means unanimous in their desire for independence. On November 4, 1775, the assembly of New Jersey declared reports of colonists seeking independence "groundless," as if the reality of the idea could be legislated out of existence. On November 9, the Pennsylvania assembly instructed its delegates to the Continental Congress to "dissent from and utterly reject any propositions ... that may cause or lead to a separation from our mother country or a change of the form of this government."

At the conclusion of the Second Continental Congress, John Dickinson of Pennsylvania drafted the so-called "Olive Branch Petition" to King George III, reiterating the colonial grievances but also professing attachment "to your Majesty's person, family, and government, with all devotion that principle and affection can inspire" and beseeching the king to interpose his "royal authority and influence ... to procure us relief from our afflicting fears and jealousies." Adams and the other New Englanders, as well as radicals like Jefferson, objected to the Olive Branch Petition; Adams observed in a letter that it "gives a silly cast to our doings." Nevertheless, he and the other members of the Continental Congress endorsed the document, which was sent off to London— where King George haughtily refused even to receive it. Instead, on August 23, 1775, His Majesty proclaimed "our Colonies and Plantations in North America, misled by dangerous and designing men," to be in a state of rebellion, and he ordered "all our Officers … and all our obedient and loyal subjects, to use their utmost endeavours to withstand and suppress such rebellion."

It was to be war. However, given the leisurely pace of eighteenth-century transportation and communication, it was November before Congress learned that its olive branch had been spurned. On December 6, Congress issued a tepid response to the rejection of the "Olive Branch Petition," reaffirming allegiance to the Crown even as it disavowed the authority of Parliament.

Despite the temporary recoil of New Jersey and Pennsylvania from independence, other colonies were eager to write constitutions for themselves, each one essentially a de facto declaration of independence. Massachusetts and New Hampshire each asked the Continental Congress to write a model constitution for it and the other colonies. When the Congress declined, the colonies began to take the issue of independence out of its hands and into their own. One by one, the colonies drew up the constitutions of independent states.

Although it had become clear by the end of 1775 that a revolution was indeed under way, the question of independence was still up in the air. What finally crystallized popular opinion in favor of complete and immediate independence was neither a fresh British outrage nor a new military battle, but a forty-seven-page pamphlet published on January 9, 1776, and written, according to the title page, "by an Englishman."

Benjamin Rush, the most highly respected physician in America and a delegate to the Continental Congress, persuaded Thomas Paine, a newly arrived immigrant from England (he settled in Philadelphia in November 1774), to write a popular pamphlet on the subject of independence. When Paine had completed it, Rush gave it a title: *Common Sense*.

Common Sense was neither lawyerly nor statesmanlike. It contained no original political theory, but it nevertheless made the argument for independence more simply, thoroughly, and persuasively than any document before it. Paine hammered eloquently at two central themes: that republican government was inherently and inescapably superior to government by hereditary monarchy, and that equality of rights was the chief birthright of humanity, which no just government could fail to support and defend. Then he did even more. "O ye that love mankind!" Paine cranked up his peroration:

> *Ye that dare oppose not only the tyranny but the tyrant, stand forth! Every spot of the old world is overrun with oppression. Freedom hath been hunted round the globe. Asia and Africa have long expelled her. Europe regards her like a stranger, and England hath given her warning to depart. O receive the fugitive, and prepare in time an asylum for mankind!*

With these words, Thomas Paine transformed a quarrel between colonies and the mother country into an international event of central importance to all humanity. The outcome of the American struggle for independence, he argued, would determine the fate of all humanity as either slave or free. The American Revolution would be a revolution for the world, for history, and for the future. In less than three months, 120,000 copies of *Common Sense* were sold. Probably more than half a million copies were distributed before the end of the Revolution.

"Every post and every day rolls in upon us Independence like a torrent," John Adams wrote in a letter of May 20, 1776, following the appearance of *Common Sense* and George Washington's victory in the siege of Boston, which sent the British army fleeing into Canada. Shaking off the vestiges of its ambivalence, Congress authorized privateers—merchant ships authorized to raid and capture British vessels—and then embargoed exports to Britain and the British West Indies. On March 3, Congress sent Silas Deane to France to negotiate for aid. On March 14, it moved against colonial Loyalists, ordering that they be disarmed. Then, on April 6,

Congress opened all American ports to the trade of all nations except Britain.

Now, one after the other, the colonies voted for independence. On May 15, 1776, the Continental Congress enacted a resolution recommending to "the respective Assemblies and Conventions of the United Colonies, where no Government sufficient to the exigencies of their affairs has been hitherto established, to adopt such Government ...." Less than a month later, on June 7, Richard Henry Lee of Virginia introduced another resolution: "That these United Colonies are, and of right ought to be, free and independent States ... and that all political connection between them and the State of Great Britain is, and ought to be, totally dissolved."

The final debate over independence got under way on July 1, 1776, with Pennsylvania's Dickinson urging delay while John Adams and Lee just as passionately urged immediate action. On that day, South Carolina and Pennsylvania voted against independence, while the Delaware delegation was divided, and New York, in the process of reorganizing its government, abstained. The vote, then, stood at nine to four in favor of independence. Desiring no less than an overwhelming majority, however, the radicals of Delaware sent Caesar Rodney to make a Paul Revere–like midnight ride from the colonial capital at Dover to the Congress in Philadelphia, eighty miles away. He arrived, breathless and mud-splattered, just in time to swing the Delaware vote to independence. This, in turn, moved South Carolina's delegation to change its vote to endorse independence, as did Pennsylvania. New York again abstained, but the majority, on July 2, was indeed overwhelming.

The Continental Congress had been preparing for this moment. Three weeks earlier, with the introduction of Lee's resolution of independence, it had appointed a committee to draft a declaration of independence, naming to it John Adams, Benjamin Franklin, Robert Livingston, Roger Sherman, and Thomas Jefferson.

As a prime mover of revolutionary activity in Massachusetts, the very cradle of the revolution, Adams was a natural choice. Franklin, at seventy the oldest of the committee, was already a figure of international reputation, known as a scientist, inventor, writer, editor, and politician, and emerging as a brilliant statesman. Livingston, scion of a distinguished New York family, carried into the work assigned him his colony's reservations regarding independence. Sherman, of Connecticut, was trained as a cobbler but had educated himself through omnivorous reading and had become a legislator, economic theorist, and the author of a series of almanacs based on his own astronomical calculations.

Jefferson was decidedly the junior member of the committee. His 1774 *Summary View* had been considered too radical by many of the early proponents of colonial reform. But it seemed far less radical now—and, besides, no one could deny its eloquence. The committee turned to Jefferson to write the first draft.

In an 1822 letter, Adams recalled that Jefferson at first demurred when the task was presented to him. Jefferson "proposed to me to make the draught," Adams recalled, to which he replied, "I will not." Jefferson protested: "You should do it."

"Oh! No."

"Why will you not? You ought to do it."

"I will not."

"Why?"

"Reason enough."

"What can be your reasons?"

"Reason first—You are a Virginian, and a Virginian ought to appear at the head of this business. Reason second—I am obnoxious, suspected and unpopular. You are very much otherwise. Reason third—You can write ten times better than I can."

At this, according to Adams, Jefferson capitulated: "Well, if you are decided, I will do as well as I can."

To be chosen to write the Declaration of Independence was an honor, to be sure, but perhaps not so great a one as we might imagine. At the time, no one thought the document needed to be particularly momentous. All that was required is that it be legally defensible, a justification that would stand up to the scrutiny of the foreign powers—most notably France, to which the United States would have to appeal for aid in battling an empire that commanded the world's mightiest army and navy.

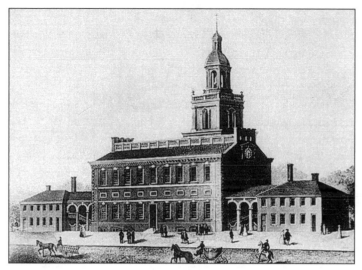

Early engraving of Independence Hall, Philadelphia, where the Declaration of Independence was signed on July 4, 1776.

(Collection: National Archives and Records Administration)

Years later, writing to Henry Lee in 1825, Jefferson explained what he had tried to accomplish in writing the Declaration. It was not to "find out new principles, or new arguments, never before thought of ... but to justify ourselves in the independent stand we are compelled to take" and to "appeal to the tribunal of the world ... for our justification."

> *Neither aiming at originality of principle or sentiment, nor yet copied from any particular previous writing, it was intended to be an expression of the American mind, and to give to that expression the proper tone and spirit called for by the occasion. All its authority rests on the harmonizing sentiments of the day, whether expressed in conversation, in letters, printed essays, or in the elementary books of public right, as Aristotle, Cicero, Locke, Sidney, etc. ....*

Of the authors Jefferson enumerated, the Declaration owed its most direct debt to the seventeenth-century British philosopher John Locke. Locke had enumerated the basic rights of human beings as life, liberty, and property. Jefferson, of course, wrote of "inalienable rights" to life and liberty but then changed Locke's *property* to the "pursuit of happiness." In this change, some later commentators have remarked, Jefferson most keenly captured "the American mind," suggesting that he believed that all Americans were driven first and foremost by the pursuit of happiness.

Perhaps. In any case, that phrase survived intact the extensive revision to which Congress subjected Jefferson's first draft. But another provision was ruthlessly stricken. Jefferson's draft included a condemnation of King George III specifically for having "waged cruel war against human nature itself, violating its most sacred rights of life [and] liberty in the persons of a distant people who never offended him, captivating [and] carrying them into slavery in another hemisphere, or to incur miserable death in their transportation thither." This passage on slavery was medicine too strong for his fellow Southern slave holders—and for most Yankee traders, too, who thrived on the so-called triangular trade by which New Englanders transported simple manufactured goods to Africa in exchange for slaves. The slaves were, in turn, transported to the West Indies, where they were traded for rum and molasses, which was sold back in New England.

The changes that Congress introduced served generally to soften and dilute the Declaration, and each change seems to have caused great pain to the author. He was hurt most, however, by the striking of the slavery clause. This meant that the United States of America would fight for its liberty and for the "inalienable rights" of humankind, but it would do so as a slave nation. More immediately, it left the Declaration with a gaping hole in its logic, which must also have mortified the eminently rational Jefferson.

"We hold these truths to be self-evident," Jefferson had written, "that all men are created equal ...." If all men are created equal, and Africans are men, slavery was clearly a violation of the self-evident truth of natural right. Congress, however, was not disturbed. It was manifestly more important to placate the South than to follow the dictates of strict logic, let alone strict morality. Belatedly, four score and *six* years later, the assertion that all men are created equal would serve as one of the principles upon which Abraham Lincoln would craft the Emancipation Proclamation.

*Reading of the Declaration of Independence from the East
Balcony of the Old State House, Boston, July 18, 1776. This
print made in 1930–31 by the George Washington Bicentennial
Commission.*

Despite its adulteration by Congress, the Declaration of
Independence, signed by the members of that Congress on July 4,
1776, gave the American Revolution unified direction and sweeping inspiration. Published to the world, it did indeed explain the

American struggle to the world, much of which instantly sympathized with and supported the cause. On July 9, John Adams wrote to Samuel Chase, a Maryland signer of the Declaration, that "the river is passed, and the bridge cut away …. The Declaration was yesterday published and proclaimed …. The bells rang all day and almost all night."

Part Three

The Practical
Visionary

Chapter 8

Designing Virginia

What could have put Thomas Jefferson closer to the heart of American independence than writing its great declaration? It was to be not only the seed document of the United States, but, as Jefferson intended, it also would be a *world* document, a justification—in the international arena of 1776 as well as for all time—of the violent enterprise that Americans had decided to undertake. Little wonder that, at the end of his life, Jefferson would include the Declaration of Independence in the brief resumé of achievements that he directed to be chiseled into his headstone.

And yet, in 1776, Jefferson wished he were somewhere other than Philadelphia, doing other things than writing the Declaration of Independence. Sitting in Philadelphia, composing the Declaration and deliberating the fate of what we today call the nation, he felt himself left *out* of the real action. Today, thanks to what Jefferson and the others assembled in Philadelphia accomplished, we call ourselves Americans. But Jefferson called himself a Virginian, and he agonized about being in Philadelphia while the leaders of *his* country, Virginia, were in Williamsburg declaring Virginia's independence and creating a new commonwealth.

Despite his physical absence, Jefferson refused to be left out of the process. He had been asked on June 11, 1776, to draft the Declaration of Independence. By this time, he had already completed two drafts of a constitution for Virginia. On June 13, even as he sat down to the task of composing the Declaration, he sent a *third* draft of the Virginia constitution to George Wythe in Williamsburg.

As Jefferson saw it, the stakes were very high. While he was away in Philadelphia, Virginia conservatives led by George Mason had already hammered out a draft constitution of their own. It called for no taxation without representation, and it provided for such rights as free elections, freedom of the press, trial by jury, the elimination of blanket warrants, excessive bail, cruel and unusual punishment, and all hereditary offices. Yet it was a conservative constitution in that it set a stringent property-owning qualification for voting, to ensure that political power in Virginia would always rest in the hands of the large landowners and prosperous planters. Even in the absence of hereditary offices, Virginia would remain the domain of the ancient landed gentry. In contrast to this, Jefferson's draft sought, first and foremost, to broaden the franchise. His constitution still set property ownership as a prerequisite for voting, but it reduced the amount of land required to fifty acres—and then it set aside a reserve of free public land to ensure that every white male would possess sufficient acreage to qualify him to vote.

Unlike Mason and the other conservative revolutionaries, Jefferson wanted to establish democracy on the broadest possible footing. At the outset of a great struggle for liberty, he was determined to create what John Adams called a "government for which men will fight." Over the course of three weeks, even as he framed the Declaration of Independence, Jefferson developed in his three draft Virginia constitutions the very political and philosophical principles that he would express most eloquently in the Declaration itself. His object was to systematize and guarantee a government in which all authority would clearly, ultimately, and finally be derived from the people—a government flowing from the governed and instituted for their benefit.

Jefferson's plan to provide every Virginia man with sufficient land to entitle him to vote was not merely a device to extend the franchise. It was the foundation of a radically redesigned society, part and parcel of what historians have called Jefferson's romantic agrarianism. He proposed to transform Virginia into a realm of independent farmers, legally bound to one another as citizens of a commonwealth, yet also self-sufficient enough to need bow to "no superior whatever."

Land was to be the foundation of Jefferson's democratic Virginia. Not only would it foster a society of free farmers, but it also would provide buffer zones to eliminate or minimize border disputes with other states, and it would serve as a safe haven for Indians. Jefferson's constitution provided for the just and equitable treatment of Native Americans, and Jefferson saw in land the means of instituting such treatment. Like many others of his time and place, he believed that the proximity of whites and Indians would inevitably produce conflict. Separate the two peoples, give each sufficient land, and conflict would be eliminated. Justice and equality could prevail.

Jefferson's draft constitution aimed at accomplishing even more. It provided for the liberalization and encouragement of immigration from abroad and for streamlining procedures for naturalization. His constitution also asserted the absolute authority of civilian government over military authority, and it eliminated such feudal holdovers as primogeniture and other practices that tended to prevent property from passing out of family hands. The penal code of Virginia was to be rendered more rational and humane, with capital punishment radically curtailed so that it would apply only to "murder, & those offences in the military service for which [the General Assembly] shall think punishment by death absolutely necessary." As for the form of government, it would be divided into three branches, legislative, executive, and judiciary, each of which would possess powers that checked and balanced the powers of the others.

As for slavery—as usual, it presented the great moral and political dilemma. Slave-owning Jefferson despised slavery, even as he continued to profit by the labor of slaves. He understood as well as any Virginian that it was possible to have moral qualms about slavery yet resist its abolition. Given his way, would Jefferson have written a constitution abolishing slavery? It is not likely. In any event, Jefferson knew that he was *not* being given his way. A constitution abolishing slavery would never be enacted by a majority of Virginians. In his third draft, therefore, he contented himself with a provision that did nothing more than discourage the further importation of slaves. If slavery was inherently evil and cruel, the most evil and cruel aspect of slavery was the slave trade—and that, at least, Jefferson sought to end.

Jefferson's anxiety over his absence from Virginia proved justified. His draft constitution arrived in Williamsburg too late to be considered in its entirety. Instead, the conservative document that George Mason had created was ratified, although some of Jefferson's provisions were given consideration as amendments. In addition, the preamble that Jefferson had composed, a denunciation of the acts of King George III, identical to the catalogue of the king's offenses included in his original draft of the Declaration of Independence, was adopted almost verbatim. Despite these contributions to the Virginia constitution, Jefferson was disappointed that he had been denied the opportunity to shape more directly the independence of his "country." His disappointment was compounded by the frustration that he felt over the congressional editing and dilution of his Declaration of Independence.

Looking to the immediate future, Jefferson decided that he could still make a deeper mark on the course of Virginia independence than he could in the Continental Congress. Jefferson was typical of most of his fellow patriots. He believed that a colonial union was essential for fighting and winning the revolution; however, it was not the *union* for which Americans were fighting. Massachusetts men fought for Massachusetts, South Carolinians for South Carolina, Virginians for Virginia, and so on. The Continental Congress was an expedient way of coordinating colonial efforts in the prosecution of the war. Perhaps it would survive once independence had been won; perhaps not. Perhaps a genuinely *United* States would emerge from the war; perhaps not. Whatever happened, any *union* would always be subordinate to the particular "country" from which each colonist came—Massachusetts, South Carolina, Virginia, whatever. If Jefferson succeeded in remaking Virginia, the other states could always choose to follow suit, but he decided that, whatever others in other states did or did not do, *he* would take his stand and make his mark in Virginia.

Portrait of Thomas Jefferson by Rembrandt Peale, engraved in
Philadelphia about 1801.

Jefferson had been elected to the Continental Congress for a term of one year. As that term drew to a close, Jefferson wrote to Edmund Pendleton, president of the Virginia Convention, informing him that he would not seek another term. He went even further, pleading with Edmund Randolph to explain to the Convention that he wished to leave the Congress. Despite the campaign that he mounted against himself, Jefferson was reelected—only to be released in September and allowed to return to Virginia because his chronically ailing wife, Patty, was again ill. Just how ill? That she was destined to die young attests to the precarious state of her overall health, but on this occasion, the source of her illness may have been nothing more or less than longing for her absent husband. Almost exactly nine months after Jefferson's return to Monticello, Patty gave birth to a son, the couple's first.

Jefferson was doubtless delighted to be back at Monticello that September of 1776. But he had no intention of staying. Shortly before he left Philadelphia, Edmund Pendleton, now speaker of Virginia's brand-new House of Delegates, asked him to come to Williamsburg to rewrite Virginia's entire penal code. Here was a chance to recover much of the opportunity he had lost when the delegates failed to adopt his draft constitution. Three weeks after he returned to Monticello, Jefferson bundled himself, his wife, three-year-old Patsy, and personal servants into carriages for the 150-mile trek to Virginia's capital city. He would serve as a delegate while he worked on the penal code.

The prospect of redesigning Virginia's laws from scratch must have been enormously appealing to Jefferson. But no sooner had he settled in Williamsburg than he received a dispatch from John Hancock, president of the Continental Congress, asking him to join Benjamin Franklin and Silas Deane as "commissioners at the Court of France"—advocates of the revolutionary cause, charged with securing French support in the struggle for independence.

Jefferson greatly admired Franklin and had even asked him to persuade Congress to appoint him to the French commission. Now, however, he was clearly torn—not only between the commission and the opportunity to stay at home and refashion Virginia's laws, but also between his duty to the Revolution and to his delicate wife. In the end, he pleaded that "circumstances very peculiar in the situation of my family" prevented him from serving in Europe.

Having declined the commission, Jefferson did not look back. Instead, he set to work on what biographer Willard Sterne Randall called the task of "almost single-handedly invent[ing] a country, the Commonwealth of Virginia, the largest of the new American states and a closely watched example for the others."

During the next three years, Jefferson immersed himself in legal research and modern philosophy, emerging with 126 new laws for a new country. Some of the legislation blasted away at Virginia's feudal property laws, demolishing the concepts of entail and primogeniture, which had for so long kept Virginia's great landed dynasties all powerful. Some of the laws modernized the commonwealth's criminal and civil codes, generally injecting penal statutes with humanity and mercy. Other laws were aimed at educating the citizens of Virginia, providing for an extensive system of free public education—as Jefferson reasoned, an ignorant people could not be expected to govern themselves effectively.

Jefferson devoted particular labor to crafting the *Virginia Statute of Religious Freedoms*, a work of which he was sufficiently proud to include, with the Declaration of Independence, among the few achievements tallied on the epitaph that he composed for his headstone. An eloquent piece of legislation, its main thrust was disestablishment—the complete separation of church from state. No longer would Virginia subsidize Anglicanism or any other religion. Moreover, Jefferson's law made it clear that freedom of religion was "one of the natural rights of mankind." Appreciating that some future legislature might attempt to repeal the act, he sought to foreclose that eventuality: "[I]f any act shall be hereafter passed to repeal the present or to narrow its operation, such act will be an infringement of natural right."

Jefferson was designing a democracy. For him this meant creating a government derived from the will and consent of the governed. But Jefferson also understood that designing an enduring democracy—one that would not merely reflect, for good or ill, the momentarily prevailing whim of the majority—called for laws that looked not only *to* but also *beyond* the will and consent of the governed. In monarchies, this was easy: All laws flowed from the king. In theocracies—or in any government with a state-sponsored religion—this was also easy: All laws flowed from God, or, more precisely, from God's will as interpreted by the state. In a democracy, however, a new, transcendent basis of law had to be identified. Jefferson therefore defined a basis of "natural right" (as he called it in the *Virginia Statute*) or "self-evident" truths and "inalienable rights" (the terms he used in the Declaration of Independence).

> "No man shall be compelled to frequent or support any religious worship, place, or ministry whatsoever, nor shall be enforced, restrained, molested, or burthened in his body or goods, nor shall otherwise suffer, on account of his religious opinions or belief; but ... all men shall be free to profess, and by argument to maintain, their opinions in matters of religion, and ... the same shall in no wise diminish, enlarge, or affect their civil capacities."
>
> —*from the* Virginia Statute of Religious Freedoms

And nature played another role in Jefferson's democratic law giving. In sweeping aside the musty traditions of primogeniture and entail, which artificially maintained dynasties built on property, Jefferson declared that he was clearing the way for the growth of an "aristocracy of virtue and talent which nature has wisely provided for the direction of the interests of society." For Jefferson, a law was right and effective if it promoted rather than hindered the expression of natural virtue and talent, allowing natural genius to flower in service to society and government. In an artificial aristocracy, power and authority are conferred on the privileged few, regardless of their natural talents or lack thereof; in a *natural* aristocracy, he said, "virtue and talent" are "scattered with equal hand through all [social and economic] conditions."

> A great planter descended from a line of great planters, if
> he is a boob, has no place in the leadership of government,
> whereas the humblest farmer, if he is naturally endowed
> with virtue and talent, may become a great legislator.

Effective laws both permit and encourage such an ascent
of the humble and the privileged alike.

The creation of so many magnificent laws was an extraordinary—indeed, unprecedented—achievement for one man. Jefferson's legislative colleagues were not quick to enact them, however. By 1785, only half of Jefferson's proposed laws had been passed. With the able assistance of James Madison, however, most of the rest of the laws were at last enacted by 1786, including the all-important *Virginia Statute of Religious Freedoms*.

Jefferson accomplished his great three-year labor during the height of the American Revolution, yet, almost eerily, Virginia remained mostly peaceful during the early years of the war. During that period, most of the action was up north. What anguish intruded on Jefferson's solitary labors was personal, not national. His son, born on May 28, 1777, died on June 14 and was buried without having been given a name. Patty Jefferson was soon pregnant again: On August 1, 1778, she gave birth to Mary—also called Maria or Polly—who became a particular delight to her father. Indeed, by the time he finished drafting the laws of Virginia in 1779, Jefferson was increasingly drawn (as he had been in the past) to the quiet life at Monticello. Let the war rage wherever it raged, and let the legislators argue over his hard work. Jefferson, now thirty-six, would play with his daughter, sleep with his wife, tend his orchard and garden, and cultivate his vineyard.

When he confessed this fantasy of quiet withdrawal to Edmund Pendelton, the Speaker of the House of Delegates brought him up short: "You are too young to ask that happy quietus from the public life." And so Jefferson allowed himself to be presented before the House of Delegates as a candidate for governor of Virginia. Patrick Henry had already served three one-year terms in that office, the maximum allowed. Jefferson ran against John Page and Thomas Nelson Jr., both good friends of his. Without campaigning or lobbying the delegates, Jefferson was elected on the second ballot, June 1, 1779.

An architect of the revolution, Jefferson had been so far virtually untouched by the war. Shortly before his election as governor, in the spring of 1779, Jefferson had arranged for the Hessian commander, Maj. Gen. Baron von Riedesel, who had been sent down from Saratoga, New York, as a prisoner of war, to rent the house of his friend and neighbor Philip Mazzei, who was on a European trip. Jefferson liked the cultivated German baron, whose daughters he encouraged to play with Patsy. Up north, the Hessians, German mercenaries in the British service, were particularly hated and feared for their fierce and gratuitous cruelty in combat. Jefferson, however, found their commander a delightful neighbor and particularly relished playing violin duets with one of Riedesel's young subordinates, Baron de Geismar.

Pleasant conversation with a baron, little girls at play, duets with a young musician: Could *these* be the elements of war? All too soon, Governor Jefferson would find out.

Chapter 9

Flight and Despair

The great nineteenth-century humorist Mark Twain once quipped that "poverty is no disgrace—but it's no honor, either." Much the same could be said of the office of governor of revolutionary Virginia. Thanks in no small part to the efforts of Jefferson himself and other legislators, the chief executive of what was in effect the largest independent nation in North America had very little power. Years of autocratic government under all-powerful royal governors had prompted the architects of independent Virginia to reduce the governor to little more than an administrator and figurehead while investing the true executive authority in the House of Delegates.

Not that the House of Delegates had much muscle to flex. A vast "nation" claiming territory westward to the Mississippi, Virginia still wasn't much of a military power. Its navy boasted three sailing vessels and four rowed galleys, none of which had a sufficient complement of sailors to make up a full crew. It managed to raise eleven battalions of land troops, but most of these were sent north to serve with the Continental army. It had a militia of fifty thousand men, but these were untrained frontiersmen, not disciplined, well-armed soldiers. Popular lore has long extolled the backwoods pluck and cunning of the American frontiersman as superior in combat to the British redcoat. In some frontier theaters of the war, this mythology has a grain of truth, but in battles fought on larger scales and out in the open, the undisciplined backwoods-men repeatedly proved no match for well-trained, well-equipped European soldiers.

In short, Governor Jefferson's Virginia was highly vulnerable. Except for action against Norfolk at the beginning of the war, the British had so far left Virginia alone. Before he assumed office, Jefferson had the peace and quiet to remake Virginia's laws and enough spare time to entertain Hessian POW officers and their families. But Virginia's peace was an illusion. Jefferson may have seen no battles and heard no gunfire, but his country was indeed under attack. The British fleet had begun a blockade that would soon strangle the Virginia economy. Just a month before Jefferson's election, a British flotilla sailed into Hampton Roads unopposed and deposited one thousand eight hundred British regulars at Portsmouth, which they seized and used as a base of operations from which to raid the Eastern Shore. Largely unopposed, the British troops razed a number of coastal Virginia towns, captured one hundred thirty ships of all kinds, and destroyed three thousand barrels of tobacco as well as military and naval provisions. They did all of this at a leisurely pace over sixteen days, losing not a single man in the process.

British strategy at the time required the troops to return to New York, so no attempt was made to occupy Virginia. But the point had been made: Virginia was ripe to fall into enemy hands. As the blockade tightened, Virginia's economy withered. The British understood that the only cash crop that mattered to Virginia was tobacco. Keep it from being exported, and the rebellious colony would soon be without funds to finance a war. Blithely, in response to the blockade, the House of Delegates authorized the printing of paper money in 1777, a scheme that Jefferson himself had endorsed, believing that Virginia's credit would be more than adequate to back the paper it issued. In 1779, however, as he took office, that paper money was depreciating daily. Virginia presses churned out more, which only devalued the currency further. Hard-pressed Virginians, most of whom had joined the Revolution because it promised to end taxation without representation, now refused to pay the taxes they owed Virginia. When Jefferson took office, half of Virginia's counties had failed to meet their tax quota obligations. To make up for the shortfall, Virginia officials had to levy higher taxes, which only provoked more resistance. Worst of all, even when taxes were paid, they were paid in ever-depreciating paper currency.

Against this backdrop of military unpreparedness and economic ruin, Governor Jefferson was expected to administer the laws of Virginia. He had no legal authority to make appointments, to veto laws, to dissolve the House of Delegates, or even to call out the militia. What elements of government did not fall directly into the hands of the House of Delegates were entrusted to an eight-man Council of State, which worked directly with the governor but was elected by the delegates, not appointed by him. Thus, the governor was unmistakably subordinate to his Council. Still, Jefferson managed to make an ally—actually, an admiring protégé—of one member, James Madison, who gave him the edge he needed to push through various directives. Jefferson also engineered the delegates' approval for the creation of a Board of War and a Board of Trade, over which he would have considerable authority. These were later replaced by three individuals: a commercial agent, a commissioner of the navy, and a commissioner for the war office, all of whom answered to the governor and were appointed by him, albeit with the advice and consent of the Council of State.

By means of Madison, the commercial agent, and the military commissioners, Jefferson leveraged every bit of power he had. He exercised all of his ingenuity as well to generate revenue where, to all appearances, there was none. He proposed a Land Office Act to allow the sale of large tracts of Virginia's western wilderness to pioneer homesteaders. Jefferson shepherded the act through the House of Delegates, and, once in place, it was at first spectacularly successful in raising revenue. Settlers poured in not only from eastern Virginia, but from all over the United States. In this way, Kentucky and the Ohio country were rapidly settled. But soon it became clear that not everyone was happy.

States that had no vast tracts of public lands to offer protested the drain of population and revenue from their precincts, while Congress complained that Virginia had effectively opened up vast tracts to shelter deserters from the state militias and the Continental army. A more serious wartime effect of Jefferson's Land Office Act was the creation of a new frontier that required defense, which meant spreading wholly inadequate defensive forces even more thinly than they already were. Perhaps Jefferson would have endured the protests from other states and from Congress had the Land Office Act in the long run succeeded in making up for currency depreciation. But despite great demand for the purchase of public land, the income fell far short of what Virginia needed.

Not to be daunted, Jefferson cast about for other sources of revenue. He created legislation to allow him to confiscate Loyalist property. The man who had modernized Virginia's archaic body of feudal laws now invoked escheat and forfeiture, legal concepts dating to the Norman Conquest, to snap up the property of those Virginia landowners considered British subjects rather than Virginia citizens. The medieval kings of England had used escheat and forfeiture to claim the property of those who rebelled against the Crown; now Governor Jefferson used this same process to acquire the property of those deemed loyal to the Crown. The problem was that the funds generated by the sale of confiscated property were paid in depreciated Virginia currency, which meant that, yet again, the income received made hardly a dent in Virginia's burgeoning debt.

On May 4, 1778, Congress had ratified a Franco-American alliance. Jefferson's hope was that the French navy would now supply adequate force to break the British naval blockade of Virginia, which would then be free to export its tobacco and thereby soon achieve economic self-sufficiency. But the actions of the French navy were repeatedly disappointing and ineffectual. The British blockade endured, the tobacco rotted on wharves and in warehouses, and yet another source of revenue was denied his state. In considerable desperation, Jefferson sent a number of emissaries to Europe, among them his friend and neighbor Philip Mazzei, to seek loans from various sources, including Italian princes and other heads of state. The loans failed to materialize.

The governor had one last card to play. Although the British blockade of Virginia effectively prevented the state from exporting any commodity in quantity, it did not entirely choke off imports. In a strategy that at first seems paradoxical and self-defeating, Jefferson persuaded the House of Delegates to complete what the British had started. He proposed an embargo on imported manufactured goods. By cutting off imports, he intended to force Virginians to develop their own domestic manufacturing industries—and, quite rapidly, this is precisely what they did.

Jefferson saw in this program of industrialization not only an opportunity to revive Virginia's economy, but also a way to aid the war effort. Observing that America's reliance on foreign sources for artillery presented a grave danger, he proposed a deal with a French munitions firm to build and operate a cannon factory at Westham, on the James River, far enough inland to be safe from British coastal raiders. It was a brilliant plan, and the House of Delegates was willing to push it forward. Unfortunately, the French government blocked him by refusing to allow French munitions workers to emigrate. Denied a major arms works, Jefferson instead converted a small foundry already standing at Westham to the manufacture of cannon, small arms, and ammunition. Its output was modest, but it was better than nothing.

Throughout his frustration, Jefferson repeatedly returned his gaze to the direction that seemed always to offer hope: the West. Even before he had become governor, he did all he could to develop the western counties of Virginia, and he worked with fellow Virginians George Mason and Richard Henry Lee to sponsor an expedition led by George Rogers Clark to secure for Virginia the Old Northwest—the region north of the Ohio River and east of the Mississippi. This would open trade with the Spanish at New Orleans via the Mississippi and Ohio rivers and would promote settlement beyond the Appalachian Mountains. That the expedition was illegal—only the Continental Congress had the power to authorize it—bothered Jefferson not at all. He arranged it so that Clark would obtain funding, supplies, and manpower from Virginia in the guise of providing for the defense of Virginia's Kentucky counties. As further inducement to Clark and his men, Jefferson arranged for them to receive a bounty in the form of vast grants of western land.

The expedition that Jefferson backed not only resulted in Virginia's annexation of the Old Northwest and the Illinois country, but it also produced important military victories in the frontier region. In February 1779, Clark captured the British outpost of Fort Vincennes (in present-day Indiana), in the process making a prisoner of the royal lieutenant governor of Canada, Sir Henry Hamilton. Among the local Indians, Hamilton had earned the grisly sobriquet "Hair Buyer" because, it was said, he paid bounties for the scalps of rebel settlers. When Hamilton was transported to Williamsburg as a prisoner of war, Jefferson treated him very differently from the way he had treated the Hessians and other prisoners of war. He ordered him confined to the Williamsburg jail, in leg irons. Uncharacteristically, Jefferson made no attempt to investigate the truth of the many hearsay stories of Hamilton's atrocities. He simply accepted them as fact and treated his prisoner accordingly, nearly wrecking George Washington's ongoing prisoner-exchange negotiations with the British. It was October 1780 before Jefferson finally sent Hamilton to British headquarters in New York, where he was exchanged for a high-ranking American officer.

British governor Henry Hamilton directed Indian raids against American settlements. During negotiations after the fall of Detroit, troops under George Rogers Clark intercepted a war party on its way to present Hamilton with American scalps. Clark had the Indians bound to a fence and tomahawked in full view of the British fort. Hamilton immediately surrendered. Clark clapped him in irons, to which he indignantly responded, "You must renounce all pretensions to the character of an officer or a gentleman."

Hamilton denied paying for American scalps, and he did treat American prisoners with utmost courtesy. Daniel Boone was his prisoner, and he not only judged him a man of "great humanity," but visited him when Jefferson held him prisoner. Released in 1780, Hamilton served as lieutenant governor of Quebec and later of Bermuda and Dominica.

Thomas Jefferson's harsh treatment of a royal official caused great controversy and, in some quarters, outrage. To those who thought they knew Jefferson well, it all seemed drastically out of character. Yet, on the contrary, it probably reached to the heart of the man as, before all else, a westerner. For Jefferson, Hamilton symbolized the cruel forces that sought to prevent the westward settlement and expansion that he believed was the destiny of America. When it came to the West, Jefferson, whose genius lay in his ability to blend the practical with the visionary, became almost entirely visionary. The region excited his hopes, his dreams, and his imagination, lifting him above his stature as the minimally powerful governor of an all-but-bankrupt state in the throes of war against the mightiest nation on earth. Driven by his dream, Jefferson expanded his state into a region far too vast to defend in time of desperate war.

Part and parcel of Jefferson's western vision was his campaign to move the capital inland from coastal Williamsburg to Richmond. He sold the idea to the House of Delegates as a means of putting the capital out of reach of British warships—which was indeed a prudent move—but he cherished two more profound reasons for moving the capital. First, Richmond was not part of the aristocratic Tidewater and was much more accessible to farmers and Piedmont planters like himself. Second, Richmond was a clean slate. As a capital, Williamsburg had one hundred sixty years of history; in Jefferson's view, the city reflected not the values of a new democracy in a new world, but it was encumbered by the corrupt and corrupting trappings of the Old World, the airs of the very aristocracy from which the nation was fighting to free itself.

When the Jefferson family moved to Richmond in the spring of 1780, they found themselves in a quiet rural village of eighteen hundred people. As Jefferson beheld it in imagination, however, it was a great shimmering capital city centered on six majestic public squares, each of which was the setting for a great public building. Over a ten-year period, he would design just such a capital.

If the move to Richmond was motivated largely by Jefferson's vision, it also proved timely for more immediately practical reasons. The War for Independence had been a long shot from the beginning, the proverbial contest between David and Goliath. Despite sharp, early patriot defeats during 1776–77 in Canada,

New York, and Philadelphia, there had also been stunning and invigorating victories during those years at Boston, Trenton, Princeton, and Saratoga. In 1778, France formally joined the cause of independence, raising American spirits even higher. But by the close of 1779, the tide of war had apparently turned against the patriots. Militarily, the French alliance was a daily disappointment, and this was apparent not only to the Americans, but to the British as well.

Early in the war, British strategists pulled out of New England, reasoning that revolutionary fervor burned too brightly hot to be extinguished there. They decided instead to target regions in which support for independence was weaker and loyalists to the Crown were still willing to fight for their king. In 1776, the British tried an attack on Charleston, South Carolina, only to be stunned by the strength and will of the city's resistance. Having failed to take Charleston, the British left much of the South alone for the next few years and concentrated instead on defeating a would-be American invasion of Canada and destroying the rebels in the Middle Atlantic region. But by 1779, when the vaunted Franco-American alliance had repeatedly failed, most notably in its effort to clear out loyalists from Savannah, Georgia, the British decided that the time had come to return to the South in earnest.

The strategy of divide and conquer had always served the imperial British forces well, and it was decided that a combined strategy of severing New England from the Middle Atlantic colonies while simultaneously cutting off the South from both of these regions would surely throttle the rebellion. Accordingly, British commander Sir Henry Clinton returned to Charleston, which fell on May 12, 1780, after a long and bitter siege in which almost all of the troops Virginia had contributed to the Continental army were either killed or made prisoner.

The fall of Charleston seemed suddenly to kick all the props out from under the South. British and Loyalist forces under the command of the brilliant and utterly ruthless Banestre Tarleton triumphed in the Carolina backcountry. On August 16, 1780, Horatio Gates and his Continentals, personally dispatched by Washington to rescue the South, suffered an ignominious defeat at

Camden, South Carolina, and retreated deep into Virginia. Jefferson, who had just commenced his second one-year term as governor, found himself listening helplessly to Gates's demands that he supply reinforcements. It must have been a depressing encounter: the defeated general pleading with a powerless governor. Jefferson had to tell Gates that all of Virginia's Continental army troops had shipped out—indeed, had mostly been lost at Charleston—and that he, as governor, could not call up the militia on his own authority. Worse, even the Council of State could not order a mobilization of militia unless Virginia itself were attacked. The best Jefferson could offer was to give Gates whatever Virginia Continentals were released from the hospital after recovering from wounds or illness.

Jefferson's personal seal. The motto reads, "Rebellion to tyrants is obedience to God."

Jefferson was all too aware that Virginia would probably be attacked soon. The governor wrote directly to the commander of French forces in America to appeal for troops. When a British landing actually came, at Newport News on October 20, 1780, Jefferson asked the Council of State for permission to create a regular standing army for Virginia.

He was refused. That was frustrating enough, but even more frustrating was having been refused something that he didn't even really want. For Jefferson to request the creation of a standing army required a great sacrifice of ideology. The imposition of a British standing army had been one of the causes of the American Revolution, and Jefferson believed that standing armies were inherently dangerous. But these days, he found himself willing to make ideological sacrifices if he thought that doing so would win the war. After having spent years engineering the westward expansion of Virginia, even circumventing the Continental Congress to do so, Jefferson recognized that the western land claims of his "country" had created a crisis for the struggling United States.

In 1777, Congress had drafted the Articles of Confederation, in effect the first constitution of the United States, although it did not so much forge a nation as it created a "firm league of friendship" among thirteen sovereign states. Loose as it was, Jefferson recognized that unity and concerted action provided by the Articles were crucial if any of the states were to prevail in the Revolution. Yet some of the states put off ratifying the Articles because Virginia's vast land claims would make her disproportionately powerful in any confederation. Maryland, Virginia's landpoor neighbor, objected most stridently. Facing the multiple crises of 1780, Jefferson boldly broke the deadlock by offering to cede his state's vast claims north of the Ohio River—not to Maryland or any other state, but to the federal government. This at once cleared the way for ratification of the Articles of Confederation, which took place the following year, thereby creating a federal government *and* giving that federal government the tangible substance of land.

The Virginia cession was essential to the birth of the nation, but the irony of it cannot have escaped Jefferson. Thomas Jefferson, enemy of standing armies, had gone before the Council of State, hat in hand, to request the establishment of a standing army. Now, Thomas Jefferson, citizen and governor of Virginia, who dreamed of transforming his "country" into a great western realm, who loathed central government and believed instead in a society of independent farmers, had helped create and establish a central government by giving to it much of the western land that Virginia claimed.

In the midst of titanic frustration and great anxiety, Jefferson became a father again. On November 30, 1780, Lucy Elizabeth was born. In seven years of marriage, Patty Jefferson had given birth five times. Of these children, little Jane had died in 1775, less than a year after her birth, and an unnamed son died about two weeks after he was born in 1777. Lucy Elizabeth seemed to thrive, but the labor and delivery had left Patty weak and unwell. The burden of his wife's precarious health, combined with the pressures of the war, induced Jefferson to ask his friend John Page to relieve him as governor immediately. Page declined, asking him to endure for eighteen months, after which his third one-year term would expire and he would be debarred by law from serving another.

The next month, Jefferson faced his most serious crisis as governor. Benedict Arnold, the bold American officer who, frustrated in his climb to a top American command, had turned traitor, led into Virginia an invasion force of Loyalists, foreign mercenaries, and Continental army deserters, together with a band of Scots and Hessians. Jefferson had known that full-scale invasion was just a matter of time, but when it finally came, it came as a total surprise. On December 31, 1780, Jefferson learned that twenty-seven ships had entered the Chesapeake. Not knowing whether these were British or French, the governor alerted Baron von Steuben, whom Washington had assigned as commander for Virginia, and also instructed the commander of the Virginia militia to do whatever he deemed necessary. Jefferson did not want to sound a false alarm, however, so he held off on calling out the militia or convening an emergency meeting of the Council of State until he had additional intelligence.

Two days went by before that intelligence reached him: The fleet was indeed British, and, having entered the James River, it had landed at Jamestown. Stunned by this belated information, Jefferson scrambled to get the Council of State together, but the required quorum of four could not be found. On his own doubtful authority and in the absence of a quorum, he called out the militia. He directed that all military supplies and government records still at Williamsburg be transported to Westham, site of Virginia's small cannon foundry. He ordered the large contingent of British prisoners held in Charlottesville transferred to Frederick, Maryland, fearing that the invaders intended to liberate them.

Jefferson did not panic, although he might have, had he realized that *he*, personally, was a prime target of the invasion. Jefferson may have thought of himself as an impotent governor of little value, but the British saw him as the author of the insolent Declaration of Independence, and there was a price on his head.

By January 4, the British ships had moved up to Westover, the great plantation of the Byrd family, just twenty-five miles from Richmond. Arnold's men disembarked and were on the march toward the capital, bringing terrible and gratuitous destruction along the way. A mere two hundred Virginia militiamen were gathered to protect Jefferson and the government at Richmond.

The governor knew a lost cause when he saw one. He evacuated his family and himself from the capital, taking the time to personally supervise the removal of many tons of gunpowder and other materiel to keep them out of enemy hands. He was barely a jump ahead of Arnold and his men, who rode into Richmond on January 5. They searched in vain for the governor, ransacking his rented house, looting his beloved library, capturing or destroying whatever state papers they found, and appropriating for sale ten of Jefferson's slaves. They then turned their attention to the rest of the town, destroying warehouses and stores of tobacco and capturing ten ships as well as a number of open boats. Arnold sent a detachment to Westham, where troops destroyed the foundry, twenty-six cannon, and three hundred ten barrels of gunpowder. Other military stores nearby were also looted or destroyed.

Jefferson understood that Arnold's action was a hit-and-run raid, and he knew that Arnold would not attempt to occupy the capital. Indeed, on January 6, the governor reentered Richmond to survey the damage, which was bad enough. Added to it was the injury that the raid had inflicted on the morale of the wholly undefended populace of Richmond.

Thomas Jefferson was profoundly depressed. His wife was ill. Virginia was vulnerable. His capital had been invaded and sacked. And he himself was now subject to attack from the public and from political enemies, who blamed him for not having called up the militia in time, for not doing something more to provide for the defense of the state, and, most of all, for having fled in the face of the enemy. Patrick Henry would never have "cowered in a barn" the way Jefferson was said to have done.

To answer these innuendoes and charges, Jefferson was as powerless as he had been to mount an effective defense of Virginia. His only response, out of sheer frustration and in violation of the very laws of Virginia that he had been instrumental in creating, was to appeal to Gen. J.P.G. Muhlenberg of the Continental army to assemble a squadron of bounty hunters to find and take Benedict Arnold.

"I will undertake," Jefferson wrote to the general, "if they are successful in bringing him off alive, that they shall receive five thousand guineas among them and ... their names be recorded with glory in history." If Arnold were killed "and America ... deprived of the pleasure of seeing him exhibited as a public spectacle of infamy and vengeance," Jefferson said, the reward would be reduced to "2,000 guineas, in proportion as our satisfaction would be reduced."

So far from order and reason had the great American apostle of order and reason been pushed.

Chapter 10

The Hermit of Monticello

"A disgrace." So Baron Friedrich Wilhelm von Steuben, the gallant and outspoken Prussian general who had volunteered his services to George Washington and the cause of American liberty, branded Thomas Jefferson's "flight" from Richmond. The Council of State exonerated the governor for having chosen to avoid capture, but many others, friends and political enemies alike, called the act cowardly. How deeply these accusations wounded Jefferson is not known. He neither spoke nor wrote of his feelings about them. In any event, he was too busy to brood; he was scrambling to scrape together equipment, clothing, food, and arms for Virginia's Continentals and militia. This required assembling his Council of State, but, incredibly, he could rarely summon the requisite quorum. The members were scattered throughout Virginia, desperately trying to keep their own plantations operating.

In these bleak times, on April 15, 1781, Lucy Elizabeth, aged five months, became the third Jefferson child to die. Her mother, who had never recovered from the pregnancy, labor, and delivery, now sunk into a deep depression and required frequent visits from the doctor. The following year, Jefferson would express the prevailing sentiment of the moment in a letter to James Madison: "I think public service and private misery are inseparably linked together."

On April 17, 1781, Jefferson moved himself and his family back to Monticello. He salvaged whatever he could of Virginia's government records and temporarily moved the capital to

Charlottesville, a short distance from his home. With most of the members of his Council of State absent, Governor Jefferson could barely govern. About the time of Lucy's death, he had decided definitely not to accept a third term. Accordingly, on June 1, 1781, upon the expiration of his second term of office, Thomas Jefferson resigned as governor of Virginia.

Afflicted by the frustrations of public service and the pains of private misery, it is little wonder that Jefferson chose this moment to quit. But the timing was hardly propitious. Just as Jefferson was in the process of leaving office, Lord Charles Cornwallis, British commander in charge of the south theater, was leading 7,200 redcoats in a new invasion of Virginia. By the time Cornwallis attacked Richmond, Jefferson and the House of Delegates had left, although the Delegates had not yet reassembled at Charlottesville. George Washington had done all he could to defend his home state, but that was not much: He detached just nine hundred Continentals under the dashing Marquis de Lafayette to defend Virginia. Lafayette, outnumbered more than seven to one, begged the outgoing governor to call up the militia.

Panoramic view of Monticello, photographed about 1912.

"It is not in my power to do anything," Jefferson told the young Frenchman. And so Lafayette retreated to save his army. In the meantime, Jefferson issued a recommendation to the delegates that they name as governor Gen. Thomas Nelson, commander of Virginia's militia. Confessing his own inadequacy in military matters, Jefferson observed that "the union of the civil and military power in the same hands at this time would greatly facilitate military measures." Then he made one final plea as governor, this time to George Washington. He asked the commander of the Continental army to come home and to take command in Virginia, for surely that would rouse and rally the Virginians to stand against the British and drive them out. Of course, Washington could do no such thing, although he did explain to Jefferson that the pressure he was applying to the British in the North was partly intended to force them out of the South. It is doubtful that this glimpse of the big strategic picture afforded Jefferson little comfort.

Although Benedict Arnold had failed to bag Jefferson in Richmond, Banastre Tarleton, the British army's master of the brutal hit-and-run raid, led a detachment of two hundred fifty Loyalist cavalrymen on a ride to Charlottesville to capture him there. It is not likely that the British had learned of Jefferson's resignation as governor, but even if they had, the author of the Declaration of Independence would still be a great prize.

We think of history as the record of important men, women, and nations doing great or terrible things and putting into action momentous plans and grand designs. Often, however, history turns on the consequences of some chance encounter in an obscure corner. Capt. Jack Jouett, a Virginia militiaman, was soothing himself with a drink at a tavern along the road to Charlottesville when he heard the crescendo of approaching hoof beats. A quick look confirmed that it was Tarleton and his British Legion. Jouett slipped out a back door, quietly mounted his horse, and pounded out the forty miles to Monticello in a midnight ride as important as Paul Revere's.

Apparently, the sight of the breathless Jouett and his lathered horse in the wee hours did little to alarm Jefferson. He quietly thanked the captain and calmly awakened his wife and several house guests, including members of the House of Delegates. No one rushed. All took the time to eat breakfast. After the meal, Jefferson dispatched the legislators to ride down the mountain to Charlottesville to awaken their fellow delegates while he personally and methodically directed his servants to hide various valuables. He was still giving directions when a neighbor burst in with the news that the British Legion was at the foot of Jefferson's "little mountain."

Now Jefferson swung into action. Gathering up Patty, eight-year-old Patsy, and two-year-old Polly, along with a pair of maids, he bundled them off in a fast, two-horse open carriage called a phaeton. He ordered the driver to drive hard for Blenheim, one of the Carter mansions, on Carter's Mountain. As for himself, Jefferson mounted his fastest steed, the majestically named Caractacus, and rode off—calmly, at first. He carried with him a collapsible spy glass and paused to look toward Charlottesville. Through the lens, he saw a typical sleepy morning in the temporary capital. Jefferson reflected. He knew what it was like to lose valuable papers; the Shadwell fire, back in 1770, had taught him that cruel lesson. With everything looking normal in Charlottesville and fearing that the British would ransack or even burn Monticello, he decided to ride back to his home to retrieve his most important documents.

He began to gallop back, only to realize that he had somehow dropped the short sword that figured as an important wardrobe accessory for gentlemen of the time. The weapon was more ceremonial than defensive, but it was costly, and it would also be unseemly for a man of Jefferson's station to appear in public without it. There was nothing to do but ride back in the other direction once again and look for it. So Jefferson turned away from Monticello, found his sword, and then looked through his spy glass again. This time he saw the streets of Charlottesville swarming with Loyalist troops. Focusing the telescope down the road, he saw cavalrymen charging up the mountain to Monticello. Leaving his papers to their fate, Jefferson spurred Caractacus on to join his wife and children.

According to Jefferson's house slaves, the master had not been gone five minutes before Capt. Kenneth McLeod, leading a detachment of Loyalist dragoons, reached the top of Monticello. One of the dragoons shoved a pistol into the chest of Martin Hemings, Jefferson's butler, demanding to know where Jefferson hand gone. When Hemings refused to answer, the dragoon told him he would be shot.

"Fire away, then," the slave Hemings responded.

Instead, the troops made themselves comfortable in Jefferson's mansion for the next eighteen hours in case he returned. They helped themselves to some of the master's fine wine, but, fortunately, they were under strict orders to loot nothing in the house. This order did not, however, extend to all of Jefferson's domain. The main body of British troops, under Lord Cornwallis, advanced into Elk Hill, a Jefferson property along the James River. The troops destroyed fields of corn and tobacco and burned barns. They appropriated cattle, sheep, and hogs as food. They took horses as cavalry mounts, save those that were too young to ride; these they butchered where they stood. For good measure, the troops burned Jefferson's fences so that whatever animals escaped seizure or destruction would simply run away.

Throughout all of this, Jefferson was relatively safe with his family—first at the Carters' Blenheim and then at Poplar Forest, his own summer retreat in Bedford County—even as seven Virginia delegates and Thomas Walker, Jefferson's neighbor and a member of the Continental Congress, were taken prisoner by the British. Once again, Jefferson's reputation had been badly tarnished. It was not a pretty picture: The war raged, Virginia was invaded, and Jefferson resigned office, then fled, leaving his state without a government. The impression that he was in hiding was made even stronger by a riding accident that occurred shortly after his narrow escape from Monticello. The spirited Caractacus reared up and threw him; Jefferson severely fractured his left wrist and was unable to ride for the next six weeks. He convalesced at Poplar Forest, inviting accusations of cowardice that would periodically shadow him for the rest of his life.

Yet even now it should have been clear to the despairing Jefferson that he had more political friends than enemies. Congress again asked him to go to Europe, along with John Adams and John Jay, to join Benjamin Franklin as one of the ministers plenipotentiary, charged with negotiating peace with the British. Once again, Jefferson was presented an opportunity to shape his nation's destiny. Once again, he was torn between the needs of Patty, whose health remained precarious, and the call of his nation. After four weeks of agonizing, he decided that he must stay with his wife and family. Moreover, after attending one more meeting of the House of Delegates (to attempt to clear his good name), he decided, as he wrote to his cousin Edmund Randolph, that he would take "final leave of everything" political or diplomatic and retire "to my farm, my family and books, from which I think nothing will ever more separate me."

Even before he and his family left Poplar Forest to return to Monticello, Jefferson turned his attention to a set of twenty-three questions that had been sent him by François de Marbois, secretary of the French legation stationed at Williamsburg. Most of the questions concerned Virginia's natural history, its animal and plant life, and its geology. Disgusted with politics, despairing over his reputation, and wracked with anxiety over the condition of his wife, Jefferson sought solace in writing about the natural glories of the place he loved. The manuscript rapidly metamorphosed into an eloquent, poetic, and romantic vision of Virginia as a kind of latter-day Eden. Yet, for all its romance, the book that became *Notes on the State of Virginia* was based on rigorous scientific observation, much of it made firsthand by the author himself. The book was driven, too, by a patriotic passion, which never died in Jefferson, despite frustration, disappointment, and despair.

At the time, the French naturalist Comte Georges de Buffon was considered the greatest of all natural philosophers, and his theories were accepted worldwide by scientists and others almost without argument. Among these theories was an assertion that the plant and animal species—including humankind—of the New World had undergone a "degenerative process" that made them smaller, weaker, and generally less vital than their Old World counterparts. In *Notes on the State of Virginia*, Jefferson, the avid amateur naturalist, presented data that he had gathered over many years. Far from being smaller and less robust than European species, American species were typically larger than what the Old World had to offer. In contrast to Buffon, who presented no hard data to back up his theory—after all, he had never even visited America—Jefferson presented comparative weights and measurements of a vast assortment of American versus European species.

Comparing native "quadrupeds" of Europe and America in Notes on the State of Virginia, *Jefferson refuted Count Buffon with statistics like these:*

Bear, in Europe 153.7 lbs., in America 410 lbs.

Beaver, in Europe 18.5 lbs., in America 45 lbs.

Otter, in Europe 8.9 lbs., in America 12 lbs.

Martin, in Europe 1.9 lbs., in America 6 lbs.

Flying squirrel, in Europe 2.2 lbs., in America 4 lbs.

Cow, in Europe 763 lbs., in America 2,500 lbs.

The discussion of flora and fauna led Jefferson also to confront Buffon on the subject of Native Americans and African Americans, both of whom the Frenchman had labeled degenerate. Jefferson defended the character of the Indian, emphasizing not only his physical prowess, but also his moral nature, including his great bravery, his devotion to his children, and his loyalty to his friends. As to blacks, there is no denying that Jefferson himself believed them inferior in most ways to whites. Without doubt, he shared the almost universal racism of his age. Yet, in *Notes on the State of Virginia*, he did not invidiously compare white and black. Instead, with a frankness that he would never permit himself in a political statement or the text of a proposed law, Jefferson denounced slavery, declaring that it had produced indolence among Southern whites—"For in a warm climate, no man will labor for himself who can make another labor for him"—and asking, "Can the liberties of a nation be thought secure when we have removed their only firm basis, a conviction in the minds of the people that these liberties are the gift of God? ... Indeed, I tremble for my country when I reflect that God is just, that his justice cannot sleep forever." The slave-owning Jefferson continued to believe that slavery was inherently wrong.

Jefferson's answers to Marbois's twenty-three questions became a thick manuscript. He turned it over to the Frenchman in December 1781. Doubtless, composing the work had served an important emotional purpose for its author. His great anxiety over Patty's health had increased markedly when he learned that she was again pregnant. It is true, however, that he, like his fellow Americans, had less reason to be anxious about the state of the Revolution at this moment. On October 17, 1781, the Franco-American siege against the army of Lord Cornwallis at Yorktown had ended with Cornwallis's surrender. Although the war would not formally end until the Treaty of Paris was concluded in 1783, Yorktown marked the practical end of the American Revolution and virtually ensured that independence had been won. For Jefferson, whose resignation as governor had come on the very eve of victory, this fact must have been bittersweet indeed.

But his colleagues would not let him retreat into Monticello, natural history, and his *Notes*. In December, the Virginia House of Delegates elected Jefferson as a delegate to the Continental Congress. He had not asked to be nominated—and he certainly had not asked for what the delegates did next. Even though they thought highly enough of him to elect him to Congress, they also voted to hold an inquiry into his conduct during his second term as governor. Although Jefferson's political foes instigated the inquiry, his friends covertly supported it; they were confident that the former governor's name would be cleared. Jefferson, however, saw nothing positive in the action. Years later, he recorded in his memoirs that "the inquiry was a shock on which I had not calculated." Adding to the shock was the fact that the inquiry was spearheaded by his much-admired colleague and friend, Patrick Henry—it was a betrayal that Jefferson would never forgive.

Even as he declined to accept his election to the Continental Congress, Jefferson took his seat in Virginia's House of Delegates. On December 19, 1781, he announced that he was prepared to answer all charges against him. This might have been one of the great confrontations in American history except that, by this time, there was really very little to confront. The assumptions of Jefferson's friends had been correct: The facts, once revealed, exonerated the ex-governor. Speaker of the House John Tyler had already reviewed the work of a committee appointed to investigate Jefferson's conduct and had concluded that the charges stemmed from "groundless ... rumors." Anticlimactically, Jefferson insisted on presenting his full defense nevertheless. After listening politely, the delegates passed a resolution, which had already been written, not only clearing Jefferson's good name but also thanking him for his "impartial, upright, and attentive" service as governor. Thus vindicated, Jefferson left the House of Delegates to return to Monticello. Subsequently reelected, he refused to serve.

Returned to his mountaintop, Jefferson responded to correspondence from Charles Thomson, secretary of Congress and a member of the American Philosophical Society, asking him to offer *Notes on the State of Virginia* to a broader audience by making several copies of it. Jefferson demurred at first because he felt that the work needed revision and amplification. So he decided to revise and amplify it. The book, which had taken only a few months to draft, now consumed three years in revision and expansion. It grew to genuine book length, much too long to make multiple copies of by hand. Accordingly, in 1785, Jefferson ordered the printing of a private and anonymous edition of two hundred copies for distribution primarily to friends. Later, as we will see, it became something of an international best-seller and has never been out of print since its first commercial publication in 1788.

Composing the first draft must have provided much-needed emotional relief for Jefferson in a time of private and public affliction, and the work of revision and expansion must have helped take his mind off the condition of his wife, which continued to deteriorate as her pregnancy progressed.

The birth of a daughter, named Lucy Elizabeth, after the child they had most recently lost, brought no improvement in Patty's health. It is said that the newborn weighed more than sixteen pounds, making for an especially difficult delivery. Just two days before the birth, Jefferson had angrily responded to Speaker John Tyler's demand that he take his seat in the House of Delegates or face being "seized" and compelled to attend. He wrote to James Monroe, protesting the House's demand for the *"perpetual ...* services of all its members" and, through Monroe, reminding his colleagues that he had already "dedicated to them the whole of the active and useful part of my life." He pleaded now for "mental quiet" as his wife lay gravely ill.

Patsy Jefferson, ten years old at this time, grew ever closer to her father and recalled, years later, how he nursed his wife: "For four months that she lingered, he was never out of calling. When not at her bedside, he was writing in a small room which opened immediately at the head of her bed."

During his vigil, before she slipped into a coma, Patty Jefferson asked Thomas not to remarry. It was request made not from selfishness, but because she could not stand the thought of her daughters being raised, as she had been, by a stepmother. Jefferson gave his promise. He would never remarry. Then, as his wife lost consciousness, her breathing becoming labored and stertorous, the blood drained from Jefferson's ruddy face, and he collapsed.

It took an hour to revive him. It was September 6, 1782. Shortly after Thomas Jefferson came to, Martha "Patty" Jefferson was dead at age thirty-three.

Before Patty's death, the prospect of becoming the hermit of Monticello was very appealing to Thomas Jefferson. To write, to read, to think, to play music, to farm, to tend his garden, to cultivate his vineyard, all in quiet company with wife and children— what delight could be greater? Now he was indeed the hermit of Monticello, but, at thirty-nine, he was also devastated, bereft of interest in all that had formerly delighted him. He wrote to his sister-in-law a month after Patty's death: "Were it not for the infidelity of deserting the sacred charge left me"—three children and six nieces and nephews—"I could not wish [life's] continuance a moment."

The needs of this "sacred charge," followed soon by the needs of his country, roused him from what he described as a "stupor of mind." Before the year came to a close, a new smallpox epidemic swept across Virginia. Jefferson accepted the invitation of his friend Archibald Cary to bring his children to Ampthill, Cary's estate outside of Richmond, where he had arranged to give inoculations. Jefferson personally nursed the children through the post-inoculation symptoms, and he was still at Ampthill on November 25 when he received a letter from the president of the Continental Congress, Robert R. Livingston. At the suggestion of James Madison, Jefferson's friend and devoted protégé, Congress had again appointed Jefferson minister plenipotentiary to France to continue negotiating a treaty of peace with Britain.

In the past, such offers had brought with them an agony of indecision. This time, Jefferson replied the very next day: "I will employ in this arduous charge, with diligence and integrity, the best of my poor talents, which I am conscious are far short of what it requires."

As if awakened from a long, dull sleep, Jefferson now moved with remarkable speed. Lucy Elizabeth and Maria were put into the hands of his sister-in-law, while his own sister Martha and her children were sent back to Monticello to live. Patsy, to whom Jefferson was now more fiercely devoted than ever, would come with him to France. Father and daughter set off for Philadelphia, the first leg of the journey, on December 19.

Chapter 11

Back to Politics

In Philadelphia, Jefferson briefed himself on international relations by studying the papers of the secretary of foreign affairs of the Continental Congress. Characteristically, while he was in Philadelphia, he mixed politics with his other great passion, natural science, by attending a meeting of the American Philosophical Society, to which he had recently been elected. After a warm reunion with James Madison, Jefferson and Patsy set off for Baltimore to rendezvous with the French frigate *Romulus*, which would transport them to France.

The winter of 1782–83 was bitter cold, and Baltimore Harbor was packed with ice. Jefferson and his daughter arrived to discover that the *Romulus*, ice locked, couldn't budge. Even if it could break free, the French vessel would then have to run a gauntlet of at least twenty-five British men-o'-war blockading the mouth of the Chesapeake. Charlestonian Henry Laurens, sent by Congress in 1780 to negotiate a war loan with the United Netherlands, had been captured by a British blockader on the Banks of Newfoundland. He was sent to England and imprisoned in the Tower of London, charged with high treason. Laurens was held incommunicado for fourteen months by a British government reluctant to condemn him as a rebel, lest prisoners held by the Americans suffer reprisals, but also unwilling to release him, lest he accomplish his mission. Laurens was finally exchanged for Cornwallis and was released on November 30, 1782, just in time to join Franklin, Adams, and Jay in hammering out preliminary articles of peace with Britain. His confinement in the Tower, however, had broken his health.

Like all Americans, Jefferson was well aware of Laurens's plight, and he understood the very real danger of being captured by the British, a prospect that must have loomed as all the more dreadful because he was accompanied by Patsy. Yet he was willing to risk it because his greater fear was that the war would be over and a final peace would be concluded before he could reach Paris. Accordingly, as soon as word came that the *Romulus* had broken free of the ice, he and Patsy boarded a small boat to overtake the French ship. But whereas the large warship had been big and heavy enough to penetrate the ice floes, Jefferson's little craft was soon locked in by the frozen tide. It could go nowhere until the tide came in again— and, by that time, the only possible direction was back to shore. Jefferson had literally missed the boat.

He returned to his Baltimore lodgings and wrote to Congress for new instructions: He could travel to Boston and take a ship from there, he could wait for the British to dismantle the blockade as the war continued to wind down, or he could attempt to sail to France under a flag of truce.

Days and then weeks dragged by as Jefferson awaited a reply. He used his time to reflect on the current condition of the nation. It was apparent to him that, as victory and independence drew nearer, the states were suffering a kind of malaise, betwixt and between a commitment to union and a desire for independence from one another.

When the war began, Jefferson had come down squarely on the side of state autonomy within the loosest of unions. Lately, however, he had come to see that the existence of autonomous states would lead to "internal contests" destined to destroy America and that "no remedy [is] so likely to prevent [such contests] as strengthening the band which connects us." As governor of Virginia, he had had a long and bitter lesson on the wages of powerlessness. Perhaps his frustration in the icebound harbor of Baltimore had brought those lessons freshly home. In any event, he now believed that a Continental Congress was a fine thing, "but we have done nothing [to] enable [Congress] to enforce [its] decisions."

Therefore, Jefferson wrote to Edmund Randolph that the decisions of Congress likely would not be enforced: "The states will go to war with each other in defiance of Congress. One will call in France to her assistance, another Great Britain, and so we shall have all the wars of Europe brought to our doors."

Jefferson had shed most of his fear of strong central government. The Continental Congress had begun at the outset of the Revolution as a forum in which the individual states might better coordinate their actions in time of war. Jefferson saw that it must now mature into a governing body composed of the representatives of the states but taking precedence over those states.

At last, Jefferson received the instructions of Congress. Since March, he had heard rumors that a peace treaty had been signed in Paris. Actually, only the Declaration for Suspension of Arms and Cessation of Hostilities had been signed, on January 20, bringing an end to the shooting. The definitive Treaty of Paris would not be signed until September 3, 1783, but Congress had already decided that Jefferson's services were no longer required in Paris; he was informed of this on April 4, 1783.

For the third time in his political life, Jefferson had lost the opportunity to shape his nation's destiny abroad. With feelings of anticlimax and disappointment, he returned with Patsy to Monticello. He found consolation in a stopover at Richmond, where his House of Delegates colleagues gave him a most cordial and enthusiastic welcome. He was happily stunned to discover that he was not only forgiven for anything that he may have done or failed to do as governor, but that he was downright popular. Even more gratifying was the news that the College of William and Mary had decided to award him an honorary doctor of civil laws degree, praising his skill "both in private and public law," his "exceptional love for his country," and concluding that "all the fine arts seem to foregather in one man." The college further recognized the essential integrity of Jefferson, who did "everything with regard to conscience." For "a deed well done," the presentation document declared, "he seeks his reward not from popular acclaim but from the deed itself."

And so, returning to Monticello in April 1784, Jefferson decided to draw on his freshly discovered "popular acclaim," not seeking a reward, but looking to accomplish a most important deed. No man knew more than Thomas Jefferson about how a state should *not* be governed. Back in 1776, his draft constitution for Virginia had arrived too late for consideration by the House of Delegates (Chapter 8, "Designing Virginia"). As a result, a conservative document had been adopted instead, one that had proved as inadequate to the needs of Virginia as the Articles of Confederation were now proving to the needs of the United States. Entirely on his own, Jefferson began drafting a new constitution for his state, which he hoped would get the support of his followers in the House of Delegates.

The new document was no mere rehash of what he had composed earlier, but it was a refinement and elaboration of the 1776 draft. It included a new statement of the doctrine of balance of powers, the division of government into legislative, executive, and judicial branches, each with distinct but interlocking powers and none taking precedence over the others. As the former governor of Virginia, Jefferson knew the evils of powerlessness; as a revolutionary patriot, he knew the evils of power unbalanced and unchecked. The tripartite government that he developed incorporated the system of checks and balances that is so familiar to us today. Also familiar is Jefferson's redesign of the House of Delegates as an assembly consisting of two houses, the equivalent of a Senate and a House of Representatives. The members of both houses were to be elected by popular vote of *all* free male citizens; completely eliminated was even the pretext of a property ownership qualification.

Not surprisingly, Jefferson devoted careful attention to the office of governor. He was to be elected by both houses of the assembly but would serve a single five-year term and would thereafter be barred from serving again. The governor would thus get sufficient time to implement his policies but would not have a dictator's job for life. He would enjoy much more authority than Jefferson had had, including veto power, although he would share it with a Council of Revision, which included two members of the Council of State and three superior-court justices.

As in his earlier document, Jefferson provided for freedom of the press, subordinated the military to civil authority, and restricted the death penalty to murder, military offenses, and treason. Most radical were his provisions regarding slavery: First, no more slaves were to be admitted into the state. Second, slavery would not continue "beyond the generation which shall be living on the thirty-first day of December 1800: all persons born after that day being hereby declared free."

The model constitution was not adopted wholesale by the Virginia Assembly; certainly Jefferson couldn't have had high hopes that the slavery provisions would ever be enacted. However, many of the other provisions were incorporated into a new constitution for the state. Even more important, most of the principles Jefferson developed would become the framework of a new constitution for the United States. Just as the United States Constitution has served as a model for democratic constitutions in many other countries, it is also fair to say that what Jefferson crafted at Monticello in 1784 has inspired and enabled international liberty over the course of at least three centuries.

The Virginia Assembly elected Thomas Jefferson to its Congressional delegation on June 6, 1783. This time, he was eager to serve in Congress. He set off for Philadelphia, again with Patsy, now eleven years old, on October 15. But father and daughter were in for a surprise when they reached the city: Congress wasn't there. Menaced by a violent uprising of ragged, hungry Continental troops demanding their back pay, the legislators had decamped to Princeton, New Jersey, to hover under the protective wing of George Washington and a cadre of still-loyal troops stationed there. Jefferson would go to Congress in Princeton, but he first arranged for Patsy to board in the home of Mrs. Thomas Hopkinson and her son Francis, who was not only a signer of the Declaration of Independence, but the newborn republic's foremost composer and one of its most important poets.

The Hopkinsons served as Patsy's tutors, implementing an ambitious program of study that her father had drawn up. It was an unusual education for a girl of that era because it was designed to make her an independent, self-sufficient human being rather than a mere ornament to some future husband. To François de Marbois, for whom he had drawn up the original version of *Notes on the State of Virginia*, Jefferson wrote: "The chance that in marriage [Patsy] will draw a blockhead I calculate at about fourteen to one, and of course [I conclude] that the education of her family will probably rest on her own ideas and direction without assistance." Just how Jefferson had calculated the fourteen-to-one odds is not recorded, but the point was clear enough: Patsy was to be educated for independence so that she, in turn, could one day educate a family of independent, thoughtful citizens of the United States.

From Annapolis, Maryland, Jefferson wrote to his eleven-year-old daughter Patsy in Philadelphia on November 28, 1783:

With respect to the distribution of your time the following is what I should approve.

from 8. to 10 o'clock practise music.

from 10. to 1. dance one day and draw another.

from 1. to 2. draw on the day you dance, and write a letter the next day.

from 3. to 4. read French.

from 4. to 5. exercise yourself in music.

from 5. till bedtime read English, write &c.

Communicate this plan to Mrs. Hopkinson [Patsy's tutor and guardian in Philadelphia] and if she approves of it pursue it.

By the time Jefferson arrived in Princeton, Congress had decided to reconvene in Annapolis, Maryland, which was more centrally located. Jefferson set off again, settled in Annapolis, and was assigned to chair the Congressional committee charged with securing ratification of the Treaty of Paris. He worked vigorously to see the treaty through the process, for he understood how precious the document was. Britain had unambiguously yielded to the United States its independence and also had agreed to a definition of the new nation's boundaries that encompassed the entire Old

Northwest, the trans-Appalachian territory that Governor Jefferson had ceded to the federal government, which represented, as Jefferson saw it, the core of the republic's future promise. Britain asked for little enough in return: the payment of debts owed to British creditors and the restoration of the rights and property of Loyalists. But it was precisely this "little enough" that many state legislatures begrudged the British. Jefferson had an uphill climb to secure the ratification of the treaty, but ratified it was on January 14, 1784.

Securing ratification of the Treaty of Paris was only one of Jefferson's accomplishments during his two years as a member of Congress. Despite his reserved manner and his fondness for the seclusion of the study, Jefferson became the central figure of Congress under the Articles of Confederation. He was a dynamo and a compass, driving any number of Congressional committees and guiding the nation with dozens of penetrating and carefully considered reports and other papers.

Congressman Jefferson was no longer the frustrated figure frozen in Baltimore Harbor. All the energies pent up by decades of political frustration and disappointment seemed to be released in a torrent during his two years as a national legislator. Despite exhaustion and chronic migraines, he was eager to model a new nation and, perhaps, was desperately trying to hold his own loneliness at bay.

Jefferson believed that the government of the United States now had five overriding needs: to establish itself economically among nations by concluding treaties of commerce, to make the administration of government far more efficient, to establish "arsenals within the states and posts on our frontiers," to administer the western territories, and to establish an efficient system of coinage.

The last-named priority resulted in Jefferson's proposal of a currency based on the decimal system, with a dollar consisting of one hundred cents, ten dimes, and so on. Not only would this introduce a simple logic into American commerce, but it would serve as yet another declaration of independence from Britain and its irrational system of pounds, shillings, and pence. Congress was persuaded and adopted Jefferson's decimal currency system in 1785.

Portrait of Thomas Jefferson by Gilbert Stuart, published in
Pendleton's Lithography, about 1828.

(Collection: Library of Congress)

Even more important was Jefferson's 1784 *Report of a Plan of
Government for the Western Territory* and his proposed Land
Ordinance of 1784. Jefferson called for the division of the
Northwest Territory into fourteen states, with brilliant, practical
provisions for an orderly progression from territorial status to full
statehood. Settlers could form a temporary government simply by
adopting the constitution and laws of any of the original thirteen

states. When the population of a territory reached twenty thousand, a constitutional convention would meet to create a permanent government. When the population equaled that of the least populous of the thirteen original states, the territory, with its constitution already in place, would be admitted to the union as the full equal of the other states. In this way, Jefferson hoped to avoid the divisive and unjust opposition of established East versus struggling West, which had bedeviled and undermined Virginia and other colonies for so many years. Within each territory, all elections were to be by universal male suffrage, and government would be based locally. All that the territories owed to the federal government was a willingness to bear their share of the federal debt and to contribute to the common defense.

> Jefferson even took a stab at naming his proposed states of the Northwest—albeit most awkwardly. There were, for example, Metropotamia, Assenisipia, Cherronesus, and Pelisipia, in addition to Sylvania, Michigania, Illinoia, and Saratoga.

On the matter of slavery, however, law was not to be left to local determination. Jefferson's Land Ordinance of 1784 called outright for the abolition of slavery after the year 1800. The Land Ordinance came up for a vote on April 19, 1784. Predictably, the North was solidly in favor of it, while the South, except for a single North Carolina representative, voted against it. Jefferson had six states in his corner, but he needed seven. The deciding vote hung on a single representative, New Jersey's John Beatty, who, sick in bed with a cold, failed to appear at the voting session. By a single vote, on account of a runny nose, the momentous Land Ordinance fell.

Jefferson's defeated Land Ordinance would be followed in 1787 by the Northwest Ordinance, perhaps the single most important piece of legislation under the Articles of Confederation. Like Jefferson's 1784 bill, the Northwest Ordinance prohibited the extension of slavery into the territories (although it also provided for the return of any fugitive slaves who might attempt to escape into the region). That gratified Jefferson, but, in 1784, the one-vote defeat of the Land Ordinance made a freshly frustrated Jefferson anxious to leave Congress. His opportunity came just two weeks after the heartbreaking vote, when it was announced that John Jay would resign as one of the U.S. ministers to France. Jefferson rushed to fill the void. On May 7, 1784, Congress chose him to serve with Franklin and Adams to negotiate treaties of commerce with sixteen European nations and to deal with the Barbary pirates, who preyed upon American and European ship-ping off the coast of North Africa. Thomas Jefferson was going to Europe at last.

Part Four

Head and Heart

Chapter 12

The Diplomat

A mere four days after Congress appointed him minister plenipotentiary to France, Jefferson left Annapolis and the frustrations of Congress for Philadelphia. He did not, however, make haste to France. Jefferson took with utmost seriousness the term *plenipotentiary:* As a negotiator on behalf of the United States, he was to be "invested with full powers." In an era without instant communication between a representative and his nation's head of state, diplomats had to have much more independent authority than they enjoy today. In Jefferson's day, they did not so much represent their nation's foreign policy as created it on the spot.

To use such power responsibly, Jefferson decided that he should learn as much about the needs of his countrymen as he could. So, instead of departing directly from Philadelphia, he decided to travel north and leave from Boston. Along the way, he would present a questionnaire to men of business and local government. He wanted firsthand knowledge of just what Americans expected from commerce with foreign nations.

On the way to France, then, Jefferson and Patsy stopped in New York City; New Haven, Connecticut (and Yale College); Portsmouth, New Hampshire; and finally Boston. At each stop, Jefferson conferred with prominent locals and solicited responses to his questionnaire. Only then did Jefferson and Patsy, with his favorite servant, James Hemings, board the *Ceres,* which, on June 5, 1784, was off to England on its maiden voyage. The *Ceres* landed at the English port of Cowes after a swift twenty-day crossing, then Jefferson and his daughter made the channel crossing to Le Havre on June 30, 1784. Landed at Le Havre, Jefferson dispatched James Hemings with their baggage while he personally supervised the unloading of the phaeton that he had brought with him from Monticello, which transported him and his daughter to Paris.

> In addition to passing time with his daughter during the cruise, Jefferson occupied himself by reading his beloved Don Quixote, this time in the original Spanish, with the aid of a dictionary. It was typical Jefferson: Finding the opportunity, he combined learning Spanish with the pleasure of one of his favorite books. At noon each day, Jefferson noted the ship's longitude and latitude, recorded wind speed and direction, and logged the distance that had been covered. He also kept his eye out for such natural wonders as sharks and whales, which he described in several journal entries.

Their route from Le Havre to the capital followed the Seine, and everything Jefferson saw along the way contributed to a love at first sight that would grow and endure. Here was the heart of the Enlightenment, the home of Voltaire, Rousseau, Diderot, and the other *philosophes* upon whose work Jefferson had based so many of his own moral and political ideas. Here, too, was a nation of great culture and beauty—its art and music beckoning to the ardent admirer in him—the very nexus of European thought, morality, politics, and general sophistication. It was a great classroom of international diplomacy, and Jefferson was as eager a student as ever he had been in his youth. America did not yet know it, but by sending Jefferson to France, it was creating a politician and states-man of extraordinary depth and breadth.

Born and raised on the edge of the American frontier, a master of rough-and-ready local politics, a lawyer and creator of law, a key architect of American independence, a keen observer of American life, and a quintessential American, Jefferson would now learn the ways of the Old World. He would return to the United States after five years abroad to become his nation's first secretary of state, its second vice president, and its third president.

Once Jefferson and Patsy settled into comfortable lodgings on the Left Bank—he had found the first place they tried, on the rue de Richelieu, too noisy—the new minister plenipotentiary dispatched a message to Benjamin Franklin to announce his presence. His first endeavors were not directly diplomatic, however, as he set up a household appropriate to the station of a gentleman and statesman. Jefferson hired a major domo and a personal valet to supplement the services of James Hemings, and he quickly sunk a small fortune into new clothes for himself and his daughter, having been warned by Adams that "to be out of fashion [in Paris] is more criminal than to be seen in a state of nature." As much as Jefferson spent on suits, a new sword and belt, and other accouterments, he lavished even more on books. Book shops and book stalls beckoned at every turn in the French capital.

As for Patsy, Jefferson enrolled her in a highly recommended convent school, which catered to the daughters of the aristocracy. Jefferson was certainly no aristocrat, and while there is no evidence that he harbored any specific anti-Catholic sentiments, it can be assumed that he shared, at least to some degree, the eighteenth-century Protestant American's distrust of Roman Catholicism. But Jefferson never let his prejudices turn him away from a good thing. According to the Marquis de Chastellux, a French gentleman, man of letters, and amateur scientist Jefferson had befriended in America, the Abbaye Royale de Panthemont was the best school for girls in all of France.

In 1783, the Montgolfier brothers gave the first public demonstration of the ascent of a hot-air balloon. A few weeks after this, Pilatre de Rozier, a science teacher, and the Marquis d'Arlandes, an infantry officer, became the first human aeronauts when they flew in a hot-air balloon for five and a half miles over Paris. Jefferson, who had seen an unmanned ascension in Philadelphia, was treated to his first view of a manned ascension, over Paris, on September 19, 1784. He was exhilarated by the prospect of the future of air travel, which seemed to him a most appropriate expression of the human spirit.

Jefferson paid a visit to Benjamin Franklin, ensconced in his elegant quarters at Passy, on August 10, just four days after he arrived in Paris. Not until the end of August, however, did he meet officially with both of his fellow ministers, Franklin and John Adams, to get down to the work of negotiating the treaties of amity and commerce so necessary to the survival, not to mention prosperity, of their fledgling democracy. Franklin was the senior minister, officially in charge of the American delegation, and no one admired him and delighted in his conversation more than Jefferson. It was with John Adams, however, that Jefferson forged his closest working relationship in Europe.

Jefferson and Adams were an odd couple, both politically and temperamentally. Beyond question, both were liberty-loving patriots, but Adams was far more the republican and Jefferson the democrat. Whereas Adams put his faith in a body of elected lawgivers, Jefferson bestowed his directly on the people. The political gap between the two men would broaden with time, especially after Jefferson became vice president under Adams. Even more immediately striking than the political differences were the contrasts in their personalities. Adams was crusty, acidic, irascible, and blunt; Jefferson was diplomatic in the familiar sense of the word— polite, reserved, easy to get along with, and always open to conversation with anyone who offered an interesting thought. Adams was a frowning brooder. His passion for liberty sprang less from a belief in the potential greatness of humankind than from a desire to create a government that might curb the selfishness and overweening ambition that he believed to be the driving force of human nature. For Jefferson, however, liberty was an opportunity for human beings to exercise what was naturally best in them.

Maybe the cliché is as old as the eighteenth century: Opposites attract. The two men not only worked brilliantly together, with one perhaps compensating for the shortcomings of the other, but they also were friends, with their friendship built at least as much on mutual respect and admiration as on affection.

As for Adams's wife, Abigail, her regard for Jefferson was deep and sisterly. Doubtless she found his optimism a healthy tonic for her husband, even as his quietly cheerful company brought her welcome relief from the often sour companionship of Adams. During the years Jefferson and Patsy lived in Paris, they were virtually adopted by the Adamses.

Benjamin Franklin, America's senior diplomat in France and chief treaty negotiator. Jefferson, who replaced Franklin as minister plenipotentiary to France, greatly admired him.

By pushing and pulling one another, Adams and Jefferson moved steadily forward. They found they could dispute productively and disagree without being disagreeable—and one of the subjects on which they disagreed most was Benjamin Franklin. He had been in Paris since Christmas 1776 and had done more than any other man to create and preserve the Franco-American alliance that, although often disappointing, nevertheless triumphed decisively at Yorktown. Franklin was everything the modern Frenchman admired: a philosopher, a diplomat, a man of courage and passion leavened by wit, both eminently practical and an idealist, pure of intention yet worldly in his sophistication, and, not least, a lady's man extraordinaire. The French adored Franklin, lionized him, listened to him, and believed in him. Best of all, the French saw him as the very embodiment of America. In this respect, he was an ideal ambassador.

Benjamin Franklin's light burned so brightly in Paris that it was difficult for lesser lights to be seen, and a succession of commissioners dispatched by the Continental Congress to join Franklin resented this—none more than John Adams. At one point, before Jefferson was attached to the mission, dissent grew so bitter that Franklin tendered his resignation. That may have relieved his fellow ministers, but Congress's rejection of Franklin's resignation sent the others an unmistakable message: *They* were expendable; Franklin was not. The latest word was that Jefferson had been sent to Paris to replace the seventy-nine-year-old Franklin. Jefferson gave no indication that he understood this to be the case, and if either Franklin or Adams (who, after all, was senior to Jefferson) resented the prospect, neither let on.

In fact, Jefferson's presence pleased both Adams and Franklin, enabling them all to work harmoniously and productively together. It wasn't just his personality that did the trick. Jefferson brought with him instructions for a mission he himself had composed and Congress had approved. The task was ambitious, and its scope excited and energized all three commissioners. Jefferson proposed concluding free-trade agreements with a host of European powers, creating a system unencumbered by regulations, restrictions, tariffs, or duties. With the impediments removed, Jefferson argued, "every

country [could produce] that which nature had best fitted it to produce, and each ... be free to exchange with others mutual surpluses
for mutual wants." It was vintage Jefferson: The modeling of laws
and agreements not to restrict but to liberate and harmonize with
the great potential "nature" offered.

Of course, the purpose of free trade was not just philosophical
or idealistic. The development of manufacturing in the United
States, Jefferson knew, would take time, whereas the struggling
republic needed to build a sound economy *now*. If the country
lacked manufacturing at the moment, it did have an abundance of
raw materials and food crops to offer the world. These could serve
as the immediate basis of a strong economy, provided that foreign
trade restrictions and punitive tariffs did not interfere. Indeed,
whereas Gov. Jefferson had been in a great rush to develop domestic industries during the war, to make Virginia and all of America
less militarily vulnerable, he saw free trade primarily as a means of
encouraging American agriculture rather than manufacturing.
International free trade was yet another way to foster a nation of
independent farmers.

Jefferson had another motive for promoting free trade. The
commercial treaties would be concluded by the United States as a
whole, not by the individual states. This would accomplish at least
three things. First, it would make commerce a *national* issue.
Second, once commerce was a national issue, the states would be
compelled to adopt a new constitution that explicitly acknowledged the precedence of the federal union over the individual
states, and to entrust to that federal union greater authority than it
had under the Articles of Confederation. Third, the nations of the
world would recognize that they were dealing not with a loose collection of former colonies, but with a single, unified, sovereign
nation. Negotiating international free trade was yet another step
in Jefferson's journey from Virginian to American.

Capping the many benefits that free trade offered to governance
and economics, Jefferson believed that those nations agreeing to
treaties would thereby be exposed to America's revolutionary philosophy. This is not to suggest that Jefferson was a precursor of
Marx or Lenin, who saw revolution in global terms, but it did occur

to him that the more democratic republics there were in the world, the friendlier that world would be to the United States of America.

Armed with a mixture of practical economic expedience and high-minded political theory, Jefferson rolled up his sleeves and took the initiative in preparing a model treaty for his colleagues to discuss. The principal provision was free trade: the right of each signatory to carry cargo for the other and to buy and sell on terms that each nation accorded its most-favored trading partner. Beyond this, Jefferson also proposed strong stipulations of the rights of neutral nations in time of war, aimed at enabling the safe continuation of commerce, including unimpeded commerce with all the belligerents.

Delighted with the strides they had made, Jefferson and the other commissioners soon began actual negotiations with several European powers. That, however, was instantly deflating. Jefferson had assumed that many nations would jump at the chance to acquire a new trading partner, a new source of raw materials, and a new market for their goods. But the commissioners found very little interest among the major nations. Only Prussia, governed by its brilliant, visionary "benevolent despot" Frederick the Great, saw the great promise in trade with the United States. Indeed, so impressed was Frederick with the treaty that he asked to see its author, and he and Jefferson subsequently met. This single victory was sufficient to hearten Jefferson, who saw the strategic importance of U.S. access to Prussian ports in peace as well as war. Operating from these ports in wartime, American privateers would be well positioned to intercept foreign—that is, British—trading vessels coming out of Russia.

His fellow commissioners may have despaired over the otherwise almost universal lack of interest in American trade, but Jefferson seized the sole example of Prussia as a promise of great things to come. He was in a hopeful mood during his first months as a top-level diplomat in Paris: hopeful for an improvement in the precarious finances of his country, hopeful for the country's future, and hopeful, too, that he was finally beginning to leave behind the devastating loneliness brought by the death of Patty. Then, in January 1785, the Marquis de Lafayette called on him, bringing dreadful news from America. Two-year-old Lucy Elizabeth had died of whooping cough.

Writing to a friend, Jefferson could only observe the cold fact that "of six children, I have lost four, and finally their mother."

Chapter 13

Making a Place for America

The news of Lucy Elizabeth's death intensified Jefferson's loneliness, of course, but he remained steadfast in his efforts to
press forward with the trade treaties. Jefferson was not only grief-
stricken, but he was assailed by a mixture of anger with his daughter's caretakers and guilt over not having been there to take care of
her himself. These feelings greatly dimmed his outlook on Paris,
but only for a time. By the late spring of 1785, he learned that
Benjamin Franklin, aged and infirm, was returning to the United
States and that the rumors had been correct: He, Thomas
Jefferson, was to replace Franklin as American minister to France.
However, he would work alone, for John Adams had accepted an
appointment as the United States's first ambassador to the Court
of St. James's: ambassador to England.

The new responsibility, the assurance of years—perhaps even a
lifetime—of work as a diplomat revived Jefferson's spirits. He
vastly preferred serving his country in a nonelective office than in
a highly political elective one. Moreover, he enjoyed his plenipotentiary authority, which gave him a great deal of decision-making
latitude and the opportunity he had always craved to take a direct
hand in shaping his nation's destiny.

Gradually, the pain of his losses diminished, and, once again,
Jefferson found Paris a delight. Benjamin Franklin had stood
Jefferson in good stead among Parisians important in government
as well as science, literature, and the arts. Franklin attracted interesting and significant French men—and women—like a magnet,

and he willingly shared these invaluable acquaintances with Jefferson, who was now forty-two. Soon Jefferson was a regular guest in the fashionable salons of Paris. He came to understand, as Franklin above all others understood, that nations do not deal with nations, and diplomats do not deal with governments: Always, people deal with people. The French men and women Jefferson met were eager to meet *Americans*, especially Americans as accomplished and charming as Franklin and Jefferson. In turn, Jefferson understood that the influential people he moved among in the salons were his most efficient conduits to the centers of power.

> *Jefferson took the lessons of the salon home with him, drawing generously on them when he became president of the United States in 1801. His White House was celebrated for its many dinners and brilliant conversation. Jefferson paid for this entertainment out of his own pocket, but he believed that the White House dinners were far more than polite social gatherings. They were his opportunity to speak candidly and at length with the world's most influential politicians, leaders, captains of industry, scientists, artists, and authors.*

Not that Jefferson spent all of his time in the salons. He worked on his revision and expansion of *Notes on the State of Virginia*, which, as mentioned in Chapter 4, "This New Man," he printed in a private edition of two hundred copies during the spring of 1785. Jefferson was torn between a desire to circulate the book to a wider audience and a fear that its frank antislavery views would alienate Southerners, including those in his home state. The matter was more or less taken out of his hands when a French bookseller obtained a copy and was about to publish a "very abominable" translation. Jefferson sought to preempt this by authorizing a trusted French acquaintance and noted translator, Abbé Morellet, to make a faithful translation. The author also decided to add a map based on the one his father had drawn up in the 1740s. However, at his own insistence, Jefferson was to remain anonymous.

Even this edition proved to be a disappointment. After reviewing the manuscript translation, Jefferson gave Morellet an extensive list of corrections, but he resigned himself to a distorted French version reaching print. To forestall the possibility of an even worse English-language edition being retranslated and pirated from the French, Jefferson authorized a British publisher to bring out an original English-language edition in 1787, this one also including his father's map, but bearing his own name on the title page. The universal acclaim with which the book met vastly outweighed any criticism from proslavery Southerners.

His work on *Notes*, together with his appointment as minister to France, did much to lift the gloom of Lucy Elizabeth's death. Acknowledging his desire to remain in Paris for the long term, perhaps even for the remainder of his political career, Jefferson sent for his daughter Mary—whom he called Polly—and moved into larger and more sumptuous quarters. The Hôtel de Langéac did befit the rank of ambassador, even though it had been built by a duke for his mistress.

Jefferson did not expect the United States government to pay for his new lodgings. He footed the hefty bills himself, and he used his villa as the setting for meetings and dinners not only with a host of French and other foreign dignitaries, but also with an endless stream of American entrepreneurs, businessmen, scientists, inventors, painters, writers, and explorers. The roster of Jefferson's growing circle is impressive. There was John Trumbull, one of the young republic's leading painters. The Connecticut-born explorer John Ledyard was a frequent guest; his ambition was to become the "first circumabulator of the globe," and Jefferson did his best to obtain for him free passage across Russia. When Tom Paine, the renowned author of *Common Sense*, called at the Hôtel to present to Jefferson his designs for a new type of iron bridge, the ambassador used his contacts to obtain English patents for him. For Maryland-born James Rumsey, Jefferson worked to obtain rights to develop steamboats for the French service—twenty-two years before Robert Fulton launched his *Clermont* on the Hudson. The great French names of the American Revolution were also Jefferson's dinner guests: Lafayette, Rochambeau, and De Grasse.

In turn, the ambassador was received by the great French scientist Antoine Laurent Lavoisier and the mathematical philosopher Marquis de Condorcet, among many other luminaries.

Portrait of Thomas Jefferson by Rembrandt Peale, about 1805.

(Collection: National Archives and Records Administration)

Jefferson worked tirelessly to help his countrymen achieve a wider international audience or market for their inventions, ideas, products, and services. They were lucky to have such a man pulling for them; Jefferson rapidly emerged, in the opinion of many, as the most popular ambassador in the French court.

As an ambassador, Jefferson saw his chief duty as making a place in the world for America. His association with the great men of the United States and Europe was essential to making such a place, and Jefferson greatly relished their company. But he also devoted himself to some more immediately pressing problems of state.

For years, the so-called Barbary states—Morocco, Algiers, Tunisia, and Tripoli—had been sanctioning piracy in the Mediterranean, preying upon the shipping of "Christian nations" to extort tribute money in return for protection. If a nation failed to pay the required tribute, its ships were seized and their sailors imprisoned, enslaved, tortured, and held for exorbitant ransoms. The nations of Europe had long been resigned to paying tribute. If the independent United States wanted to participate in the Mediterranean trade—as the British-protected American colonies had—it, too, would have to ante up the protection money.

This was repugnant to Jefferson. To be sure, he did not suggest abandoning trade that, by his own calculation, amounted to a very large percentage of American wheat, flour, rice, and dried fish export. But, as an alternative to the humiliation of tribute payments, which undermined the twin principles of freedom of the seas and sovereignty of the new republic, Jefferson advocated the creation of a strong American navy charged primarily with the protection of American commerce. Yet again, the man who deplored the idea of standing armies found himself advocating a standing military force. In contrast, John Adams, a staunch advocate of a powerful federal government, argued that simply paying the tribute money, distasteful though it was, made more sense as a business decision.

While Jefferson, Adams, and the nation debated how best to cope with the Barbary pirates, the pressure to do *something* mounted. The great British shipping insurer, Lloyd's of London, now charged a crippling twenty-five percent premium to insure

American cargoes bound for the Mediterranean, whereas the rate for the shipping of nations that had purchased "protection" was only one and a half percent. It became clear to Jefferson that Britain had a vested interest in the continuation of the Barbary situation as a force of intimidation against a competitor for trade. When it also became clear that the Congress was not about to vote funds for a new navy, Jefferson pulled all available strings to discover the going rate for tribute money. This, however, was not easy, because European governments were unwilling to share that information with the United States. As Jefferson discovered, England was not alone in its desire to allow Barbary Coast piracy to discourage the trade of an American rival.

At last, through his friend Lafayette, Jefferson was able to get reliable figures, which revealed that the amount Congress proposed to appropriate was far too low. This notwithstanding, Jefferson did the best he could. With Morocco, he was able to negotiate, through his emissary Thomas Barclay, the release of a captured crew and even an innovative most-favored-nation trade treaty—all in return for a bribe of thirty thousand dollars, which, as these things went, was a great bargain. Elsewhere, Jefferson was less successful. Algeria flatly refused to negotiate a trade treaty, and it would accept no reasonable ransom for prisoners it held.

In 1786, John Adams, now ambassador to the Court of St. James's, recalled Jefferson's triumph with Morocco rather than his failure with Algeria when he summoned him to London to collaborate on the secret negotiation of a treaty with Tripoli. Jefferson arrived in London in March. Although the Tripoli talks soon broke down, Jefferson decided to press ahead with negotiating a trade treaty with Britain. He had already enjoyed success with the French, and he had found time to negotiate credit extensions with Dutch bankers to keep the credit of the United States sound. Encouraged by these achievements, he hoped to conclude a treaty with the British that would secure rights to participate in the British West Indies trade. However, he was met with nothing but evasion from the crown's negotiator, Lord Carmarthan.

From King George III, Jefferson received a response he considered even more pointed. Adams presented him, the author of the Declaration of Independence, at court on March 17, 1786. According to the memoir Jefferson wrote late in life, Adams and Jefferson bowed to George and his queen, Charlotte, only to have the royal couple turn their backs. For various reasons, a number of later historians have doubted that this really happened (George III was thick-headed, but rarely impolite) and have suggested that Jefferson's hatred of the British—his full-blown Anglophobia— vividly colored his recollection. In any case, the aged Jefferson made his feelings clear in his memoir: "I saw at once that the ulcerations in the narrow mind of that mulish being [George III] left nothing to be expected on the subject of my attendance." Even at the moment, in 1786, Jefferson concluded that Britain "hates us, their ministers hate us, and their king more than all other men." He wrote to the American envoy in Spain: "I consider the British our natural enemies and as the only nation on earth who wish us ill from the bottom of their soul."

In company with Adams, Jefferson did attend plays while in Britain, and he inspected the latest innovations in steam power by James Watt and Matthew Boulton, for which he professed his admiration. He also visited some of the great estate gardens in the outskirts of London, looking for ideas he might apply to Monticello and pronouncing most to his liking not the latest, highly formalized designs, but those of the older style, which were much more in harmony with nature.

It was with relief, however, that Jefferson returned to Paris in June 1786. There he could always count on being welcomed by courtier and commoner alike. The French translation of *Notes on the State of Virginia,* for all the inaccuracies Jefferson so abhorred, had increased the ambassador's celebrity. England in early spring had been cold in more ways than one. France in early summer was warm, sunny, and open-hearted, and Jefferson was persuaded more than ever that Britain and the ways of the British represented for America the dead past, whereas France, a land of philosophers and artists, with stirrings of reform and revolution in the air, would be an ally in the future of the United States.

Thomas Jefferson discovered that he was at last happy in France, and soon a young woman was to drift into his life and make him even happier—for a time.

Chapter 14

The Lover

Thomas Jefferson was never *a* lawyer, *a* governor, or *an* ambassador. He was never *one* of anything. Even as he immersed himself in negotiating trade treaties, he worked to advance the careers of fellow Americans in the interest of advancing the international standing of American commerce and culture. As he gained entry into the most important circles of French diplomacy, science, and culture, he took time to nurture American culture.

In Europe, he saw examples of the kind of classical and neoclassical architecture that he believed would be most eloquent in expressing the timeless ideals of democratic liberty for the new American republic. When he learned that, in his absence, the Virginia legislature had backed away from his own recommendations that a classical capitol be built in Richmond and had decided instead to emulate the Georgian style of the old capitol at Williamsburg, Jefferson swung into action. He secured the services of a French architect who had studied for two decades in Rome, and asked him not so much to design a building, but to serve as a front man for what were essentially his own designs based on the Maison Carée at Nîmes, France, a pristine example of a classical Roman temple. Jefferson sent his architect to draw the temple and then to create a plaster model to send to Virginia for local masons to copy.

Still inspired by classical traditions, Jefferson commissioned the great French sculptor Jean Antoine Houdon to create a life-size statue of George Washington for the Virginia capitol. He also commissioned Houdon to create a bust of Lafayette for the Virginia Assembly, and he became a good friend of the Connecticut painter John Trumbull, who was painting a large canvas depicting Adams, Jefferson, and the other signers of the Declaration of Independence. While Jefferson idealized the simple life of the American farmer as the strongest possible foundation of an American democracy, he also valued the emotional power of patriotic icons. That three centuries later we find it hard to think of the United States of America without summoning up painted and sculpted images of the "Founding Fathers" is due to men like Jefferson, who began the process of mythologizing the leaders of the Revolution while those leaders were all very much alive.

Among the classically inspired buildings Jefferson envisioned for Virginia's new capital city was a covered public market. On an August afternoon in 1786, he asked John Trumbull to accompany him on a visit to a building that he thought might serve as a model, the Halle aux Bleds, a bustling Parisian market. Trumbull invited two of his artist friends to join them, a married couple from England who were staying in Paris.

Forty-six-year-old Richard Cosway was considered England's foremost miniaturist, highly sought after by the wealthy for the portraits he painted on ivory as tokens and keepsakes. Described by some as "monkey-faced," he was, in fact, dark and diminutive. While his modest place in the history of art is secured by his miniature portraits, he had reaped much of his personal fortune from a crop of pornographic miniatures decorating snuff boxes belonging to a lengthy roster of English nobility. His money enabled him to ante up a substantial inducement to present to the widowed mother of Maria Louisa Catherine Cecilia Hadfield, who, at age twenty, became his wife.

The union was not Maria's idea. She was the daughter of an English resort owner in Florence, Italy. After a nurse the family had hired became deranged and murdered four of Maria's siblings, her distraught family sent the girl to be raised in a convent. After the death of her father, seventeen-year-old convent-bred Maria decided, understandably, to become a nun. This appalled her English Protestant mother, however, who immediately took Maria back to England. Mr. Hadfield had not left his family a great deal of money, and, although she drew the line at allowing her daughter to become a nun, Maria's mother grew concerned about how the young woman might provide a living for herself.

Maria Cosway, hand-colored lithograph of Self-Portrait, *1787. Jefferson met her in Paris and fell in love.*

(Collection: Library of Congress)

Recognizing her daughter's considerable artistic talent, she decided to introduce her to Angelica Kaufman, then the most successful female artist in England. Kaufman instantly appreciated her talent and not only trained Maria as a miniaturist, but also introduced her into an elite social circle including the likes of Joshua Reynolds and Samuel Johnson's biographer, James Boswell. Also in the circle was Richard Cosway, effete and foppish, described by one of his acquaintances as a "china mannikin" of a man.

Maria was a petite blonde with piercing blue eyes, exquisite features, porcelain-like skin, and a highly intelligent yet languid manner. Her husband was unfaithful to her with a variety of lovers, both male and female, most of them occupying lofty niches in society. How faithful Maria was is not known. To be sure, many other men were attracted to her—a fact that Cosway rather liked. If anything made him jealous, it was not her male admirers, but her growing reputation as an artist, which threatened to eclipse his.

As for Jefferson, he was smitten at first sight. Whether he had been drawn to other women since the death of his wife—to whom he had pledged never to remarry—is not known. What is clear is that Maria Cosway is the only woman Jefferson expressed interest in after Patty Jefferson's death; what is more, the attraction seems to have been mutual from the first meeting. From that time on, they sought every opportunity to be together and made the rounds of the cultural and artistic monuments of Paris, including its great parks and gardens, the Bois de Boulogne, the Jardin du Roi, and the Parc de Saint-Cloud. As countless lovers have done before and since, they strolled the banks of the Seine.

Jefferson's letters to friends at this time are peppered with oblique references to his growing infatuation. "Beauty is leading us astray," he wrote to one correspondent. To Abigail Adams in London, he wrote of living in Paris, among a singing, dancing, and *kissing* people, who "have as much happiness in one year as one Englishman in ten."

Twenty-seven-year-old Maria made the middle-aged Jefferson feel young again. One day, as lovers will, Jefferson did something foolish. On September 18, he sprinted to his carriage in the courtyard of the Hôtel de Langéac to ride off to a rendezvous with

Maria. A small fountain lay in his path, and, impulsively, he leaped over it—only to trip and go sprawling headlong. Jefferson fell on his right hand and fractured his wrist, as he had broken his left one back in 1781 (Chapter 10, "The Hermit of Monticello").

It was no minor injury, but a compound fracture, with the bone clearly visible just beneath the skin. Despite what must have been excruciating pain, the determined lover bound his injured wrist as best he could and rode off to his date with Maria. As they often did, the pair rode in Jefferson's phaeton through the cobbled streets of Paris, each cobble producing a bump that pierced Jefferson like a knife. After some hours, even this passionate swain had to surrender. He explained to Maria what had happened, and he left for home to summon a doctor.

Maria did not desert her fallen hero, but she visited him as he languished in the Hôtel de Langéac. However, her husband was about to take her back to London. On the day of her departure, against doctor's strict orders to keep to his room, Jefferson rode out to bid Maria farewell. The affair had begun in the glow of late summer and ended in the mists of mid-autumn, an apt time for such things to end—although it didn't *quite* end. For many years, the pair conducted a lively, often wistful correspondence, beginning with a remarkable letter Jefferson began the evening after seeing Maria off. It was a long dialogue between his "Head" and his "Heart," and he wrote it slowly, struggling to make his left hand take the place of his right.

Jefferson's "Heart" declared:

> *Let the gloomy Monk, sequestered from the world, seek unsocial pleasures in the bottom of his cell! Let the sublimated philosopher grasp visionary happiness while pursuing phantoms dressed in the garb of truth! Their supreme wisdom is supreme folly: and they mistake for happiness the mere absence of pain. Had they ever felt the solid pleasure of one generous spasm of the heart, they would exchange for it all the frigid speculations of their lives.*

To which his "Head" replied:

> *Do not bite at the bait of pleasure till you know there is no hook beneath it. The art of life is the avoiding of pain*

*.... The most effectual means of being secure against pain
is to retire within ourselves.*

In the "Head and Heart" letter, Jefferson wrestled with a
dilemma that was not unique to this intense but abortive love
affair. Always he was aware of being pulled in two directions,
toward engagement with society on every level and simultaneously
toward the solitude of contemplation and study atop a lonely
mountain in Virginia's Piedmont.

Early in their correspondence, Jefferson wrote to Maria of his
hope that she would one day make good on her pledge to visit him
in America. Among so much else, Jefferson wanted to show her
the Virginia wonder that was but a short distance from Monticello,
the spectacular Natural Bridge. Shortly after he wrote to her of
this, Jefferson decided to embark—alone—on another journey
that the two had spoken of taking together, a tour of Maria's native
Italy.

Jefferson had always loved all things Italian, contemporary or
classical. His Italian neighbor, Philip Mazzei, was among his closest friends, and now thoughts of Maria made the idea of seeing
Italy all the more delectable. He set off on February 28, 1797, in
his own phaeton driven by a hired postilion. His object was not
only to take in and relish all that he could, but to observe the agriculture of Italy and look for new crops that might be introduced to
America. New varieties of grapes especially interested him, but so
did olives, which grew well in poor soil and, brought to America,
might turn whole tracts now considered little more than stony
desert into useful farmland.

At one point in his trip, Jefferson even risked his life to obtain
and smuggle out of the Italian Piedmontthe local species of rice,
which he thought might take well to the upland areas of the
American South. Of course, rice was already a major crop in the
South, but the varieties grown in America were cultivated exclusively in the swampy low country of the Carolinas and required the
hard labor of slaves to plant and harvest. Jefferson reasoned that
the Piedmontese variety, grown in the drier uplands, could be cultivated by the free farmers in these areas. The very existence of this

rice in America would be one more weapon against the perpetuation of slavery.

There was, however, a problem. The Piedmontese so jealously guarded their rice that the king had made it a crime to export so much as a single grain—and not just a crime, but a *capital* crime, punishable by death. Undaunted, Jefferson bribed a muleteer to take a quantity of rice to Genoa, where he could arrange for its transport to Virginia. For good measure, he stuffed his own pockets with as much as they could carry.

In addition to his cloak-and-dagger agronomy, Jefferson engaged in secret diplomacy. The way to Italy lay through the south of France—Lyons, Marseilles (whose celebrated port he carefully studied to obtain ideas for improving America's port facilities), and Nice. He scheduled a side trip to Nîmes, for what would seem obvious reasons to anyone who knew him. Nîmes, after all, was home to the Maison Carée and the other Roman antiquities that were Jefferson's passion. But the diplomat had an ulterior motive for the detour. He secretly met with Dr. José Barbalho Da Maia, a Brazilian who wanted U.S. aid in financing a rebellion to free his nation from Spain. Jefferson explained to Barbalho that the United States was "not in a condition at present to meddle nationally in any war," but he also let him know that his nation favored any Latin American colonial uprising against a European power. In this secret meeting may be found the seed of the Monroe Doctrine of 1823—whereby President Monroe would give notice that the United States intended to regard any interference by European powers in the Americas a direct threat to the security of the United States itself.

Jefferson returned to Paris on June 10, 1787, having been absent for a little more than three months. He wrote to Maria Cosway about his journey: "I am born to lose everything I love. Why were you not with me? So many enchanting scenes which only wanted your pencil to consecrate them to fame."

One beloved person Jefferson was determined not to lose was his daughter Mary, familiarly called Polly, but also known as Maria. He had decided to send for her as soon as he was named minister to France; however, eight-year-old Polly was none too keen on joining a father she barely knew. "I don't want to go to France," she wrote Jefferson. "I want to stay [in Virginia] with Aunt Eppes." In the end, the Eppeses shipped her out by an act of subterfuge that would horrify any modern child psychologist. Her aunt took her aboard ship, along with the girl's "childminder" or maid, a fourteen-year-old slave named Sally Hemings, and the two played with her until she fell asleep. While she slept, the ship set sail.

Poor Polly. Even her companion, Sally Hemings, was little comfort. The fourteen-year-old had never ventured beyond the confines of either John Wayles's plantation, The Forest; Jefferson's Monticello; or the Eppeses' Eppington. Now she was on a ship at sea, seasick and terrified. The ship's captain comforted and looked after Polly and carried her into the arms of Abigail Adams when the vessel reached London. Jefferson, believing himself too encumbered by diplomatic duties to meet his daughter in London, had sent his French butler, Adrien Petit, to escort her and Sally Hemings across the Channel to Paris.

Jefferson adored Polly and was hurt by her initial aloofness toward him, but gradually she returned his warmth and affection, and soon vied with her older sister, Patsy, for the position of her father's favorite.

And then there was Sally.

In September 1802, James Thomson Callender, a disgruntled patronage-seeker and freelance political journalist, published in a Virginia newspaper an account of a liaison between Jefferson, then running for his second term as president, and the slave Callender called "Dusky Sally." Disappointed in his bid to secure from Jefferson a lucrative appointment as postmaster of Richmond, Callender held a grudge against the president and probably received financial support from Jefferson's enemies. For these reasons—as well as, perhaps, reluctance to besmirch a founding father—most historians over the years dismissed Callender's allegations.

In 1974, however, Professor Fawn M. Brodie published a popular and controversial biography, *Thomas Jefferson: An Intimate History*, in which she corroborated Callender by drawing on a memoir written by Madison Jefferson, who identified himself as the son of Thomas Jefferson and Sally Hemings. Brodie's book caused a stir, but subsequent historians and biographers again argued against the likelihood—in some cases, even the mere thought—that Jefferson, humane apostle of liberty, could have had sexual relations with his fourteen-year-old slave, let alone have fathered a child by her.

But on November 5, 1998, the distinguished British science journal *Nature* published the results of a study by a retired pathologist, Dr. Eugene Foster, who took DNA samples from four male lineages that bear on the paternity of Sally Hemings's children. Foster drew blood from descendants of Jefferson's uncle Field Jefferson, John Carr (grandfather of Jefferson's nephews Samuel and Dabney Carr), and Sally Hemings's sons Thomas C. Woodson and Eston Hemings Jefferson. The DNA of the Y chromosomes in these samples was analyzed. The Y chromosome is unique because it largely escapes the shuffling of genetic material that occurs between every generation. The only changes on the Y chromosome are rare sporadic mutations that accumulate over many generations. This means that male lineages can be distinguished from one another through the characteristic set of mutations carried in their Y chromosomes.

According to Foster, the analysis reveals that Thomas Woodson was not Sally Hemings's or Jefferson's son. Woodson was born shortly after Sally Hemings returned from Paris to Monticello, and Woodson family tradition has always identified him as Jefferson's son. However, if Foster's interpretation of the DNA evidence is correct, it is unlikely that Sally Hemings became pregnant by Jefferson while the two were in Paris. However, as Foster points out, the analysis does indicate that "Thomas Jefferson, rather than one of the Carr brothers [as previously thought], was the father of Eston Hemings Jefferson," who was born in 1808, when Jefferson was nearing the end of his second term as president. The DNA evidence has nothing to say about the paternity of Madison Hemings, born in 1805, because none of his living descendants came from an exclusively male line and, therefore, could not be subjected to Y-chromosome analysis.

Not everyone—including a number of scientists—agrees with the results of the DNA analysis; however, Daniel P. Jordan, a historian who serves as president of the Thomas Jefferson Memorial Foundation, Inc., issued a statement on January 26, 2000, based on expert evaluation of the DNA results and historical evidence. He concluded that "our evaluation of the best evidence available suggests the strong likelihood that Thomas Jefferson and Sally Hemings had a relationship over time that led to the birth of one, and perhaps all, of the known children of Sally Hemings."

> On April 12, 1999, some members of the DNA Study Committee of the Thomas Jefferson Foundation issued a "Minority Report" dissenting from the conclusion of the committee majority that Jefferson fathered at least one of Hemings's children. The Minority Report cites certain historical evidence that Jefferson was absent from Hemings for the fifteen months preceding the birth, in 1808, of Eston Hemings, the Hemings child said most closely to resemble Jefferson. Such an absence, the Minority Report concludes, suggests that "another Jefferson DNA haplotype carrier would be the father of Eston." (A "haplotype" is a set of genetic determinants located on a single chromosome.) The prime candidate the report identifies as Jefferson's nephew Peter Carr.

Just who was Sally Hemings? She was a woman, a mother, a slave. Her given name was probably Sarah, and she was the daughter of Elizabeth (Betty) Hemings and—many believe—John Wayles, Jefferson's father-in-law. If so, she was, therefore, Jefferson's late wife Patty's half-sister. When Wayles died in 1774, Sally became Jefferson's property and moved with her mother to Monticello by 1776.

Though a child herself, Sally was assigned to work as a "child-minder"—later, a maid—to little Polly Jefferson, which is why she accompanied her to France. It is not known whether she lived at the Hôtel de Langéac with Jefferson or at the nearby boarding school where Patsy and Polly were enrolled. Jefferson, his daughters, and Sally returned to Virginia in 1789, and Sally probably remained at Monticello after Jefferson left to serve as George Washington's secretary of state. Although she is referred to as "Maria's [Polly's] maid" in a 1799 record, her son Madison

Hemings recalled that her duties included taking "care of [Jefferson's] chamber and wardrobe, look[ing] after us children, and do[ing] light work such as sewing, &c."

Only two physical descriptions of Sally Hemings exist. The slave Isaac Jefferson remarked that she was "mighty near white … very handsome, long straight hair down her back." Jefferson's grandson Thomas Jefferson Randolph described her as "light colored and decidedly good looking."

At the time of his death, Jefferson did not have the power to emancipate any of his slaves. As part of his debt-ridden estate, the slaves were no longer his property, but were subject to creditors' claims. On his deathbed, he did plead with creditors to grant five slaves their freedom, including both Madison and Eston Hemings, but he did not include Sally in this request. Most historians believe that Jefferson's daughter Patsy eventually gave Sally Hemings "her time"—that is, allowed her a kind of unofficial freedom, presumably to enable her to remain in Virginia in an era during which the law required emancipated slaves to leave the state within a year. Madison Hemings reported that his mother lived in Charlottesville with him and his brother Eston until her death in 1835.

In all, Sally had four surviving children—five, if Thomas C. Woodson was her son. Beverly (born 1798), a carpenter and fiddler, was allowed to leave the plantation in late 1821 or early 1822 and, according to Madison Hemings, "passed for white" in Washington, D.C. Harriet (born 1801) also left Monticello in 1821 or 1822, probably with her brother, and, like him, passed for white. Madison Hemings (1805–78) moved to southern Ohio in 1836, where he worked as a carpenter and farmer. Eston Hemings (1808–c. 1853), also a carpenter, moved to Chillicothe, Ohio, around the time of Madison's move. He established a local reputation as a professional musician and then moved to Wisconsin in about 1852. There he changed his name and also passed for white. Woodson left Virginia for southern Ohio during the early 1820s and became a farmer.

Jefferson lived in an age and place in which miscegenation, sex across racial lines, was both generally decried and commonly practiced. Edward Coles was a young man of Jefferson's acquaintance who served James Madison, for a time, as secretary and who would eventually become governor of Illinois. In 1814, Coles revealed to Jefferson his plan to free his slaves in Illinois and set them up on small farms. In a letter of August 25 of that year, Jefferson tried to talk Coles out of executing his plan, on the grounds that the slaves, so accustomed to slavery, were "incapable as children of taking care of themselves." Jefferson went on to make clear his feelings regarding miscegenation: "The amalgamation of whites with black produces a degradation to which no lover of his country, no lover of excellence in the human character, can innocently consent." Did Jefferson fall in love with Sally Hemings? And was he so desperately in love—or so desperately lonely—that he overcame his apparent repugnance toward miscegenation? Or was Hemings only a sexual substitute for the absent Maria Cosway, or for Patsy, his dead wife? If Sally Hemings was the daughter of John Wayles, then she was Patsy's half-sister. Did Jefferson know or believe she was the daughter of his father-in-law? Or was Jefferson, in the intoxicating atmosphere of Paris, simply attracted to a pretty girl? And was she attracted to him?

Among all these speculations and questions, one in particular is painful: Were the feelings of Sally Hemings even relevant to Jefferson? Or did he do what masters had been doing—and felt they had the right to do—with female slaves for generations? This question, more than any other raised by the Sally Hemings controversy, most haunts admirers of Jefferson, the enlightened political thinker and patriot who wrote so eloquently and defiantly about the cruelty and injustice of slavery. That neither this question nor the others relating to the Jefferson-Hemings relationship can ever be definitively answered makes the underlying issues all the more disturbing. Whatever unease we might feel hints at just how disquieting—perhaps even agonizing—such issues may have been to Jefferson himself.

As for Sally Hemings, although she was not freed by Jefferson, she does seem to have gained as much freedom as a black woman could hope for in the nineteenth-century South, and she lived to see her children achieve as much freedom as American society in those days accorded black men.

Chapter 15

Au Revoir to Revolution

An American *counter*revolution? The grim prospect plagued Jefferson's thoughts in 1786 and 1787. John Adams passed on news he'd had from America of a ruckus in western Massachusetts. The young republic had not been kind to the veterans of the War for Independence. Demobilized Continental army troops received little of the back pay due them, and what payment they got was typically in "Continental notes," which were of so little value that the phrase "not worth a Continental" soon entered popular speech as a synonym for *worthless*. As the soldiers returned to farming, they were besieged by state governments demanding payment of taxes and threatening foreclosure on property. To make matters worse, even those states that had approved the issue of Continental notes now refused to accept them in payment of taxes.

Congress acted promptly to improve the lot of many former officers, who were compensated mainly with grants of land in the Ohio territory, but the enlisted veterans, the rank and file soldiers, were left in the lurch. In rural western Massachusetts, these veterans were especially hard-pressed. They had not been paid, their crops brought dismal prices in the postwar depression economy, and they were subject to heavy taxation endorsed by the state's conservative governor, James Bowdoin. Finding no relief from the government, farmers in western Massachusetts began banding together in paramilitary gangs dubbed "Regulators." These groups of five hundred to two thousand men, armed with clubs and muskets, marched on circuit-court sessions to intimidate the magistrates into postponing property seizures until the next gubernatorial election, which, they hoped, would see the conservative Bowdoin replaced by a more liberal governor sympathetic to their plight. For some five months, the Regulators were active in Northampton, Springfield, and Worcester as well as smaller towns. Intimidation proved an effective weapon: The Regulators succeeded in paralyzing the courts without firing a shot or throwing a punch.

The news of discontent in the West was hardly a novelty to Thomas Jefferson of Albemarle County, Virginia. What did shake him, however, was the response of certain members of the new national government, who sought to exploit the unrest as an opportunity to demonstrate the urgent need for a strong—*very* strong—central government with the power and authority to crush such a rebellion. For that is what Secretary of War Henry Knox was calling it. He reported to Congress that the Regulator movement was nothing less than a full-blown rebellion led by Daniel Shays, a former captain in the Continental army. Knox, an advocate not only of a strong central government but also of a powerful standing army, portrayed "Shays's Rebellion" as the work of radicals and anarchists who wanted to abolish private property, erase all debts, and generally incite a civil war. Knox called for a crackdown. As if to underscore the impotence of the current federal government to implement it, he joined Governor Bowdoin in an appeal to Boston merchants to privately finance a force of four thousand, four hundred volunteers under Revolutionary War veteran Gen. Benjamin Lincoln. Lincoln led his men to the Springfield Arsenal, where, on January 24 and 25, 1787, they confronted fifteen hundred Regulators under Shays and others. Lincoln fired a cannon into the Regulator band, killing three and sending the others into flight. Several "ringleaders" were arrested and tried for treason, two were hanged, and the Regulator movement came to an end. Shays fled to Vermont and, the following year, was granted a pardon.

Jefferson's miserable experience as governor of revolutionary Virginia had persuaded him of the necessity of some form of central government, but he was appalled at how conservatives like Knox inflated a local tax revolt into a civil war that they claimed would soon spread to all thirteen states. Jefferson had always hated tyranny, and his experience in Europe had shown him far more of it than he had ever seen in America. In a letter home, he wrote of how the autocratic governments of Europe "prey" on the masses. "Man," he wrote, "is the only animal which devours its own kind." The United States must not emulate Europe in the creation of oppressive government. If anything, Jefferson had a certain admiration for Shays's Rebellion. He wrote of it to Abigail Adams: "The spirit of resistance to government is so valuable on certain occasions that I wish it to be always alive." To a conservative colleague in Virginia, Jefferson observed "that the good sense of the people will always be found to be the best army."

Whatever else Shays's Rebellion was and was not, for many Americans it dramatically demonstrated the inadequacy of the federal government under the Articles of Confederation. Even if one did not heed the conservative alarm that the rebellion was a prelude to civil war, the fact that a handful of farmers in western Massachusetts could bring government to a halt was a persuasive argument for revisiting the Articles. Accordingly, in May 1787, a Constitutional Convention was convened in Philadelphia. Jefferson was shocked by the news that the convention had abandoned the idea of simply revising the Articles and, instead, had scrapped them in favor of creating an entirely new Constitution, which mandated a central government to which the states were ultimately subordinate. Revision was called for, Jefferson believed, but all that was necessary were "three or four new articles" added to the "good, old and venerable fabric" of the existing document.

To George Washington, Jefferson wrote of his greatest fear concerning the new Constitution: "I was much an enemy to monarchy before I came to Europe. I am ten thousand times more so since I have seen what they are. There is scarcely an evil known in these countries which may not be traced to their king ...." As the proposed Constitution created and then elevated the office of president of the United States, Jefferson saw the makings of monarchy. At the very least, creating a powerful chief executive seemed to him a potentially tragic overreaction to a minor disturbance in Massachusetts.

A Adams

For years, Jefferson conducted a lively correspondence with
Abigail Adams, wife of John Adams. The lithograph was
engraved after the portrait by Gilbert Stuart.

(Collection: Library of Congress)

"God forbid," he wrote to John Adams's son-in-law, William S. Smith, "that we should ever be twenty years without such a rebellion. What signify a few lives lost? The tree of liberty must be refreshed from time to time with the blood of patriots and tyrants."

As a diplomat on foreign station, Jefferson felt it his duty to make no official pronouncement, pro or con, on the proposed Constitution. His self-enforced neutrality on the subject must have been trying, but at least he comforted himself with the thought that the first president under the Constitution, should it be ratified, would almost certainly be George Washington. He had no fear that this man would be tempted to make himself a tyrant, even if he were handed the opportunity to do so. Washington, however, was but one man. What would the future bring?

> *In a letter to James Madison written from Paris on December 20, 1787, Jefferson cited two major flaws he saw in the Constitution:*
>
> First the omission of a bill of rights providing clearly and without the aid of sophisms for freedom of religion, freedom of the press, protection against standing armies, restriction against monopolies, the eternal and unremitting force of the habeas corpus laws, and trials by jury .... The second feature I dislike, and greatly dislike, is the abandonment in every instance of the necessity of rotation in office, and most particularly in the case of the President. Experience concurs with reason that the first magistrate will always be re-elected if the constitution permits it. He is then an officer for life.

If being so far from the processes of creating and ratifying the Constitution frustrated Jefferson, he did not let on. Instead, most immediately, he continued to work on finding an international remedy for what he saw as the chief cause of Shays's Rebellion and other American discontents. In 1992, James Carville, the exuberantly blunt manager of Bill Clinton's presidential campaign, framed in memorable terms the leading issue of that campaign: "It's the economy, stupid." For all his attraction to political philosophy and political idealism, Jefferson always looked for practical solutions to practical problems. Why did the Shaysites rebel? *It's the economy, stupid.*

Jefferson understood that the post-Revolutionary economic depression, which caused all Americans to suffer, hit Westerners hardest. These farmers had plenty to sell—America was a land of abundance—but they had no place to sell it. England as well as France had yet to sign commercial treaties that would open up their markets to American trade, especially in the Caribbean. Being locked out from these markets was economically disastrous, and Jefferson continued to work hard to get trade concessions.

England was Adams's responsibility, but France was all Jefferson's. On the plus side, Jefferson loved the French, and they admired and respected him. Moreover, Jefferson had cultivated an influential circle of enlightened French leaders who understood—or were coming to understand—that it was important to their country to keep the United States within the sphere of French influence (and out of Britain's) and that only by opening trade to American merchants could the ties between France and the United States be maintained. On the minus side, however, were the wails of protest rising from French merchants, farmers, workers, and sailors. They did not see the United States as a new market for goods and services, but as competition for what they had to sell.

Nor was Jefferson facing a simple comparison of pluses and minuses. All around him, he saw the signs of a French reform movement verging on revolution. He saw clearly that people were becoming increasingly alienated from their king and queen, Louis XVI and Marie Antoinette. The French government was loath to give in to the demands of merchants, farmers, workers, and sailors, but it dared not turn its back on them now, either. As revolution approached, the French government became increasingly paralyzed.

Jefferson was also constrained in what he could offer France. As was frequently the case, war loomed between Britain and France. Jefferson's emotional and philosophical inclination, of course, was to side with his beloved French against the despised English. But he knew that not only was the United States woefully unprepared for war, but it would fare far better as a neutral, enjoying profitable trade with *both* sides in any conflict. Accordingly, Jefferson couldn't make extravagant promises to French officials. Nevertheless, through dogged persistence and great diplomatic skill, Jefferson managed to wrest valuable but limited trade concessions, albeit not the sweeping, most-favored-nation trade treaty he had hoped for. Still, he succeeded in opening French ports to American rice and whale oil, and he negotiated a vast increase in the quota of tobacco that France would import from the United States.

In the summer of 1788, Jefferson watched as the old France began to crumble. Riots broke out in July and continued into the fall. Early the next year, Louis XVI consented to convene the Estates General. It was an epoch-making decision that temporarily restored order.

The Estates General was a representative assembly of the three "estates," or classes, recognized in France. Jefferson himself described these as the "Clergy, Nobles, and Commons," corresponding to the First, Second, and Third Estates. In pre-Revolutionary France, the clergy were not only representatives of the Catholic church, but they also served as judges. The nobles generally also included militarists. The commoners were really two classes, often at odds with one another: The bourgeoisie were wealthy merchants and landowners, whereas the poor encompassed rural peasants as well as urban poor. Something resembling the Estates General had existed in France, at least sporadically, since the thirteenth century, but the body had never proved effective largely because the three estates were perpetually at cross purposes and because the king was rarely eager to yield significant power to them.

Now, for the first time since 1614 and the reign of Louis XIII, a French monarch summoned the Estates General to assemble. Popular perception tends to paint Louis XVI and his wife, Marie Antoinette, as heartless aristocrats, entirely unsympathetic and unresponsive to the needs of their subjects. In fact, as Jefferson observed, Louis XVI was far less the absolute monarch than his immediate predecessors, Louis XIV and Louis XV.

Jefferson, with other foreign diplomats, was present at Versailles on May 5, 1789, when the king addressed the opening session of the Estates General. Louis's words were warm and hopeful: "Sirs, this day which my heart awaited since a long time has finally arrived and I see myself surrounded by the representatives of the nation which I am honored to command." Far from seeking to maintain the status quo, Louis made a revolutionary proposal: "The debt of the state, already immense on my coming to the throne, has accumulated during my reign …. The increase in the tax has been the unavoidable result and has been rendered more painful by [its] unequal distribution." Of the three estates, only the common were taxed, whereas nobles and clergy were exempt. Louis continued: "A general anxiousness in and an exaggerated desire for change, have taken over the public mind." His cure for these symptoms of revolution? A proposal that the nobles and clergy "renounce their financial privileges"—that is, begin to pay taxes. Louis further proposed that the two higher estates share equal representation with the Third Estate; for every vote cast by the First and Second Estates, the Third Estate would cast two. Louis believed that this would better represent the numbers of French subjects represented by the estates.

While the king understood the justice and necessity of equitable taxation and representation, the upper estates would agree to no such thing. As Jefferson observed, "The clergy will move heaven and earth to defeat the effects of this [equitable] representation." Some of the nobility, however, were willing to make the change, he observed: "The younger part of the nobility are in favor of [equality]." Jefferson was optimistic that the "more advanced [nobles] are daily coming" to join the Third Estate, thereby forming a chamber (Jefferson commented) "of upwards of 800 members." Emboldened, recognizing that it was now composed of deputies sent directly by at least ninety-six percent of the nation, the Third Estate summarily declared itself the National Assembly on June 17, 1789.

Jefferson had hoped for just such an outcome, writing to John Jay, "If the king will do business with the [Third Estate] which constitute the nation, it may well be done without priests or nobles." To James Madison, he wrote proudly that the French "nation had been awakened by our revolution. They feel their strength, they are enlightened, their lights are spreading and they will not retrograde." Yet Jefferson was also keenly aware that the creation of a National Assembly had brought the nation to a true crisis. He believed that if Louis and his ministers had the wisdom now to side with the commons, a constitutional monarchy would be the result. He feared, however, that Marie Antoinette, most of the nobles, and the clergy would oppose the king if he decided to align himself with the people. The result of such opposition would be civil war.

But suddenly Jefferson found relief for his anxiety. Locked out of its Versailles assembly hall, the National Assembly neither dispersed nor rioted, but instead it convened out-of-doors in the royal tennis court and took there the so-called "Tennis Court Oath," pledging "not to separate, and to reassemble wherever circumstances require, until the constitution of the kingdom is established and consolidated upon firm foundations." With a constitution in the offing, Jefferson concluded that the crisis was passed.

At about this time, Jefferson became more than an observer of the French Revolution. With Lafayette, one of France's liberty-loving nobles, he collaborated on a declaration of rights based on the Virginia declaration of 1776, and they then worked on the text of the French constitution. Jefferson didn't attempt simply to replicate in France the revolution that had produced the United States; he put into words a concept more radical than any he had proposed for his own country. To the final article of the draft constitution he added the right of subsequent generations "to examine and, if necessary, to modify the form of government." In short, Jefferson put forward a principle of *continual* revolution. To Madison he observed, "No society can make a perpetual constitution .... The earth belongs to the living and not the dead."

Jefferson took great pride and pleasure in the fact that his words and thoughts on the nature of government and liberty would be discussed, debated, and *used* in what he thought might be a bloodless revolution. Jefferson was correct in assuming that his work would be discussed and would be used. The French Declaration of the Rights of Man and Citizens, enacted in October 1789, was based on the Virginia Declaration of Rights as well as on the Declaration of Independence. In addition, when it was completed, the French constitution would owe much indeed to Jefferson. But the minister plenipotentiary was as wrong as a man could be in predicting a French Revolution without blood.

On July 4, 1789, Lafayette, Jefferson, and other Americans in Paris celebrated the thirteenth anniversary of United States Declaration of Independence. Four days later, Jefferson reported to the French foreign minister that his house had been robbed and that the neighborhood was in need of military protection from roving mobs. On July 12, Jefferson could look out his window and watch the Customs House, center and symbol of royal taxation, be ignited and burned to the ground. Rioters had set it ablaze after Louis had dismissed Jacques Necker, the liberal finance minister, an advocate of liberty and a friend of Jefferson's. Two days later, on July 14, word came of the storming of the Bastille.

Throughout that tumultuous summer, Jefferson, who must have agonized over the fate of a nation he loved second only to his own, looked on with the dispassionate focus of a scientist. He rode through the city, visited the Bastille—even as it was being torn down brick by brick—and did his best to remain hopeful after the National Assembly took the bold, sweeping step of abolishing all noble titles and privileges.

Back in November 1788, Jefferson had requested six months' leave to return to Virginia, primarily to take Patsy back to America and away from the convent school in which he had placed her. The impressionable girl was talking about not only converting to Catholicism, but becoming a nun. Because of changes in the government following the ratification of the Constitution, Jefferson's request had to be postponed. It came through, at last, in September 1789, and he bid *au revoir* to Paris on September 26.

He expected to return in half a year and resume his diplomatic duties. What he did not know is that, as he set sail for home, a letter from President George Washington was also traveling to Virginia. It asked Jefferson to accept appointment as the first secretary of state of the United States. Jefferson would never leave the United States again.

Chapter 16

Mr. Secretary

Jefferson had wanted to leave France earlier. Now that the revolution he had played a role in starting was underway, he was no longer so anxious to leave; however, the father in Jefferson was more compelling than the revolutionary. He believed it critically important to get his daughters back home to Virginia, where Patsy could be steered away from her aspirations to the Catholic clergy and where Polly could be schooled someplace other than a convent. Indeed, unleashed upon Albemarle's young gentlemen, Patsy, age seventeen, met a beau, fell in love, and was married within roughly two months of the family's return to Monticello. The groom was Thomas Mann Randolph Jr., the son of Jefferson's classmate from grammar school days, "Tuckahoe Tom" Randolph. Finding a suitable husband for Patsy was a great joy—and relief—for her father.

That personal mission accomplished, Jefferson would probably have preferred to think about returning to France, to observe and even fan the flames of the revolution there. But when he arrived at the port of Norfolk, Virginia, on November 23, 1789, he did what he always did when he came into a city. He read the newspaper, which contained the news that George Washington had appointed him secretary of state. Washington's appointment letter reached Jefferson two weeks later, at Eppington, where he was visiting the Eppeses.

George Washington, in a twentieth-century copy of the famed
Gilbert Stuart "Atheneum Head" portrait.

(Collection: National Archives and Records Administration)

Jefferson was not thrilled. In fact, earlier in the year, when
James Madison had written him in Paris to broach the subject of
serving in Washington's cabinet, Jefferson had demurred. Now
that the appointment was official, he waited until December 15 to
reply. Even then, he sent Washington nothing more than a tenta-
tive, reluctant acceptance, indicating that he preferred to resume
his duties as a diplomat in Paris but that he would obey the will of

his president if he thought it "best for the public good." Obey he did, but he took his sweet time doing so. Jefferson did not formally accept the appointment until February 12, 1790. Then, having accepted the position, he did not rush off for New York City, now designated the nation's capital. First he attended Patsy's wedding, which took place at Monticello, and then he let another week go by before he left for New York on March 1, 1790.

The prospect of occupying the chief position in the first cabinet of the first president of the United States struck Jefferson as neither momentous nor exciting. To begin with, his professional domain was hardly vast. In 1790, the entire United States Department of State consisted of two clerks, two subclerks, a translator, and himself. With this staff, Jefferson was expected to handle not only foreign affairs, but many domestic ones as well. Washington's entire Cabinet was much smaller than that of today's presidents. There was a secretary of the treasury, Alexander Hamilton; a secretary of war, Henry Knox; and an attorney general, who was Jefferson's own cousin, Edmund Randolph. The rest of the executive branch consisted of the vice president, John Adams, and President Washington himself. Nor was the Cabinet a powerful decision-making force, as we think of it today. Washington regarded it as simply a panel of advisers and assistants, none of whom was empowered to make on his own anything remotely resembling a policy decision. Within these constraints, Jefferson did have more autonomous authority than anyone except Alexander Hamilton; Washington admitted that he had little grasp of foreign affairs and relied on Jefferson, but he confessed to even less understanding of finance and so relied even more on Hamilton.

The new secretary of state thought he would ease into his job with a straightforward report on what he considered a straightforward issue. Under the old Articles of Confederation, Jefferson had proposed the decimal system as the basis of American currency (Chapter 11, "Back to Politics"). The scheme sailed through Congress. Now, as secretary of state, he attempted to persuade Congress to adopt a decimal standard for all linear measurement as well, which Jefferson believed would greatly simplify surveying, laying out, and selling land in the nation's frontier territories. What Jefferson proposed was not exactly the metric system (which is generally credited to a French vicar named Gabriel Mouton in 1670), because it was based not on the meter, but on the familiar English rod. Jefferson's innovation was to create new units of measure derived decimally from the rod, which was either divided or multiplied by ten. Congress seemed utterly mystified by Jefferson's proposal and tabled—permanently. Americans have been muddling through with inches, feet, yards, and the rest ever since.

Failure to understand and accept a rational system of measurement proved to be only a foretaste of the Congressional thickheadedness Secretary Jefferson had to pound against. Very soon, he also found himself blocked in his attempts to create permanent diplomatic ties with the nations of the world. Congress was reluctant to fund diplomatic missions abroad. To France, an ally in the American Revolution, Jefferson was still permitted to send a minister plenipotentiary, but Spain and Portugal were allotted mere chargés d'affaires, while Britain and the Netherlands received only one agent each. In Morocco, heart of the troublesome Barbary States, he was permitted to place a single consul. Thus, from the very first presidential administration of the United States, the forces of conservative isolationism strongly asserted themselves. Believing that connections with the world at large were essential to the survival and prosperity of the new nation, Secretary of State Jefferson fought against this tide. It was most often a losing struggle.

Nor was Congress Jefferson's only opponent in international relations. He soon found a foe in Secretary of the Treasury Alexander Hamilton. Indeed, Hamilton—and "Hamiltonism"—would become the force in American government against which Jefferson and his most intimate political protégé and ally, James Madison, would organize their own vision of government.

That Jefferson and Hamilton developed a bitter ideological rivalry is not surprising. The most profound difference in their views of government—Jefferson believed that the bulk of power should reside with the people, whereas Hamilton advocated a more authoritarian central government—can be traced to their very earliest years. Jefferson grew up in a socially prominent family and enjoyed financial security, yet in a region that also exposed him to the potential and perils of the Western farmer. Hamilton, in contrast, was orphaned at age eleven and grew up under financially constrained circumstances on the island of Nevis in the British West Indies. Jefferson was in the thick of pre-Revolutionary discontent with British rule, whereas Hamilton was raised in a place where that rule was accepted virtually without question. Jefferson had been born with significant social advantages and connections. Hamilton had had to struggle first to survive and then to attain wealth. He worked his way up through a mercantile firm on Nevis. His ability and tireless industry impressed a local benefactor, who, in 1772, financed his passage to New York and his education there at King's College (today's Columbia University). Young Hamilton soon cut short his studies to write and publish essays promoting the revolution. In 1775, he was commissioned captain of Continental artillery; then, in 1777, he became General Washington's aide de camp, serving closely with the commander in chief through the next four years. As the war wound down, Hamilton, who had already risen high through the strata of American society, married Elizabeth Schuyler, a daughter of one of New York's most prominent, influential, and powerful families.

But Hamilton did not intend to rest on his laurels. Immediately after the war, he resumed his studies, determined to become a lawyer. This, together with his connection to Gen. Washington, stood him in good stead when delegates were chosen to revise the Articles of Confederation in a convention at Philadelphia in 1787. Hamilton was in the forefront of delegates who successfully converted a convention of revision into a full-fledged constitutional convention. Hamilton and his colleagues saw the convention as an opportunity to create a much more powerful central government, and they did just that.

Whereas Jefferson's temperament and background had persuaded him that people free from tyranny were generally good and sensible, deserving ample power to govern themselves, Hamilton's early struggles seem to have reinforced a sterner, more pessimistic, and even cynical outlook. He made little distinction between "the people" and "the mob." He certainly didn't believe that tyranny and dictatorship were called for, but he insisted that the new government should have sufficient muscle to lead the people, not simply to follow their will. If this meant introducing a strong executive branch and even an element of autocracy, so be it. Whereas Jefferson fostered and applauded a people's revolution in France and deplored the hidebound monarchism of Britain, Hamilton scorned the French mob and blatantly courted close relations with the English government.

In contrast to Jefferson, who demurred and delayed when Washington appointed him secretary of state, Hamilton leapt at the opportunity to serve as secretary of the treasury. In January 1790, Jefferson had yet to formally accept his appointment, whereas Hamilton had already produced his epoch-making "First Report on the Public Credit," a sweeping three-part plan for managing the finances of the new nation.

In part one of the plan, Hamilton proposed funding the national debt by paying off the patriots who had purchased bonds to finance the Revolution. Despite current financial hardship and economic crisis, Hamilton believed that paying off this debt would enhance the reputation of the United States and establish its good credit so that it could secure loans in the future. While Jefferson agreed on the importance of building sound credit, which had motivated his efforts to conclude international trade treaties, he backed Congressman James Madison's objections that indiscriminately paying back the *current* bond holders was not the same as paying back the patriots who had financed the war. Faced with hard times, most Southerners, who had bought the bulk of the bonds in the first place, had sold the obligations to Northern speculators at a tiny fraction of their face value. Paying these speculators would enrich *them*, not reward those who had financed the Revolution. Madison proposed distinguishing between speculators and original bond holders who still held their bonds; only the original bond holders, he proposed, should be paid. Largely because tracking down the original bond holders and distinguishing them from speculators was a highly impractical project, Hamilton's funding bill passed.

John Trumbull painted this portrait of Alexander Hamilton, secretary of the treasury, arch-Federalist, and political foe of Thomas Jefferson.

(Collection: National Archives and Records Administration)

The second part of Hamilton's grand plan was assumption— a proposal that the federal government assume the debts incurred by the states since independence. At first glance, one would think that the states must have jumped at this proposal. But they did not, and Madison, with Jefferson's concurrence, again led the opposition.

177

Both men understood that Hamilton's motive was to completely subordinate the states to the federal government by assuming their debts and then taxing the entire country to pay them off. Madison countered that most of the Southern states had already paid off their war debts, whereas the Northern states had not. Why should the entire nation pay off a primarily Northern debt?

Madison's logic was persuasive, and Congress became deadlocked on the issue. With his bill imperiled and his entire financial plan in jeopardy, Hamilton appealed to his Cabinet colleague and adversary, Thomas Jefferson. Jefferson didn't like Hamilton, but he always had the ability to put the good of the nation ahead of personal feelings and philosophical instincts. He struck a bargain with Hamilton and persuaded Madison to go along with it. Jefferson and Madison would support the passage of assumption through Congress; in return, Hamilton would endorse a pledge to move the seat of the national government from New York to a federal reserve that would be acquired along the Chesapeake. Thus, in exchange for agreeing to an inherently powerful central government, the Virginians ensured that the center of that government would be adjacent to Virginia. The stage was thus set for the creation of Washington, D.C. At the time, Jefferson believed that the compromise was necessary to save the union itself; within a few years, however, he would regret having made a deal with the devil Hamilton, feeling that he had conceded far too much to the central government and thereby imperiled, if not diminished, democracy.

The final part of Hamilton's national financial plan was the creation of a national bank, chartered by the federal government but principally financed and run by private investors. While he agreed that this would be a powerful financial instrument for the economically struggling young republic, Jefferson was appalled by two major aspects of the plan. First, it would create a government-sanctioned monopoly, a highly undemocratic oligarchy that was, in effect, government by the rich. Second, the Constitution did not explicitly empower the federal government to create such an institution. In 1791, after the bank bill had passed both the House and the Senate, President Washington delayed signing the bill until he received opinions from his Cabinet on its constitutionality. Jefferson responded with a report that must be regarded as one of the key documents in American history. Its crux is this:

> I consider the foundation of the Constitution as laid on this ground: That "all powers not delegated to the United States, by the Constitution, nor prohibited by it to the States, are reserved to the States or to the people." To take a single step beyond the boundaries thus specially drawn around the powers of Congress, is to take possession of a boundless field of power, no longer susceptible of any definition.
>
> The incorporation of a bank, and the powers assumed by this bill, have not, in my opinion, been delegated to the United States, by the Constitution.

In 1791, President Washington hired French-born Continental army engineer Pierre Charles L'Enfant to plan the capital city on the Potomac. Secretary of State Jefferson communicated with L'Enfant on April 10, 1791:

Having communicated to the President, before he went away, such general ideas on the subject of the town as occurred to me, I make no doubt that, in explaining himself to you on the subject, he has interwoven with his own ideas, such of mine as he approved .... Whenever it is proposed to prepare plans for the Capitol, I should prefer the adoption of some one of the models of antiquity, which have had the approbation of thousands of years; and for the President's house, I whould prefer the celebrated fronts of modern buildings, which have already received the approbation of all good judges.

The creation of a national bank, therefore, was a step on a slippery slope leading to abrogation of the Constitution and the creation of tyranny.

Despite Jefferson's incisive analysis, President Washington signed the national bank bill into law. The matter hardly ended there, however. Jefferson's articulation of the limits of "implied powers," his insistence that all powers not specifically assigned to the federal government are to be assumed by the states or the people, became the basis of a national debate that continues to this day. Sometimes that debate took the nation in directions Jefferson never imagined, let alone intended. For while Jefferson's position (later called "strict constructionism," an insistence that the Constitution be read literally and narrowly) promoted personal and local liberty, it was also used as the foundation on which the South built its doctrine of "states' rights." This doctrine, in turn, served as a defense of slavery, a motive for the Civil War, and, later, a justification for the state-sanctioned racial discrimination and segregation that would not end until the late twentieth century.

More immediately, the issue of the national bank was the springboard from which Jefferson and Madison launched a new political party, the Democratic-Republicans, to oppose the conservative Federalists. First, however, Jefferson had to face even more conflicts with the secretary of the treasury.

In the spring of 1790, the Spanish navy seized some British vessels off Vancouver Island. A crisis quickly developed, and war between Britain and Spain loomed. As secretary of state, Jefferson took a firm hand in advising and defining a policy of absolute neutrality, not simply to avoid involvement in the conflict, but so that United States merchant vessels could "become the carriers for all parties." Beyond the profit motive, Jefferson saw the prospective war as an opportunity to assert the "natural right" of neutrals, such as the United States, to engage in "commerce with all."

It was a rational and sound policy; as secretary of state with the approval of Washington, Jefferson should have had the authority to execute it. Without consulting Jefferson (or, for that matter, Washington), however, Hamilton met a British secret agent, Maj. George Beckwith, to discuss the United States' position on relations between Spain and England. Hamilton assured Beckwith that the United States had no ties with Spain and that the U.S. government also wanted to resolve "all matters unsettled" between Britain and America—in effect, implying a desire for an alliance.

Jefferson was outraged by Hamilton's meddling—and not just because he resented trespassing on his turf. British Canada was a powerful presence in North America, as was the Spanish presence in Florida and Louisiana. Jefferson believed that these two North American colonial powers balanced one another, more or less canceling each other out, to the great benefit of their neighbor, the United States. To side with one power or the other would upset this balance, almost certainly at America's peril. Hamilton's backdoor dealings with the British subverted Jefferson's efforts to maintain balance. Fortunately, the anticipated war never broke out.

If Jefferson struggled to steer a perfectly neutral course between British and Spanish interests in North America, he advocated an out-and-out trade war to force Britain to live up to the Treaty of Paris by evacuating the forts it still maintained in the Old Northwest and to negotiate a fair commercial treaty with the United States. Jefferson persuaded President Washington to close the American mission in London, a step just short of severing diplomatic relations. He further advocated increased trade with France and other countries friendly to the United States, at the expense of England. British merchants depended heavily on salted fish from U.S. fisheries; Jefferson wanted to divert this trade mainly to France until Britain evacuated the Northwestern forts and agreed to a commercial treaty. Hamilton not only opposed this plan, but actually leaked to the British what should have been Cabinet secrets. The secretary of the treasury would do anything, it seemed, to undercut the pro-French secretary of state and drive America closer to Britain, the stable, conservative nation Hamilton favored.

Even when it came to the Barbary pirates—in particular Algeria, which was currently holding American sailors captive—Hamilton worked against Jefferson. Jefferson held that payment of ransom and tribute was not only dishonorable, but a course inherently untenable for any nation wishing to preserve its sovereignty. He recommended that Congress finance the creation of a naval force to operate in concert with the navies of other nations trading in the Mediterranean so that Barbary piracy might be stamped out once and for all. The target of such a policy was not just the Barbary pirates, however. Although it was a mighty naval power, Britain chose to pay tribute. It did not want to end Barbary piracy, but to perpetuate it—against American vessels. Britain encouraged Algeria to disrupt the trade of its rival, the United States. Hamilton, as always, took the British side and directed his supporters in Congress to defeat Jefferson's naval proposal. Ultimately, Hamilton won. Congress voted funds not for a navy, but to ransom the Algerian captives.

The conflict between Jefferson and Hamilton took place on several levels. It was personal: The two men had sharply differing temperaments and simply did not like each other. It was ethical: Jefferson believed in the preeminence of principle, whereas Hamilton was a Machiavellian who believed that a desirable end justified even questionable means. Above all, it was a contest between two political philosophies and systems of government. One of the qualities that raised Jefferson far above ordinary politicians was his ability to see that he and Hamilton did not differ just as men or as Cabinet members, but that the outcome of their argument would determine the nature and the future of the United States. And this realization revealed to Jefferson the need to create an opposition party.

Jefferson sat on the Cabinet of a president vehemently opposed to political parties. Washington believed that could only heighten factionalism at the expense of the common good of the nation. The validity of this position must have weighed heavily on the secretary of state as he decided to join Madison in creating a vehicle to express what was then called the "Whig" (borrowing the name of Britain's liberal party) position versus the "Tory"—that is, the conservative Federalist—point of view. Jefferson and Madison secretly negotiated with the poet Philip Freneau to found and edit the *National Gazette,* an anti-Hamiltonian propaganda sheet. Jefferson supported Freneau—again, secretly—by hiring him as a State Department translator, without requiring him actually to translate anything. He also agreed to feed Freneau exclusive news stories, promising him "the perusal of all my letters of foreign intelligence and all foreign newspapers" as well as other official documents. Then Jefferson and Madison used their nationwide network of contacts to create a subscription base for the *Gazette.*

By 1792, the *National Gazette* had succeeded in disseminating the anti-Hamiltonian point of view to an ever-increasing readership. Almost immediately, Jefferson became universally recognized as the leader of the anti-Hamiltonian coalition, which, by 1794, was being called the Republican Party or the Democratic-Republican Party. Geographically, the party's adherents tended to come from the South and the West, whereas the Hamiltonian crowd (the Federalists) were mainly New Englanders.

Philosophically, the differences between the Democratic-Republicans and the Federalists broadly mirrored the differences between Jefferson and Hamilton. The Democratic-Republicans were intensive democrats, as well as advocates of majority rule and what would later be called states' rights. In contrast, the Federalists favored a much more limited definition of democracy, with strong centralization of governing authority. In international relations, the Democratic-Republicans wanted to reach out to form many foreign ties, and they welcomed the radicalism of the French Revolution; the Federalists tended toward isolationism, feared and distrusted the radicalism of the French Revolution, and, if anything, felt at least a fraternal bond with Britain.

Throughout the 1790s, the Federalists would continue to dominate the American political scene, but the Democratic-Republicans would emerge as a credible opposition. Hoping to stem the tide of Federalist tyranny, Thomas Jefferson and James Madison had invented America's two-party system.

Chapter 17

Unnatural Acts

Today, politicians and the public alike frequently decry the absence of civility in campaigns and political dialogue. They long for the bygone days in which servants of the people could "disagree without being disagreeable." Whenever those halcyon days may have been (if they ever were), it was not in the 1790s.

Backed by Jefferson and Madison, Philip Freneau's *National Gazette* was vehement in the charges it hurled against Hamilton and the Federalists, just as Hamilton and the Federalists were vicious in the accusations they heaped on Jefferson and the Democratic-Republicans. President Washington, to whom the very idea of political parties was supremely repugnant, wrote confidential letters to Jefferson and to Hamilton, beseeching both men to rein in their political passions, which were creating "internal dissensions" that were "harrowing and tearing our vitals." The president's appeals were to no avail. The attacks and counterattacks continued in the press, with Hamilton writing many of them personally (under the classical pseudonym Catullus), and supporters, chiefly James Madison and James Monroe, writing on Jefferson's behalf. Although the secretary of state thought it unseemly to appear in print personally, he did nothing to stop his lieutenants from taking up the cudgels for him, and to Washington's appeal, Jefferson personally replied on September 9, 1792:

> *That I have utterly, in my private conversations, disapproved of the system of the Secretary of the treasury, I*

acknowledge & avow: and this was not merely a specula-
tive difference. His system flowed from principles adverse
to liberty, & was calculated to undermined and demolish
the republic, by creating an influence of his department
over the members of the legislature.

He was even more heated in referring to the aspersions Hamilton
cast upon his character:

I ... value ... the esteem of my countrymen, & conscious
of having merited it by an integrity which cannot be
reproached, & by an enthusiastic devotion to their rights
& liberty, I will not suffer my retirement to be clouded by
the slanders of a man whose history, from the moment at
which history can stoop to notice him, is a tissue of machi-
nations against the liberty of the country which has not
only received and given him bread, but heaped its honors
on his head.

The Democratic-Republicans backed candidates in the congressional elections of 1792, and, even more important, they mustered impressive support for opposition to a second vice
presidential term for John Adams. In those days, before the adoption of the Twelfth Amendment, each member of the Electoral
College cast two votes for president. The candidate who received
the majority was elected president, and the runner-up was elected
vice president. Once Washington was persuaded to run for a second term—and Jefferson was one of the most ardent persuaders—
no opposition was offered him, but the Federalist vice presidential
candidate, Adams, was opposed by a Democratic-Republican, New
York governor George Clinton. In the end, Adams won reelection,
receiving seventy-seven electoral votes to Clinton's fifty—which,
nevertheless, was an impressive showing for a brand-new opposition party.

Jefferson held himself aloof from direct participation in the
1792 elections, but he was nevertheless encouraged by the results.
Yet, having been instrumental in creating the new party and stal-
wartly enduring Hamilton's ideological and personal attacks,
Jefferson had no desire to pursue public life further. Although

he was a fighter, he did not like political strife, and the office of secretary of state must have seemed to him too much like the revolutionary governorship of Virginia. Subordinated to Washington, undercut by Hamilton, and repeatedly curtailed by Congress, Jefferson hardly had a free hand in steering America's course through international relations. As always happened when his leadership aspirations were frustrated, Jefferson longed to retire to his beloved Monticello.

It had taken a great deal of persuading to convince Washington to seek a second term, and when it looked as if he would not run again, Jefferson planned to resign at the end of the first president's term—so eager was he to leave office that he began packing. When Washington announced that he would run again after all, Jefferson stood firm in declining a second term as secretary of state, and he even declined to renew his tour as minister plenipotentiary in Paris. Nothing, it seemed, would come between him and Monticello—nothing, that is, except a fear that, by retiring now, in the thick of the Hamiltonian attack upon him, he would damage not only his own reputation, but that of the fledgling Democratic-Republican Party as well. Deciding that he could not afford the appearance of running away, he gritted his teeth and held on to his Cabinet post, at least for the time.

Almost immediately after Jefferson's decision to remain in office, the peace of Monticello must have seemed all the more intensely appealing. In July 1790, the House of Representatives had approved the removal of the United States capital from New York City to Philadelphia, and Congress opened its first legislative session there on December 6. In 1793, during the first year of Washington's second term, a terrible yellow fever epidemic swept through Philadelphia. As in the great plagues of the European Middle Ages, carts rumbled nightly through the streets, the corpses of victims heaped on them. Six thousand people, two out of ten Philadelphians, succumbed to this scourge, and the panicked government withdrew to the relative safety of rural Trenton, New Jersey, across the Delaware and to the south.

John Adams, print (1850–1900) made after the painting by
John Singleton Copley.

Nor was there peace in the wider world. The revolution in France, which had started so hopefully—observed, aided, and even partly inspired by Jefferson—had become a nightmare of severed heads and rivers of blood. The Reign of Terror gripped France, sending into exile—or to the guillotine—even those among the nobility who had supported the cause of liberty, equality, and fraternity. Many of these individuals had been intimates of Jefferson's social and intellectual circle in Paris. He regarded them as the very best exemplars and champions of Enlightenment civilization. Lafayette escaped the guillotine by fleeing to Belgium, only to be arrested and imprisoned by the Holy Roman Emperor Francis II. The great scientist Antoine Laurent Lavoisier, whom Jefferson had met and greatly admired, was executed in 1794, his judge declaring simply that the French Republic had no need of scientists.

By this time, too, the French Revolution had reached beyond France to engulf in war most of Europe and its colonial possessions. Hamilton and his partisans crowed: *This* was the result of the radical revolution Jefferson and his ilk supported, celebrated, and wanted to import into the United States. Still, Jefferson did not give up on the French Revolution or the French Republic. He believed that the defeat of the revolution, either by internal forces or by royalists from other countries, would ultimately threaten the American republic, encouraging the likes of Hamilton to reshape American government after the British model. Jefferson's hope, naïve though it was, was that the moderate wing of the revolution, the Girondists, would prevail against the radical Jacobins and that the result would be a fellow republic that was stable, peaceful, and friendly to the United States.

But while he feared the excesses of the Terror and yet rejoiced in each French victory over the forces of royalism, Secretary of State Jefferson once again counseled strict neutrality as war broke out between France and the First Coalition, made up of Britain, Holland, Spain, Austria, Prussia, and Russia. Jefferson would not let his personal and philosophical affinity for the French Revolution seep into his conduct of United States foreign affairs. However, he did advise Washington against making a blanket declaration of neutrality. His reasoning was that, in a world at war,

American neutrality was a thing of value and should not simply be given away, but, rather, held back. "We might reasonably ask a price," Jefferson suggested. Washington overruled him; accepting this defeat with grace, Jefferson agreed to support whatever declaration the president might make.

He was not ready to cave in, however, on the matter of honoring the 1778 Treaty of Alliance with France. Concerned that the treaty, which obligated the United States to help France defend its West Indian possessions, would drag the nation into war against England, Hamilton argued that the treaty was null and void because it had been made with the French monarchy, now deposed. Jefferson countered that treaties are made between nations, not between agents of government, and he also tried to reassure the president and his Cabinet colleagues that assistance to France in the matter of the West Indies did not obligate the United States to enter into war. In the end, Washington was persuaded, and he agreed to recognize the French Republic, to honor the treaty of 1778, and (over Hamilton's vigorous protest) to receive its ambassador, Citizen Edmond Genêt.

Washington was very particular concerning just how Genêt should be received—"not with too much warmth or cordiality"— but Jefferson chose to ignore the specification. Indeed, he was not alone in this. Many Americans welcomed the French Revolution and were thrilled and excited to greet Genêt. Doubtless encouraged by Jefferson's warmth and, even more, by the reception of the people, the French ambassador wasted no time in flouting United States neutrality provisions. He commissioned American privateers to prey on British merchant shipping in American waters and even began recruiting American volunteers for an assault by land and sea against Florida, which, at the time, was a Spanish possession.

Jefferson did not need orders from President Washington to prompt him to issue a warning to Genêt that his actions violated United States neutrality and that he must stop. Genêt, in reply, confronted Jefferson with the 1778 treaty, which, he said, gave France the right to fit out privateers on American soil and operate them in American waters, then sell any prize vessels in American ports. Jefferson refuted this, although he did suggest to Washington that captured prizes were indeed French property and could, therefore, be sold. Washington would have none of it. He summarily ordered all French-commissioned privateers out of U.S. ports.

Despite all warnings, Genêt continued for some four months to raise privateers and recruit volunteers. His activity culminated in the July 1793 seizure of the British vessel *Little Sarah*, which was towed into the port of the United States capital itself, Philadelphia, to be fitted out with heavier guns so that it might then be used as a French privateer. Hamilton joined Secretary of War Knox in moving that a battery of artillery be erected on the Delaware River to prevent the departure of the prize ship. Fearing this would provoke a war with France, Jefferson objected and proposed that the matter be referred to the Supreme Court for an opinion on proper procedure for a neutral United States. When the court refused to render an opinion, the Cabinet itself drew up "Rules Governing Belligerents." Then, on August 2, it recommended to the president that he demand Genêt's recall to France.

The French, it turned out, were all too willing to comply with President Washington's recall demand. Genêt had been sent to the United States by the moderate Girondist party, which, in the bloody rush of events, had now been overthrown by the far more radical and ruthless Jacobins. Not only did the Jacobin government dispatch a new ambassador, but it also requested that the American president not simply send Genêt packing, but extradite him. He was now deemed an enemy of France. Continuing to observe strict neutrality, Washington decided that he could not compel Genêt to return to France and certain death on the guillotine. Stripped of his ambassador's credentials, Genêt was allowed to remain in the United States. He subsequently was naturalized as a United States citizen and then settled into quiet respectability after marrying the daughter of New York governor and prominent Democratic-Republican George Clinton.

As for Jefferson, the dispute with and over Citizen Genêt had moved him once again to tender his resignation from the Cabinet. On July 31, he told the president that he intended to retire on September 30, but, at Washington's insistence, he agreed to stay on until the end of the year. Little enough was accomplished during this time, as the government largely recessed in an effort to escape yellow fever. At the eleventh hour, on December 21, Washington pleaded with Jefferson to reconsider and remain in the Cabinet. Jefferson was adamant. He fully intended to retire from public life and to embrace the sweet solitude of Monticello.

At the age of fifty, Thomas Jefferson was exhausted mentally and physically. From the beginning of 1794 through 1796, he seldom strayed more than a few miles from Monticello. He farmed and he gardened. He built a profitable business on his property producing iron nails. He designed a new mold-board plow, which was far more efficient than traditional designs and, years later, in 1805, would win him a gold medal from the Societé d'Agriculture du Département de la Seine. He invented a new kind of threshing machine driven by horsepower. And, as always, he labored over the architectural perfection of his Monticello mansion.

But, try as he might, Jefferson could not isolate himself from the rush of world events. He fended off a request that he head a special mission to Spain in 1794, but when he saw the text of the "Treaty of Amity, Commerce, and Navigation" that John Jay, as Washington's special minister, had concluded with Britain, he was sufficiently outraged to throw his support behind Democratic-Republican efforts to block its ratification by the Senate. Jay's Treaty laid a firm foundation for Anglo-American trade, secured a renewed promise of the British evacuation of the frontier forts in the Old Northwest, and secured at least the limited right of American ships to trade in the British West Indies. Jefferson and others who objected to the treaty protested that it conceded so much to the British that it was really a covert treaty of alliance "between England and the Anglomen of this country against the legislature and people of the U.S." Despite the protests of Jefferson and many others, Jay's Treaty was ratified in 1795, bringing a short-lived improvement in U.S.–British relations and a precipitous decline in relations between America and France, which, like Jefferson, saw the treaty as a covert Anglo-American alliance.

Jay's Treaty was not the only act of Washington's second term that provoked Jefferson's Democratic-Republican ire. Back in 1791, Alexander Hamilton had successfully urged Congress to enact a federal excise tax on spirits distilled in the United States. Opposition to this federal tax was both rapid in coming and intense in feeling. The focal point of protest was western Pennsylvania, where federal tax collectors were harassed, threatened, intimidated, and even assaulted. A number were tarred and feathered, as were certain distillers who chose to cooperate with the revenue officials. Finally, on July 16, 1794, a band of about five hundred tax protesters attacked the home of Gen. John Neville, Allegheny County's inspector of the excise. Neville did not meekly submit to the attack, but he defended his home with the aid of a small detachment of U.S. Army regulars. Two of the attackers were killed and six were wounded. Outnumbered, however, Neville and his men made their escape, leaving the house to the mercy of the mob, which looted and burned it.

The attack on Neville briefly emboldened the protesters, who assembled at Braddock's Field, near Pittsburgh, on August 1, 1794. The protesters were almost six thousand strong, but within two days the six-thousand-man "army" dissolved and dispersed. This did not satisfy President Washington, who announced on August 7 that he was calling out the militia to restore order, to enforce the excise tax, and to crush the "Whiskey Rebellion." Simultaneously with this show of force, Washington dispatched to western Pennsylvania a team of commissioners to offer amnesty to all those who agreed to swear an oath of submission to the United States. Although organized violence was at an end, few came forth to swear the oath. At last, therefore, on September 25, Washington ordered 12,950 militiamen and volunteers from Pennsylvania, New Jersey, and Maryland to march to Pittsburgh. This large force managed to apprehend and arrest a small number of participants in the Whiskey Rebellion, but the majority of the prominent protesters fled and hid.

In the meantime, Jefferson protested what he called the excessive and irresponsible use of military force, which, he believed, had been intended not so much to restore order as to demonstrate the willingness—and the capacity—of the federal government to enforce submission to its authority.

In view of Jay's Treaty and what he deemed the dangerous precedent set by the suppression of the Whiskey Rebellion, Jefferson allowed Madison to talk him into offering himself as the Democratic-Republican's first candidate for the office of president of the United States. Because Washington absolutely refused to stand for a third term—establishing a tradition that would not be interrupted until the four terms of Franklin Delano Roosevelt— Jefferson's opponent was John Adams, his longtime friend but, increasingly, his ideological nemesis.

Not that Adams and Jefferson ever had to face off in a campaign. Adams considered it beneath his dignity to make a direct appeal to the American people. He felt that having served as Washington's vice president was sufficient qualification for the office of president. This suited Jefferson, who never even left Monticello. Yet the supporters of both candidates did debate and argue and harangue. The flashpoint issue was Jay's Treaty, but, not for the last time in American politics, the sharpest focus of the contest was the contrasting images of the candidates: Adams, representing a continuation of the dignified greatness of Washington; Jefferson, the defender of the rights of the people.

Adams's supporters—never Adams himself—attacked Jefferson's dismal record as governor of Virginia (an arguable position). They also accused him of having opposed the Constitution (he had done no such thing), having quit as secretary of state when the going got too rough (it was a job he never relished to begin with), and wanting to import wild French radicalism into the United States (a vast oversimplification). In the end, it was a stunningly close election, with Adams winning by just three electoral votes, seventy-one to Jefferson's sixty-eight.

But then things got even more interesting. As mentioned earlier, before the Twelfth Amendment changed the electoral process, the president and vice president were elected separately. The Federalist vice presidential candidate, Thomas Pinckney, received forty-eight votes, while Aaron Burr, the Democratic-Republican, received thirty. By a substantial margin, Jefferson had received more votes than Pinckney and, therefore, as runner-up, had been elected vice president. Jefferson was under no obligation to accept his election, but, perhaps because he knew Adams as a man and a friend, he believed that he could work productively with him, despite the political and ideological gulf that separated them.

Jefferson was sworn in as vice president of the United States at Philadelphia, in the Senate chamber, on March 4, 1797. The day before, he had been sworn in as president of the prestigious American Philosophical Society—a scientific honor that, in Jefferson's eyes, probably eclipsed his entry into the vice president's office. Certainly, Jefferson's service with the society would give him far more pleasure and satisfaction than the next four stormy years as a Democratic-Republican vice president in the Federalist administration of an increasingly conservative Adams.

The first crisis came just two months after Adams took office, when it was learned that the recently created five-man executive body of France, the Directory, had high-handedly refused to accept the credentials of Charles Cotesworth Pinckney, sent as the new American minister to France. President Adams responded with an indignant speech, which, in the bitter climate of Franco-American relations created by Jay's Treaty, Jefferson feared would bring on war between the former allies.

While Adams and the Federalists stirred anti-French feelings in America, relations between Vice President Jefferson and his old friend the president, already strained to the breaking point, took a sudden turn for the worse. A private letter Jefferson had written more than a year earlier unexpectedly found its way into print. Sent to Philip Mazzei after ratification of Jay's Treaty, the letter was a denunciation of Washington as well as Adams. It called them advocates of an "Anglican monarchical and aristocratical party," and it criticized the royalist tone of the Washington-Adams administration. Without Jefferson's permission, Mazzei had given the letter to a Florentine newspaper, which printed it in Italian. It was subsequently translated into French by a French newspaper, and, from this version, it was retranslated into English by none other than Noah Webster, who printed it in his Federalist *Minerva* with the intention of embarrassing Jefferson and the Democratic-Republicans.

But it did not embarrass Jefferson, and it embarrassed his supporters even less. If anything, the Democratic-Republican press trumpeted Jefferson's assessment of the Federalists as counterrevolutionary Anglophile monarchists, and Jefferson, seizing the moment of his unintended "exposure" to the electorate, dropped any further pretense of secrecy as to his political position. He now personally took up the reins of the Democratic-Republican Party as its unquestioned leader. It was an unmistakable signal that, come the next election, he intended to challenge the Federalist candidate for president, no matter who it might be.

Having brought to a head the dispute between rival ideologies, Jefferson soon found himself confronting another crisis over Democratic-Republican letters. A Federalist associate justice of the Supreme Court published a presentment of a federal grand jury finding concerning circular letters from a number of Democratic-Republican members of Congress, chief among them Representative Samuel J. Cabell. According to the grand jury, the letters disseminated "unfounded calumnies" against the government of the United States. In the presentment, Cabell and others were further accused of using the letters to undermine "the peace, happiness and independence of these United States."

Jefferson was appalled and alarmed that the Federalist administration would so blatantly use the judicial branch as a means of suppressing criticism of the government—free speech. Publicly, Jefferson vigorously made his views known. Secretly, he drew up a petition, circulated in his home congressional district, condemning the grand jury's presentment as a violation of free speech and calling for the impeachment of the jury. In the end, the Virginia House did vote condemnation of the jury's action, but it did not proceed further against the jury because no charges were actually filed against Cabell or the others.

As it turned out, the grand jury's presentment was only a prelude to much more dangerous Federalist abuses to come. More immediately, however, it was the crisis in Franco-American relations that became urgently critical. After Pinckney was rebuffed by the Directory, President Adams sent to Paris a commission consisting of Pinckney, John Marshall, and Elbridge Gerry to attempt to heal the growing breach in Franco-American relations by concluding a new treaty of commerce. Incredibly, French Prime Minister Charles Maurice de Talleyrand-Perigord sent three agents to greet the American commissioners in Paris in October 1797 and told them that before a treaty could even be discussed, the United States would have to loan France $12 million *and* pay Talleyrand a personal bribe of $250,000.

On April 3, 1798, an indignant Adams submitted to Congress the correspondence from the commission, which designated the French agents as "X," "Y," and "Z." Congress, equally indignant, published the entire portfolio, and the public learned of the "XYZ Affair." As Jefferson watched Americans of various political stripes unite in outrage, it was clear to him that the Federalist government of the United States was spoiling for war against its erstwhile ally. Indeed, by the time the XYZ Affair came fully to light, French naval operations against the British in the West Indies were already beginning to interfere with United States shipping.

In the hostile climate created by the XYZ Affair, Congress authorized the rapid completion of three great frigates, the *United States*, the *Constellation*, and the *Constitution*, and funded the arming and training of some eighty thousand militiamen. Congress also commissioned one thousand privateers to capture or repel French vessels, and George Washington himself was recalled from retirement to command the army. On May 3, 1798, what was now an undeclared war—historians would dub it the American-French Quasi-War—became the occasion for the formal creation of a U.S. Department of the Navy. During July 1798, Lt. Stephen Decatur, commanding the sloop *Delaware*, captured the French schooner *Croyable* off the New Jersey coast. (Renamed the *Retaliation*, the vessel would be retaken by the French in November 1798 off Guadaloupe.)

In the summer of 1798, while the Quasi-War was being fought, the Federalist-dominated Congress passed the Alien and Sedition Acts. These included the Naturalization Act (June 18, 1798), which required immigrants seeking U.S. citizenship to be resident in the country fourteen years instead of the originally mandated five; the Alien Act (June 25), which authorized the president summarily to deport any alien he regarded as dangerous; the Alien Enemies Act (July 6), which authorized the president, in time of war, to arrest, imprison, or deport subjects of any enemy power; and, most outrageous of all, the Sedition Act (July 14). This prohibited any assembly "with intent to oppose any measure ... of the government," and it forbade printing, uttering, or publishing anything "false, scandalous, and malicious" against the government.

In and of itself, the Sedition Act was clearly counterrevolutionary, an infringement on the Constitutional rights to peaceable assembly and to free speech. But what made all of the dangerous Alien and Sedition Acts even more insidious was the fact that many of the leading Democratic-Republicans were recent refugees from turbulent Europe and had not been resident in the United States for anything approaching fourteen years. Whatever else the Alien and Sedition Acts were intended to accomplish, they were squarely aimed at reducing the power base of the Democratic-Republican Party. It was as if the present-day GOP managed to pass laws explicitly to suppress the Democratic Party, or vice versa.

Jefferson declared that if the Alien and Sedition Acts were allowed to stand, "we shall immediately see attempted another act of Congress, declaring the President shall continue in office during life, reserving to another occasion the transfer of the succession to his heirs, and the establishment of the Senate for life." Jefferson set to work on a series of resolutions attacking centralized governmental authority and promoting the sovereignty of the states. He wanted a state legislature to publish the resolutions, to give it the weight of the people represented by a governmental body. On November 22, 1799, Kentucky (which had become a state in 1792) published Jefferson's resolutions. On December 24, 1798, Virginia had already published ideologically similar resolutions, drafted by James Madison.

Both sets of resolutions held that the Alien and Sedition Acts were unconstitutional and, therefore, not binding on the states. Jefferson's original draft of the "Kentucky Resolutions" boldly maintained that a state had the right not only to judge the constitutionality of acts of Congress, but also to "nullify" any acts it determined to be unconstitutional. The concept of nullification was too radical for the Kentucky legislature to accept, and it was suppressed in the final draft. However, the nullification principle was *implied* in both the Kentucky and Virginia resolutions. What Jefferson had articulated was the position that the United States was founded on a compact among the states, not among the people. The powers enumerated in the Constitution as the prerogatives of the federal government Jefferson did not challenge, but, he held, acts beyond the central government's constitutionally enumerated powers were inherently unconstitutional and, therefore, had no binding force on the states.

The Kentucky and Virginia resolutions did not succeed in bringing about the immediate repeal of the Alien and Sedition Acts, but they clearly set forth the Democratic-Republican opposition to autocratic power, and they ensured that, even in an atmosphere of international crisis, the Alien and Sedition Acts would be short-lived. The Sedition Act was repealed in 1801, and the Alien and Naturalization Acts expired without renewal in 1802. Only the Alien Enemies Act occasionally resurfaced in American political life, most notably during World Wars I and II.

The Kentucky and Virginia resolutions were a bold and timely defense against a Federalist retreat into the tyranny that supposedly had been defeated in the American Revolution. They also made Jefferson a popular political figure at the expense of the Federalists. But it is also true that the concept of nullification would linger to haunt American history. In the decade before the Civil War, South Carolina's John C. Calhoun would echo—and distort—Jefferson to assert that the states could override and "nullify" *any* federal law they judged unconstitutional. As the basis for states' rights, nullification thus became a wedge that drove North and South apart and brought about the violent disintegration of the American union during 1861–65. In writing to preserve American democracy, Jefferson inadvertently planted the seeds of what could have been its destruction.

Part Five

President of the United States

Chapter 18

Jefferson and Burr

As vice president, Thomas Jefferson learned the lesson that all who occupied that office in the future would learn: Barring the death of the president, the vice president has very little power indeed. During Jefferson's lonely vice presidential "watch," the Federalists significantly aggrandized the central government, enacted legislation to suppress dissent, did their best to strangle the Democratic-Republicans in the cradle, destroyed good relations with France, and created a standing army and navy.

Jefferson himself had wanted to create a navy to combat the Barbary pirates, but the Federalists finally built one to fight the French and end any possibility of alliance with revolutionary France. Paradoxically, the Federalists found themselves supporting a revolution—this one in Haiti, led by former slave Toussaint Louverture, against French colonial rule. A revolution to *fight* France readily found favor with the government of John Adams. In addition, the rapidly assembled U.S. Navy acquitted itself brilliantly against the established French naval forces in the course of the Quasi-War. On February 9, 1799, the freshly commissioned USS *Constellation* captured the French frigate *Insurgente*, and additional exchanges took place at sea sporadically through 1800, mainly in the Caribbean. Of ten major engagements, the French recapture of the *Croyable/Retaliation* (Chapter 17, "Unnatural Acts") was the only American loss.

Against the background of diminished domestic liberty and disintegrating relations with the nation he loved second only to the

United States, Jefferson not only decided to run for president, but he did so with an enthusiasm that he had never before exhibited in pursuit of a political office. In keeping with the precedent set by Washington and Adams, however, his enthusiasm did not extend to public campaigning. Instead, he worked through James Madison and others to get out the Democratic-Republican message, and that message—indeed, the entire party platform—was the work of Jefferson.

The Democratic-Republicans, Jefferson wrote to Madison, wanted peace—with France *and* with England. They intended as well to cherish and cultivate the Union (despite the stand Jefferson himself had taken in the "Kentucky Resolutions," asserting a state's right to overrule and nullify federal acts it deemed unconstitutional). The party wanted to disband the standing army "on principles of economy and safety"; Jefferson said nothing about disbanding the navy, which he considered useful in defending America's right to freedom of the high seas. Protest would also play a key role in the Democratic-Republican agenda where unconstitutional laws such as the Alien and Sedition Acts were concerned. Jefferson understood that, in creating an opposition party, he was advocating a kind of second revolution. However, he wanted to ensure that this one would take place without bloodshed. To Madison, Jefferson left the task of working out the details within the broad ideological strokes he had painted.

The Alien and Sedition Acts were a worthy issue against which to define the Democratic-Republican Party; however, they also presented Jefferson's campaign with practical problems. Intended to suppress Democratic-Republican opposition to the Federalist regime, the acts sometimes succeeded in doing just that. Jefferson worked secretly to secure financial assistance for loyal Democratic-Republican newspaper editors and publishers who were being prosecuted under the Alien and Sedition Acts. Indeed, Jefferson himself, although a sitting vice president, risked prosecution under the acts when he personally distributed anti-Federalist pamphlets and other matter.

The Federalists used the judiciary, especially U.S. Supreme Court Associate Justice Samuel Chase, to hunt down and prosecute cases of "seditious libel." While using the legal system against the opposition, they also resorted to personal attacks on Jefferson. Scandal as a political weapon is hardly new to American politics, and the Federalists during the campaign of 1800 slung mud in quantities that make today's so-called "politics of personal attack" look positively polite.

Jefferson was vulnerable on at least two points. There were charges that he, like other Southern slave owners, slept with his female slaves and even maintained what his enemies called a "Congo Harem." More specific charges of miscegenation, bearing on the case of Sally Hemings, would not emerge until Jefferson was already in office and beginning to campaign for a second term. More important in his first presidential bid were charges of radical atheism. Jefferson had made no secret of his deism, a religious-philosophical position that did not reject belief in God but that did eschew sectarian religion and argued that, while God created humankind, He did not intervene providentially in human affairs. The Federalists made no nice distinction between deism and total unbelief, however. They painted Jefferson as an atheist, pure and simple, who wanted to infect America with the very godlessness that had driven France through its anarchical reign of terror. Federalist preachers denounced Jefferson from their pulpits, declaring that a vote for him was "no less than a rebellion against God." Once the leaps had been made from deism to atheism to French "Jacobinism," it was a short hop to a nation in which (according to the Federalist-sympathizing Hartford *Connecticut Courant*) "murder, robbery, rape, adultery and incest [would be] openly taught and practiced."

Jefferson never defended himself personally against charges like these; to enter the campaign fray was considered beneath a candidate's dignity. His supporters vigorously defended him, however, and, in turn, accused Adams and the Federalists of all species of tyranny.

Jefferson, following Adams's lead and the custom of the time, held himself aloof from the campaign, but it was nevertheless highly organized by Madison and his other supporters. They stirred the people with journalism and speeches. They worked hard to get out the vote. At this point in American history, the division between the popular vote and the electoral vote was sharper than it is today. In the majority of the states, the electors were chosen by the legislature, not by popular vote. The Democratic-Republicans managed to push through reform in Virginia, which put the election of electors in the hands of the people. Jefferson's popularity in his home state, the most populous state in the union, ensured him a win here. Elsewhere, the Democratic-Republicans skillfully mustered support in the state legislatures.

In contrast, the Federalists put their faith in the legacy of Washington, who had just died in 1799. That legacy, they believed, would carry the day. Most of the Federalists refrained from vigorous campaigning, organizing, and political maneuvering—except for the wily Alexander Hamilton. New York was about to change from the legislative to the popular election of presidential electors, but, for the upcoming election, the state was still using the legislative method. Aaron Burr, a New York Democratic-Republican, campaigned hard in New York City and ensured that the bustling town would send enough Democratic-Republicans to the state assembly to create a majority. Hamilton sought to outmaneuver Burr by prevailing on New York's Federalist Governor John Jay to call the assembly into special session before the election, while it still had a Federalist majority, to change the election method immediately and thereby circumvent the purpose of a Democratic-Republican legislative majority. Hamilton chided Jay not to be "overscrupulous," but Jay, a man of law, refused to sidestep the law. He would call no special session for partisan purposes. Thus the stage was set for a Democratic-Republican victory in New York.

Defeated here, Hamilton settled on another tactic. He decided that it could actually be politically expedient for Jefferson to triumph over Adams. After all, Adams was insufficiently Federalist to suit him, and he believed that he could more effectively oppose Jefferson in office than he could Adams. It would be a joust between mortal political enemies, which, come the *next* election, in 1804, would put Hamilton in striking distance to become a Federalist champion far more capable than Adams of defeating Jefferson and the whole Democratic-Republican program.

Jacques Jouvenal's bust of Aaron Burr, Jefferson's vice president, political enemy, and would-be emperor of the West.

(Collection: ArtToday)

The loss of Virginia and New York, coupled with Hamilton's opposition, was a severe blow to Adams and a major boost to Jefferson. Nevertheless, the vote was extremely close. When the

Federalists were very narrowly defeated in South Carolina, the numbers thrust the two Democratic-Republican candidates into the lead: Jefferson and Burr were tied, with seventy-three electoral votes each, whereas Adams trailed with sixty-five. Charles Cotesworth Pinckney, the Federalist candidate for vice president, received sixty-four electoral votes, and John Jay received one vote.

The tie between Jefferson and Burr would have to be resolved by the House of Representatives as it was constituted before the election—that is, with a Federalist majority. Although the Democratic-Republicans had put up Burr as their candidate for vice president, he now refused to promise that he would not accept election to the presidency if the House chose him. Many of the Federalist legislators, especially those who had just been voted out of office, were eager to get revenge on Jefferson.

Politics, the old saying goes, makes strange bedfellows. It would be difficult to find two more bitter political enemies than Jefferson and Hamilton. Difficult, but not impossible: Hamilton's hatred of Burr went beyond differences between Federalist and Democratic-Republican ideologies. Their political rivalry was personal and longstanding.

> *Born in Newark, New Jersey, in 1756, Aaron Burr came from a prominent family and, like Hamilton, served on George Washington's staff during the Revolution. Unlike Hamilton, he rubbed Washington the wrong way and was soon transferred out of the commander-in-chief's staff. Burr became a prosperous attorney in New York, with an impressive political power base. During the 1790s, he organized a political coalition opposed to Philip Schuyler, a New York arch-Federalist and Hamilton's father-in-law. Burr's triumph over Schuyler took on the aura of a personal vendetta, and Hamilton came to resent Burr on every possible level. Presumably for these reasons, Hamilton decided to work against Burr and for Jefferson.*

The Federalist-dominated House of Representatives cast ballot after ballot in an effort to break the tie between Jefferson and Burr. While this lengthy process was underway, Hamilton busily contacted his Federalist colleagues. He "confided" to them that Jefferson was a dangerous man, but at least he had "pretensions to character." Burr, it was true, shared Jefferson's radical political opinions, but, in contrast to Jefferson, he had "nothing in his favor. His private character is not defended by his most partial friends." Hamilton churned out a number of letters expressing these and similar sentiments about Burr and sent them to Federalist congressmen as the balloting continued. At last, on the thirty-sixth ballot, on February 17, 1801, the House elected Thomas Jefferson the third president of the United States. Jefferson ultimately owed his victory to Alexander Hamilton, his nemesis.

That was one unpleasant irony. Another was the fact that President-elect Jefferson also faced the prospect of serving at least four years with a vice president he had never liked and now had ample reason to distrust, resent, and despise. Before the Twelfth Amendment, there was no way to distinguish between presidential and vice presidential candidates on ballots. The candidate with the most electoral votes became president, while the runner-up became vice president; however, simultaneously with the introduction of the two-party system, it was unmistakably understood which candidate the nominating party *intended* for president and which for vice president. It was, therefore, always clear that Jefferson was the Democratic-Republican candidate for president and that Burr was the party's candidate for vice president. Burr's refusal to release votes to Jefferson, while perfectly legal under the Constitution of that time, was nothing less than a double-cross, the kind of Machiavellian maneuvering that Hamilton detested in Burr (though he was quite capable of the same). Throughout his presidency, Jefferson would keep his vice president at arm's length, making no pretense to cordiality or collegiality, and, in fact, effectively freezing him out of the Democratic-Republican Party.

As for Jefferson's old friend John Adams, he was too pained by his defeat to attend the new president's inauguration. Adams had moved to Washington, D.C., after it officially become the capital city of the United States on June 1, 1800. He quietly slipped out of the city on the morning of the inauguration, March 4, 1801, before the ceremony, without greeting his successor.

In terms of spectacle, Adams didn't miss much. Whereas both he and his predecessor, George Washington, had ridden in splendid carriages to the place of inauguration, rolling regally as part of a great parade, Jefferson casually walked from his boardinghouse on New Jersey Avenue and C Street, allowing himself to be escorted partway by a detachment of Alexandria, Virginia, militia officers. He had donned no uniform or formal attire, not even a gentleman's sword. Rather, he wore the era's equivalent of an ordinary business suit.

Jefferson's message was clear: The days of the imperial presidency were over. And there was more symbolism, for those who cared to see it. The new capital city was largely Jefferson's idea, and the Capitol building was still unfinished, save for the Senate Chamber. For that reason, the Senate Chamber was chosen as the place of inauguration—though Jefferson would doubtless have preferred the more democratic House of Representatives, had that chamber been ready. What must certainly have pleased him, though, is the climb he and the inaugural party had to make to reach the Capitol. Jefferson had specified that the building housing the federal legislature should occupy a hill so that it would be higher than the president's mansion. As Jefferson conceived of American government, the people's representatives, not the chief executive, were to hold the dominant place.

After Chief Justice John Marshall administered the oath of office, President Jefferson delivered his inaugural address. He spoke with a humility that did much to salve the wounds created by a bitter struggle between competing ideologies and personalities. It set the tone for an administration that hoped to put aside partisanship, or at least put front and center the common causes of American government and American potential. To the packed Senate Chamber, in a speech he knew would be widely published, Jefferson confessed his feelings of inadequacy to the task for which his "fellow citizens" had chosen him:

> A rising nation, spread over a wide and fruitful land, traversing all the seas with the rich productions of their industry, engaged in commerce with nations who feel power and forget right, advancing rapidly to destinies beyond the reach of mortal eye—when I contemplate these transcendent objects, and see the honor, the happiness, and the hopes of

this beloved country committed to the issue and auspices of
this day, I shrink from the contemplation, and humble
myself before the magnitude of the undertaking.

Utterly indeed, should I despair, did not the presence
of many whom I here see remind me, that in the other
high authorities provided by our constitution, I shall find
resources of wisdom, of virtue, and of zeal, on which to
rely under all difficulties.

Thus President Jefferson put himself in his place—as a president, not a monarch; as a man, as much a follower of the will of the people as a leader of the people; and as an authority among other authorities, all of whom had the welfare of the nation in their minds, hearts, and deeds.

He acknowledged the vehemence of the contest that had brought him to this chamber, a contest that "has sometimes worn an aspect which might impose on strangers unused to think freely and to speak and to write what they think." Jefferson gently warned those "strangers" not to be deceived about the essential unity of a politically boisterous America: "This being now decided by the voice of the nation, announced according to the rules of the constitution, all will, of course, arrange themselves under the will of the law, and unite in common efforts for the common good." This, naturally, was an easy enough sentiment for the victor to express, but Jefferson continued:

All, too, will bear in mind this sacred principle, that
though the will of the majority is in all cases to prevail,
that will, to be rightful, must be reasonable; that the
minority possess their equal rights, which equal laws must
protect, and to violate which would be oppression.

Let us then, fellow citizens, unite with one heart and
one mind. Let us restore to social intercourse that harmony
and affection without which liberty and even life itself are
but dreary things. And let us reflect that having banished
from our land that religious intolerance under which
mankind so long bled and suffered, we have gained little if
we countenance a political intolerance as despotic, as
wicked, and capable of as bitter and bloody persecutions.

The man who, more than any other single American of his time, had created and defined the Democratic-Republican opposition to the reigning Federalism of the United States, declared:

We have called by different names brethren of the same
principle. We are all republicans—we are all federalists.
If there be any among us who would wish to dissolve this
Union or to change its republican form, let them stand
undisturbed as monuments to the safety with which error
of opinion may be tolerated where reason is left free to
combat it.

The full genius of Jefferson was expressed in this, one of the greatest speeches in American history. It is at once full of timeless eloquence and resounding principle, yet it is also very much a speech that speaks to the needs of the moment. It is, as Jefferson always was at his best, a synthesis of high idealism and practical good sense. Its doctrine is immortal, but its expression is intensely timely and human: "I know, indeed, that some honest men fear that a republican government is not strong enough." Thus he penetrates to the human heart of the controversy between Federalist and Democratic-Republican. Then he appeals to the head, to reason, to logical good sense:

But would the honest patriot, in the full tide of successful
experiment, abandon a government which has so far kept
us free and firm, on the theoretic and visionary fear that
this government, the world's best hope, may by possibility
want energy to preserve itself? I trust not.

I believe this, on the contrary, the strongest govern-
ment on earth. I believe it is the only one where every
man, at the call of the laws, would fly to the standard of
the law, and would meet invasions of the public order as
his own personal concern. Sometimes it is said that man
cannot be trusted with the government of himself. Can
he, then, be trusted with the government of others? Or
have we found angels in the forms of kings to govern him?
Let history answer this question.

Having made his case for a democratic-republican form of government, Jefferson closed with a sketch of the government he proposed to preside over. It would be a deliberately minimalist government, designed to harmonize with nature, which had situated the United States geographically far "from the exterminating havoc of one quarter of the globe" and which had provided a "chosen country, with room enough for our descendants to the thousandth and thousandth generation." The American people, as Jefferson saw them, were inherently a moderate people, who valued one another not for any station conferred by birth, but by "our actions and [our] sense of them," and who were "enlightened by a benign religion, professed, indeed, and practiced in various forms, yet all of them including honesty, truth, temperance, gratitude, and love of man ...." What more, Jefferson asked, "is necessary to make us a happy and prosperous people? Still one thing more, fellow citizens—a wise and frugal government, which shall restrain men from injuring one another, which shall leave them otherwise free to regulate their own pursuits of industry and improvement, and shall not take from the mouth of labor the bread it has earned."

He continued, "About to enter, fellow citizens, on the exercise of duties which comprehend everything dear and valuable to you, it is proper that you should understand what I deem the essential principles of our government." And Jefferson went on to declare his intention to preside over a government of "equal and exact justice to all men, of whatever state or persuasion, religious or political." He pledged to pursue a policy of "peace, commerce, and honest friendship ... with all nations—entangling alliances with none." He promised to support "state governments in all their rights" and to cherish the "right of election by the people—a mild and safe corrective of abuses which are lopped by the sword of revolution where peaceable remedies are unprovided."

Rather than a large standing army, he called for a "well-disciplined militia—our best reliance in peace and for the first moments of war, till regulars may relieve them." He asserted the absolute "supremacy of the civil over the military authority; economy in the public expense, that labor may be lightly burdened; the honest payment of our debts and sacred preservation of the public faith; encouragement of agriculture, and of commerce as its hand-maid; the diffusion of information and the arraignment of all abuses at the bar of public reason." He called for freedom: of the press, of "person under the protection of the *habeus corpus*," and of trial by jury. He called, most of all, for a continual recollection of what the American Revolution had been fought to attain, all that the "wisdom of our sages and the blood of our heroes have been devoted to" attain; these things "should be the creed of our political faith—the text of civil instruction—the touchstone by which to try the services of those we trust."

Rarely has any leader in any time or place expressed the situation of his people and his intentions toward them so clearly and confidently as Jefferson did on March 4, 1801. His extraordinary inaugural speech was a fitting prelude to four years of American evolution, greatness, and harmony, which few who thronged that Senate Chamber, having come through a difficult and divisive political campaign, could have hoped for, let alone predicted.

Chapter 19

A Second Revolution

The Federalists had done their best to paint Thomas Jefferson as a wild-eyed "Jacobin" radical. His eloquent, frank, eminently rational, and intensely human inaugural address was anything but Jacobin, however. If *Vice President* Jefferson had quickly discovered what every future United States vice president would learn—that the scope of his office is severely limited—so *President* Jefferson understood what just about every successive president has seemed to understand: It is best to enter the office of the president through the center of the doorway rather than risk a sharp bump by veering too far left or right. For some Democratic-Republicans, the tenor of the inaugural speech was too centrist. Jefferson had raised his voice in a call to national unity, whereas many in his party longed to hear the battle cry of a new revolution—and were disappointed.

They need not have been. For a new revolution is precisely what Jefferson set about—quietly, almost gently, without divisive slogans or discordant claims of victory. Within four days of taking office, the new president ordered prosecutions under the Sedition Act immediately stopped, and he directed that fines already collected be refunded without delay. His next order of business was appointing his Cabinet, which he did without so much as a nod to the Federalists. Levi Lincoln as attorney general, Revolutionary War commander Henry Dearborn as secretary of war, and Robert Smith as secretary of the Navy were all good Democratic-Republicans, but they were hardly party leaders. More aggressive were Jefferson's appointments to the departments of state and the treasury. He made his most trusted political ally, James Madison, secretary of state, endowing that role with much more power than Washington had given it. Indeed, Jefferson's entire Cabinet more closely resembled those of modern presidents than Washington's and Adams's. For Jefferson, a Cabinet was not a body of mere assistants and administrators, whose duties were limited to reporting to the president and then executing his policies. Instead, the Cabinet was now a panel of advisers and makers of policy.

James Madison, the Jefferson protégé and ally who co-created the Democratic-Republican Party, in a twentieth-century copy of the painting by Gilbert Stuart.

(Collection: National Archives and Records Administration)

As much as Jefferson would rely on Madison, he gave, if any-thing, even greater autonomy to his treasury secretary, Albert Gallatin. Next to Madison, Gallatin was the most thoroughly committed Democratic-Republican in the Cabinet. In fact, Jefferson believed that the Federalists had aimed the Alien and Sedition Acts directly against him. He had been born in Geneva, Switzerland, to a venerable and noble family and had been edu-cated at the prestigious Geneva Academy. Offered a lucrative com-mission as a lieutenant colonel by the Landgrave of Hesse, a position that would have put him in command of "Hessian" mer-cenaries against the Americans in the revolution, he declined, sac-rificing his entire inheritance because he had resolved "never to serve a tyrant." His family was outraged at his refusal to accept the Landgrave's commission, so he escaped, secretly taking passage for America.

Gallatin took up residence first in Boston and then taught French at Harvard University before moving to Virginia in 1785. From there, he settled finally in Pennsylvania, where he success-fully ran for the state assembly. After his election to the United States Senate, Federalist Senators challenged his seat on the grounds that he did not meet citizenship requirements; he had taken an oath of loyalty to Virginia but had never been formally naturalized as a citizen of the United States. Before he was rejected, however, Gallatin demanded from Secretary of the Treasury Alexander Hamilton a statement of the national debt as of January 1, 1794. He further demanded an accounting that dis-tinguished the money received under each branch of the revenue and expended under each appropriation. Washington had given Hamilton free rein in the treasury, and it had become something of his private reserve. The accounts Gallatin demanded provided the first comprehensive picture of the nation's finances, a picture most government officials had ever seen. The people of Pennsylvania returned Gallatin to Congress, this time to the House of Representatives, for which citizenship requirements were less strin-gent, and Gallatin immediately became a member of the new Standing Committee on Finance, precursor to the modern House Ways and Means Committee.

In July 1800, Representative Gallatin issued a report titled "Views of the Public Debt, Receipts and Expenditure of the United States." It was a brilliant, eye-opening analysis of the fiscal operations of the government under the Constitution, and it was highly critical of Hamiltonian spending policies. Acting on the strength of his report, Gallatin shepherded through Congress measures to hold down appropriations, particularly those for military purposes. In response to his efforts, the Federalists launched an all-out attack against him, in particular questioning his loyalty on account of his foreign birth and accusing him of plotting to weaken the United States by reducing military and other expenditures. As Jefferson saw it, the Alien and Sedition Acts were wielded as a weapon in these attacks—an attempt to silence the perceptively critical Gallatin by whatever means necessary.

Impressed by Gallatin's ideology as well as his analytical genius, Jefferson turned him loose on the nation's finances. His chief assignment was to reduce the national debt as quickly and as steeply as possible. Gallatin set to work immediately and was soon able to report to Jefferson the disheartening news that, as of January 1, 1801, the United States was more than eighty million dollars in debt. However, he also had a plan to cut this mountain down to size. In perfect harmony with Jefferson's inaugural promise of "a wise and frugal government, which shall ... not take from the mouth of labor the bread it has earned," Gallatin called for spending cuts, particularly in the military. As for revenue, the two main sources for the reduction of the national debt would be capital gained through the sale of public lands and revenue brought in through custom duties—taxes on imports. During his first year in office, Gallatin reduced the national debt by more than two million dollars.

One problem the Adams administration had not bequeathed to Jefferson was its Quasi-War with France. That had been resolved in part through the brilliant performance of the United States Navy, then in its infancy, but even more because Napoleon Bonaparte had assumed the leadership of the French government in a coup d'etat of November 9, 1799, that overthrew the Directory. In contrast to the government of the Directory,

Napoleon sought rapid reconciliation with the United States. His eyes, after all, were on the world, and he realized that he urgently needed the support of neutral Denmark and Sweden to lend legitimacy to his new government. How could he expect to get this support if his nation pursued a policy that failed to respect the rights of a *neutral* United States? Therefore, Napoleon's negotiators quickly agreed to a treaty, concluded in 1800, that affirmed the right of the United States, as a neutral nation, to trade with whomever it wished.

Yet no sooner was the Quasi-War with France ended than the long struggle against Barbary piracy flared up anew. Ever since his European service as a treaty commissioner and then as minister plenipotentiary to France, Jefferson had wanted to deal once and for all with the Barbary pirates. A man of peace whose very idea of government was founded on minimizing the military, Jefferson had nevertheless always believed that only a military solution would bring a permanent end to the depredations in the Mediterranean. Each time he had proposed such a solution, however, he was met by objections that the cheaper and more expedient course was to continue to pay the same ransoms and tribute monies other nations paid.

Now he was president, and he immediately assembled a naval squadron at Norfolk. Before sending it off to Tripoli, however, he convened his Cabinet and put before it two questions. First, should the squadron be sent to deal with the pirates? Second, did the president, with Congress adjourned, have the authority to commit an act that might lead to war?

The Cabinet was unanimous in its opinion that the squadron should be sent. This was enormously gratifying to Jefferson, who believed not only that paying tribute money was dishonorable and permanently damaging to national sovereignty, but that it could also never be anything more than a stopgap measure. What the Cabinet members disagreed about was the president's authority to act without congressional approval. Attorney General Levi Lincoln expressed the gravest doubts, arguing that, in the absence of a congressional declaration of war, U.S. warships could legally do nothing more than defend themselves; they could not act aggressively.

The rest of the Cabinet, however, led by Gallatin and Secretary of the Navy Robert Smith, ultimately agreed with Jefferson that he had the authority to act against the Barbary pirates.

Again, Jefferson found himself in a paradoxical position. A man of peace, he was advocating acts of war. A believer in the subordination of the executive branch to the legislative, he was about to exercise—and thereby define for the future—an executive prerogative that neither Washington nor Adams, those Federalist "monarchs," had ever seized upon. Without consulting Congress, President Jefferson ordered the squadron to set sail for the Mediterranean, to locate Barbary pirate vessels, and to destroy them wherever they might be found. Jefferson did allow that Congress would want to review his action when it reconvened in seven months, and, at that time, it would have to decide whether to continue profitably navigating the Mediterranean or relinquish that trade to other nations.

The Barbary Wars would span 1801–15, with the most concentrated action directed against Tripoli in the Tripolitan War of 1801–05. Jefferson did not send the Navy out alone. With customarily brilliant diplomacy, he organized a coalition with Sweden, Sicily, Malta, Portugal, and Morocco to oppose Tripoli in a show of force that persuaded Yusuf Qaramanli, Tripoli's pasha, to back down immediately. For the next two years, one U.S. frigate and several smaller U.S. Navy vessels patrolled the Tripolitan coast. This mission proceeded successfully until the frigate USS *Philadelphia* ran aground in October 1803 and was boarded by Tripolitan forces, which captured three hundred U.S. sailors, took the ship as a prize, and prepared to use it against the Americans.

In February 1804, however, Lt. Stephen Decatur, with great daring and exquisite stealth, entered Tripoli Harbor and burned the *Philadelphia*. Following this action, Commodore Edward Preble increased the intensity of the ongoing bombardment of Tripoli while William Eaton, U.S. consul at Tunis, proposed an alliance with Ahmed Qaramanli, the brother Yusuf had deposed in 1795. Eaton also recruited an army of Arabs and Greeks to join a contingent of United States Marines and support the restoration of Ahmed as ruler of Tripoli. Eaton's force captured the city of Derne in 1805, just as the Jefferson government concluded a treaty of peace with Yusuf on June 4, 1805. The treaty ransomed the prisoners for sixty thousand dollars and, although it made no explicit mention of the subject of tribute, put a de facto end to the practice of tribute payment by establishing free and unhindered commerce between the United States and Tripoli. Although the treaty was concluded at the start of Jefferson's second term in office, it was justly celebrated as one of the great triumphs of his first.

While the U.S. Navy squadron sailed off to do battle with foreign enemies, Jefferson turned his attention to matters at home. The conciliatory tone of his inaugural address notwithstanding, Jefferson had no intention of allowing his predecessor to get away with having installed a substantial slate of Federalist judges just before he left office. Jefferson wanted to dismiss these "midnight appointees" but was blocked from doing so by the Judiciary Act of 1801. Jefferson did replace Federalist district attorneys and marshals, who, unlike the judges, were not protected by the Judiciary Act. Fellow Democratic-Republicans urged him to broaden his sweep by replacing Federalist office-holders generally. At first, Jefferson resolved to replace any who were found guilty of misconduct or malfeasance, but he could not, in fairness, bring himself to replace those he considered "good men, to whom there is no objection but a difference in political principle." Under unremitting pressure from his own party, full of men who craved lucrative patronage positions in the government, Jefferson agreed to achieve a balance between Federalist and Democratic-Republican appointees. But, at present, he would go no further.

He still went further than his Federalist opponents wanted him to. Adams had left behind him a number of obstacles to hinder the installation of a Democratic-Republican government. The Judiciary Act he had sponsored reduced the number of Supreme Court seats to five, thereby ensuring that Jefferson could not install a Democratic-Republican justice. Simultaneously, the act increased the number of federal circuit courts, thereby enabling Adams to install more Federalist judges, marshals, and other judicial officials. Jefferson campaigned for the repeal of the Judiciary Act, managing to get a repeal motion introduced in the Senate, only to have it blocked by the ever-antagonistic Vice President Aaron Burr, acting in his capacity as president of the Senate. After much arm twisting, the act was finally repealed on March 8, 1802, and replaced by a new Judiciary Act, which restored a sixth Supreme Court seat and greatly reduced the number of federal circuit courts, thus pulling a number of offices out from under many of Adams's midnight appointees.

Jefferson was not always immediately successful in transforming government by removing Federalists from it. For example, just two days before Jefferson's inauguration, Adams, under the Judiciary Act of 1801, had appointed William Marbury justice of the peace for Washington, D.C. In that final rush of appointments, however, Adams had not actually distributed this and other appointments. After repeatedly dodging Marbury's attempts to secure his appointment, in February 1803, Jefferson formally directed Secretary of State Madison to withhold the appointment. The president argued that it was invalid because it had not been distributed before the repeal of the 1801 Judiciary Act under which it had been signed and sealed. Marbury responded by petitioning the Supreme Court for a writ of mandamus, an order to the secretary of state to distribute the commission.

Chief Justice John Marshall was a Federalist, but he was also committed to the rule of law and the stewardship of the fledgling Supreme Court. He knew that if he issued the writ, he would put the court in direct opposition to the president, a condition of government he did not want to create. On the other hand, if he denied the writ, he would forever compromise the authority of the Supreme Court by deferring to the president's will. The brilliant Marshall found a third course. He ruled that Marbury had been wrongfully deprived of his commission, but he also declared that Section 13 of the Judiciary Act of 1789, which empowered the Supreme Court to issue writs of mandamus and under which Marbury had filed suit, was unconstitutional. The provision added to the Supreme Court's "original jurisdiction" by improperly allowing into the court a case that should be heard by a lower court. In an apparent victory for Jefferson, Marbury's suit was thrown out. Yet it was a victory that, far from diminishing the Supreme Court, enhanced it.

The case of *Marbury v. Madison* forever established the right of the Supreme Court to "judicial review." Ever since Marshall's decision, the Supreme Court has functioned to set aside statutes of Congress that it judged unconstitutional. Whether or not Jefferson fully realized or approved of it at the time, Marshall had established a major federal power. Jefferson had focused on balancing the executive against the legislative branch of government. Marshall's decision ensured that the third branch, the judiciary, would also participate forcefully in this system of "checks and balances." Although Jefferson was not directly responsible for it, judicial review must stand as one of the most profound achievements of the first term of his administration.

Most historians agree that *Marbury v. Madison* was more important for establishing the principle of judicial review than for its outcome with regard to Marbury and the other midnight appointees. For Jefferson, however, the overriding issue was the midnight appointees and how they and other Federalists might be purged from the government. As the months and years of his first term flew by, Jefferson abandoned his earlier ideal of achieving balance between Democratic-Republican and Federalist appointees. He became increasingly determined to carry out a bloodless revolution, replacing as many Federalists as he could to change the composition of the government dramatically.

Perhaps the president's accelerated zeal was driven by a realization that he was not merely ousting members of a rival political party. He was acting as he had when, during the Revolution, he wrote out of Virginia statutes the feudal land-tenure laws of entail and primogeniture, laws intended to perpetuate the power not of a political party, but of an entrenched and exclusive social class. The Federalists who lost their posts, either through termination, replacement, or, where necessary, the elimination of jobs and even entire government departments, were overwhelmingly the sons of the wealthy—America's aristocrats, a ruling class who came to their position through accident of birth rather than by personal achievement. The people who replaced the Federalist old guard were, for the most part, self-made and certainly not the sons of any aristocracy.

Jefferson saw the Federalists as the constituents of an aristocracy and the Democratic-Republicans as members of a meritocracy. Whatever their geographical origin, they were the equivalent of the hard-working Piedmont people Jefferson had known in Albemarle County. The old-line Federalists, in contrast, were like the self-satisfied Tidewater aristocracy of prerevolutionary Virginia. The Federalists, like the Tidewater upper crust, were the power elite. Jefferson intended to come down squarely on the side of the have-nots, the aspirants to greater equality.

Again, metaphorically, Jefferson's peaceful revolution looked westward, away from the complacent establishment and toward that up-and-coming portion of society on the frontier of America's future. The first American Revolution had started in the cities and villages of the coastal Northeast and the southern Tidewater. The *second* American revolution—the chief business of Jefferson's first term—was rooted in the West as a state of mind, a social and political orientation, and, as we will see in the next chapter, a very real American place.

Chapter 20

The World Beyond the River

In his inaugural address, Jefferson remarked upon his nation's good fortune at possessing "room enough for our descendants to the thousandth and thousandth generation." But even as he said these words, he was keenly aware that the United States didn't actually possess all the room the continent offered. As much space as the nation had, it was also hemmed in. To the north was British Canada; to the south and west were the possessions of Spain. Aside from Canada, the greatest North American territory in foreign hands was the Louisiana Territory, which, following the French and Indian War, France had ceded to Spain.

In 1800, Napoleon Bonaparte secretly reacquired the Louisiana Territory in exchange for parts of Tuscany, which Napoleon pledged to conquer on behalf of Spain. Napoleon further pledged that France would maintain Louisiana as a buffer between Spain's other North American settlements and the United States. But no sooner was the Secret Treaty of San Ildefonso concluded than Napoleon summarily dropped his Tuscan campaign. Enraged, Spain opened a dispute with France and refused to honor the secret treaty. In 1802, even though France asserted possession of the Louisiana Territory, it was Spain that closed the Mississippi River to American trade.

This created a major crisis for the Jefferson administration. The president could not tolerate the disruption of western trade, but he was also loath to support France's claims on the territory against those of Spain. As much as Jefferson loved the French, he was fully aware that Napoleon's France was *not* the hopeful and idealistic France that he had known during the early months of the French Revolution. The idea of helping a rapacious conqueror like Napoleon establish himself in America's vast backyard was hardly more appealing than yielding to Spain and abandoning the West. And there was even worse: Assume that France, even under Napoleon, did not pose a threat. The ongoing warfare between France and England was bound, sooner or later, to result in the *British* seizure of the Louisiana territory. To be hemmed in by the British on the north *and* the west was intolerable.

In search of a resolution to this crisis, Jefferson appointed James Monroe minister plenipotentiary and envoy extraordinary to France and Spain to make an offer for the purchase of the port city of New Orleans and Florida. As usual, Jefferson's vision looked far beyond the immediate problem. His intention was not only to reclaim the right to Mississippi River navigation, important as that was, but also to capitalize on a discovery that had been made years earlier, in 1790, when Captain Robert Gray found and named (after his ship, the USS *Columbia*) the Columbia River on the Pacific Northwest coast. Jefferson believed that once the United States established a presence at the mouth of the Mississippi, the nation's claim on the Columbia River would acquire enormous value. The United States could then also claim the vast territory lying *between* the Mississippi and the Columbia. Jefferson had high hopes for Monroe's mission.

In the meantime, Napoleon agonized over the plight of one of his large armies, bogged down in the West Indies. That army was making little headway against West Indian rebels led by Toussaint Louverture and was wasting away in the malarial climate. Napoleon decided to withdraw from the hemisphere and consolidate his forces in European campaigns of conquest. This decision suddenly rendered Louisiana more of a French military liability than an asset; if France wasn't willing to defend it, then surely it would fall, most likely to England. Even as Monroe was crossing the Atlantic, Napoleon's minister Talleyrand asked the resident U.S. foreign minister, Robert R. Livingston, how much Jefferson might offer, not for New Orleans alone, but for the entire Louisiana Territory.

Livingston stalled until Monroe arrived, briefed him on the vastly expanded scope of negotiations, and then presented him to Talleyrand. Monroe proceeded to make perhaps the greatest real-estate deal the world has ever seen. For sixty million francs—about fifteen million dollars—he acquired ninety thousand square miles of trans-Mississippi territory for the United States, a per-acre price of four cents—*three* cents, if one discounts from the purchase price $3,750,000, which represented U.S. assumption of claims of American citizens against France. As a result of the Louisiana Purchase, the nation instantly grew by one hundred forty percent. The vast territory would one day contain Missouri, Nebraska, Iowa, Arkansas, North and South Dakota, Kansas, Minnesota, Montana, most of Louisiana, and portions of Colorado and Wyoming. A Treaty for the Cession of Louisiana was concluded on May 2, 1803, and was antedated to April 30.

Triumphant though it was, the treaty did present two significant problems. For one thing, it was not absolutely clear just what had been purchased. The borders of the territory were very vague, and it was never specified whether West Florida was included. (East Florida remained in Spanish hands.) A second problem was that the United States Constitution did not explicitly give the federal government the right to purchase territory in this manner. As a strict constructionist, Jefferson might have questioned whether the Louisiana Purchase was constitutional. For that matter, as a president pledged to fiscal responsibility, he might have questioned whether the nation could afford to increase its debt by a whopping fifteen million dollars. In the end, of course, Jefferson questioned neither of these points—and the Senate, recognizing a bargain when it saw one, also approved the treaty and the purchase by a vote of twenty-four to seven.

It had all happened so quickly that even the visionary Jefferson did not fully grasp what he had done. Primarily, he had seen the purchase as a means of avoiding war by creating vast distances between the United States and its European colonial neighbors. Secondarily, a large western territory also seemed to Jefferson the best place for the eventual peaceful relocation of Indians currently living east of the Mississippi. "Indian removal" is something historians associate primarily with the Andrew Jackson administration and the Indian Removal Bill of 1830; however, Jefferson contemplated such a removal three decades earlier and asked his secretary of war, Henry Dearborn, to make some preliminary plans for it.

Soon enough, though, Jefferson saw what many of his fellow citizens had seen immediately: Whatever else the Louisiana Purchase meant, it meant cheap land and the opportunity for any number of citizens to live out their American dreams. Jefferson also realized that, as a vast inventory of public land, the Louisiana Purchase would allow the nation to raise revenue in the manner Secretary of the Treasury Gallatin had prescribed, by selling land and thereby offering a wonderful alternative to burdensome taxes.

Beyond this, the new territory made the United States a truly continental nation. It must have seemed to Jefferson the fulfillment of a national destiny as well as of his own, which he saw as intimately bound up with that of America. Raised near the frontier, Jefferson had grown up looking west. When it came time to build his Monticello, there was no question that he would set down his house facing west. And now, by purchasing so much trans-Mississippi land, he directed all of the nation to the vast land beyond the Blue Ridge and the Appalachians, beyond even the great Mississippi River.

> With the Louisiana Purchase, the nation instantly grew by one hundred forty percent. The vast, ninety-thousand-square-mile territory would one day contain Missouri, Nebraska, Iowa, Arkansas, North and South Dakota, Kansas, Minnesota, Montana, most of Louisiana, and portions of Colorado and Wyoming.

Grade-school history typically presents a straightforward chronology of the Louisiana Purchase. The territory was acquired in 1803 and was followed logically in 1804 by the Lewis and Clark Expedition to explore it. In truth, Jefferson's insatiable scientific curiosity had outrun politics and diplomacy. He had proposed funding an expedition to the Far West as early as 1792, and, early in 1803, while contemplating the purchase of only New Orleans, Jefferson engineered in

Congress the appropriation of twenty-five hundred dollars for such an expedition. Congress, of course, wasn't about to provide funding for mere curiosity, so the president proposed a more potentially lucrative reason for the trek: to search for a "Northwest Passage" to the Pacific.

The quest for a water "passage to India" across the North American continent can be traced at least to the 1534 voyage of the French navigator Jacques Cartier, who explored the St. Lawrence River with the express purpose of finding a passage to China. In 1566, Britain's Sir Humphrey Gilbert published *A Discourse to Prove a Passage by the Northwest to Cathia* (Cathay, or China), which, eleven years later, indirectly led Sir Francis Drake to sail his famed vessel, the *Golden Hind*, down the Atlantic coast of South America, around Tierra del Fuego, and northward, just beyond San Francisco, California. But Drake's fellow sea dog, Martin Frobisher, was the first Englishman to set out in deliberate search for the passage in 1576, discovering an inlet in Baffin Island, now known as Frobisher Bay, which he believed was the opening of the Northwest Passage.

Meriwether Lewis (left; in an engraving by Charles Balthazar Julien Fèvret de Saint-Mémin) and William Clark (right; in a early-twentieth-century book illustration), the intrepid explorers Jefferson sent into the territory of the Louisiana Purchase.

(Collection: ArtToday)

Two more Frobisher voyages, in 1577 and 1578, failed to find the passage, but this did not discourage another Englishman, John Davis, from making three voyages of his own between 1585–87. He was followed by Henry Hudson, who, during 1610–11, explored the bay that would be named for him. It was an inland body of water so vast that Hudson was sure it had to be the mouth of the fabled passage. His crew, less sure, mutinied, casting him and a few loyal men adrift and to their deaths. Yet the drive to find a Northwest Passage was so powerful that, between 1612–15, Englishmen Thomas Button, Robert Bylot, and William Baffin made additional voyages to the Hudson Bay—looking not only for the Northwest Passage, but for any sign of Henry Hudson.

So it was not terribly difficult to persuade Congress early in 1803 to revive the age-old search by modestly funding an expedition. Jefferson approached the legislative body secretively, probably to make the idea seem all the more valuable. He promoted the expedition as a search for the Northwest Passage and as a means of opening the fur trade to the United States. The expedition, Jefferson argued, would prevent foreign trading companies from monopolizing this valuable source of revenue. The finalization of the Louisiana Purchase, when it unexpectedly came, simply added to Jefferson's momentum.

Jefferson never had any doubt about who would lead the "Corps of Discovery." When he became president, he hired his Albemarle County cousin, Army captain Meriwether Lewis, as his private secretary. Jefferson became almost a second father to the twenty-seven-year-old Lewis, whose own father had died when he was eighteen. He saw in Lewis intelligence, courage, and loyalty and came to rely on him more as an aide than as a secretary. The young man also shared Jefferson's abiding interest in natural science and had accompanied the president on rambles along the Potomac's overgrown banks and into the woods outside of Washington. When Lewis eagerly agreed to lead the expedition to the Far West, before Jefferson had secured Congressional appropriation and well before the Louisiana Purchase was contemplated, the president found the money to finance a year of study for Lewis in Philadelphia. At Jefferson's direction, Lewis prepared himself with courses in botany, zoology, and medicine. Given free rein to choose whomever he wished as co-captain of the expedition, Lewis tapped his close friend William Clark. The younger brother of George Rogers Clark, frontier hero of the American Revolution, William Clark was also an Army officer; the pair had served together in 1795.

Except for assigning the actual conduct of the expedition to Meriwether Lewis, Jefferson did not refer management of the project to some "science adviser," as a modern president would. A man of science himself, still serving happily as president of the American Philosophical Society, Jefferson himself was the administration's science adviser, and he wrote a long and detailed letter of instruction to Lewis. It listed the equipment and supplies he would be provided with: "Instruments for ascertaining, by celestial observations, the geography of the country through which you will pass .... Light articles for barter and presents among the Indians, arms for your attendants, say from ten to twelve men, boats, tents, and other traveling apparatus, with ammunition, medicine, surgical instruments and provisions ...."

Jefferson made it clear that Lewis would have the authority to recruit from the Army volunteers for the mission, and he assured Lewis that the ministers of Spain, France, and England had all agreed to permit the expedition free passage through their territories. Then he defined the object of the expedition: "to explore the Missouri River, and such principal streams of it, as, by its course and communication with the waters of the Pacific Ocean, whether the Columbia, Oregon, Colorado, or any other river, may offer the most direct and practicable water-communication across the continent, for the purposes of commerce." He outlined the route that was to be taken, and he charged Lewis to make "observations ... with great pains and accuracy," especially where navigation and science were concerned.

Of particular interest to Jefferson was establishing contact with the Indians and gathering detailed information concerning them:

- The names of the nations and their numbers
- The extent and limits of their possessions
- Their relationships with other tribes or nations

- Their languages, traditions, and monuments
- Their ordinary occupations in agriculture, fishing, hunting, war, arts, as well as their tools
- Their food, clothing, and domestic accommodations
- The diseases prevalent among them, and the remedies for those diseases
- Moral and physical circumstances that distinguish them from the tribes already known
- Peculiarities in their laws, customs, and dispositions
- Any articles of commerce that they may either need or furnish themselves

In addition, Jefferson wanted detailed data on the following:

- The soil and topography of the country and its growth and vegetable productions, especially those not of the United States
- The animals of the country, especially those not known in the United States, including any that were deemed rare or extinct
- The mineral productions of every kind, particularly metals, limestone, pit-coal, and saltpetre
- Bodies of water, including mineral water (also notes on the temperature of mineral water)
- Volcanic appearances
- Climate, including information on temperature; the proportion of rainy, cloudy, and clear days; lightning, hail, snow, and ice storms; frost; winds prevailing at different seasons; the dates at which particular plants appeared or lost their flowers or leaves; and times of appearance of particular birds, reptiles, or insects

Manned, equipped, and personally charged by the president of the United States, the Lewis and Clark expedition—officially the United States Corps of Discovery—left St. Louis on May 14, 1804, and reached central North Dakota in November. The Corps wintered among the friendly Mandan Indians, from whom they gathered information on what lay ahead. Accompanied by a remarkable young Shoshoni woman, Sacagawea, who served as translator and guide, the Corps explored the Rockies and reached the Continental Divide on August 12, 1805. By this time, Lewis and Clark were convinced that the Northwest Passage did not exist. Considering the wonders they beheld and recorded, that hardly mattered now. The expedition pressed on, reaching the Columbia River and the Pacific Ocean in November 1805.

The expedition's second winter was spent on the Northwest coast. The return east began in March 1806 and ended at St. Louis on September 23. Jefferson's preparation, his choice of Lewis, and the leadership of Lewis and Clark ensured that all but a single man returned safely. The unfortunate member of the Corps of Discovery who died succumbed not to an accident of the trek, but to a ruptured appendix. Given the state of medicine at the time, he died in the wilderness as he would have died in a Philadelphia or New York sickroom. Nothing could have been done for him.

Although Lewis and Clark did not bring President Jefferson and the nation news of a Northwest Passage, the twenty-seven-month, eight-thousand-mile odyssey returned a wealth of data meticulously and vividly recorded in Lewis's journals. The expedition had discovered 122 animal species and subspecies, as well as 178 previously unknown plants. Valuable contact with important Indian tribes had been made, and the foundation for a profitable fur trade had been established. Most of all, the United States had done more than simply lay claim to land from sea to shining sea. Intrepid agents of the nation had embraced and explored that land, making it possible for others to follow.

The return of Lewis and Clark came during Jefferson's second term in office. He would be propelled to that second term thanks in no small part to the Louisiana Purchase, which was enthusiastically and proudly welcomed by almost all of the American people. As for his own party, Jefferson cleaned house. He had so successfully written Aaron Burr out of the party that not one of the 108 Democratic-Republicans who caucused in March 1804 cast a vote to put him on the ticket. When they also refused to put him up as a candidate for the New York governorship, Burr ran anyway.

In the course of the campaign, Alexander Hamilton cast the familiar slurs on Burr's character, and Burr challenged Hamilton to a duel, which took place at Weehawken, New Jersey, on the morning of July 11, 1804. Witnesses reported that Hamilton fired first, in the air, and that Burr, in cold-blooded contrast, took careful aim, fired, and hit Hamilton in the stomach. The wounded man was taken across the river to a house on Jane Street in Manhattan, where he died after lingering for many agonizing hours. Although some later historians have speculated that Hamilton's pistol discharged prematurely—that he actually intended to kill Burr—Burr was charged with premeditated murder by the states of New Jersey and New York. He evaded prosecution by returning to Washington, D.C., where, as sitting vice president, he claimed immunity.

When Jefferson offered himself as a candidate for reelection, he remarked that the Federalist calumnies heaped upon him made it necessary to "throw myself on the verdict of my country." That verdict turned out to be a landslide. In November, Jefferson took 162 electoral votes to Charles Cotesworth Pinckney's paltry fourteen, carrying every state except for Connecticut and Delaware, both resolutely Federalist strongholds. He had faced reelection confidently and with an even greater sense of mission than he had when he ran for his first term. He had begun his revolution in government; a second term would give him the opportunity to ripen and develop that revolution.

If he was anxious about anything after his virtually unanimous nomination in March, it was strictly personal. Mary—the daughter he had always called Polly and sometimes Maria—had given birth to a daughter on February 15, 1804. "A thousand joys to you, My dear Maria," he wrote to her. But he feared that anything but joy would be her lot. Twenty-four-year-old Polly was frail, the labor and delivery had been hard, and, like her own mother before her, she fell desperately ill.

As soon as Congress adjourned, Jefferson set out for Monticello, to which Polly had been taken to convalesce. He arrived on April 4: "I found my daughter ... so weak as barely to be able to stand, her stomach so disordered as to reject almost every thing she took into it, a constant small fever, & an imposthume [abscess] rising in her breast," he wrote to Madison. On April 13, he wrote to his friend again: "Our spring is remarkably uncheary. A North West wind has been blowing three days .... My daughter ... rather weakens." On April 17, Jefferson wrote in his account book: "This morning between 8 & 9 o'clock my dear daughter Maria Eppes died."

To John Page, his friend of many years, Jefferson wrote some two months after Polly's death: "Others may lose of their abundance, but I, of my want, have lost even the half of all I had. My evening prospects now hang on the slender thread of a single life"—by which he meant his surviving daughter, Patsy.

Jefferson could take some comfort in the unfamiliar feeling of political security. With both Burr and Hamilton, his two greatest political enemies, out of the way, and backed by a popular mandate few presidents would ever again enjoy, Jefferson believed that he could look forward to the rich promise of his second term.

Chapter 21

A Sadder Sequel

In democratic style, Jefferson had walked to his first inauguration. The journey to his second more closely resembled a funeral than an inaugural procession. Jefferson was still in mourning for his daughter, and he did not walk, but rode to the March 4, 1805, inauguration in a carriage. He was dressed in black from head to toe.

The American people, however, had nothing to grieve over. The nation overwhelmingly backed the president, who had reduced or eliminated Federalist taxes and who had added an internal empire to America. The first inaugural address had been about promise, Jefferson explained, whereas the second concerned performance.

"You best know," he addressed his fellow citizens, "whether we have done well or ill." Jefferson reminded his hearers that his first administration had seen a reduction in the central government, including a reduction in burdensome taxes, and if the Louisiana Purchase had added massively to the national debt, the "extension [of our national territory] may possibly pay for itself before we are called on [to pay for it through taxes], and in the meantime, may keep down accruing interest; in all events, it will repay the advances we have made."

To those who might still disapprove of the purchase, Jefferson was gently logical:

> The larger our association, the less it will be shaken by
> local passions; and in any view, is it not better that the

*opposite bank of the Mississippi should be settled by our
own brethren and children, than by strangers of another
family? With which shall we be most likely to live in harmony and friendly intercourse?*

While Jefferson was not reticent about reviewing the achievements of his first term, he was careful not to claim too much credit.
This was less from a sense of modesty than from ideology. Jefferson
had been a strong chief executive, but he did not want to appear
overly strong, nor did he want to aggrandize the office of president,
as he felt Washington and Adams had done. In outlining the
achievements of his first term, Jefferson declared, "I do not mean,
fellow citizens, to arrogate to myself the merit of the measures; that
is due, in the first place, to ... our citizens at large" and to the legislators they have elected.

Having given credit to the people and the legislators, the
reelected president went on to define the meaning of his first term.
He did not use the word *revolution*, but he presented the sum of the
last four years in just this way. His first term had been an "experiment ... fairly and fully made," conducted before all the world, to
discover "whether freedom of discussion, unaided by power, is not
sufficient for the propagation and protection of truth." The Alien
and Sedition Acts, defensive, coercive bastions of Federalism, had
constituted a counterrevolution. Tearing them down, along with
many of their Federalist supporters, had been the primary thrust of
Jefferson's revolution:

*... the experiment ... prove[s] that, since truth and reason
have maintained their ground against false opinions in
league with false facts, the press, confined to truth, needs
no other legal restraint; the public judgment will correct
false reasonings and opinions, on a full hearing of all
parties ....*

For the success of his first term and the triumphant outcome of
the great "experiment" of that first term, Jefferson offered not self-
congratulation but, "contemplating the union of sentiment now
manifested so generally, as auguring harmony and happiness to our
future course," he offered "to our country sincere congratulations."

Jefferson's celebration of freedom of the press—of national expression untrammeled by any Sedition Act—is all the more remarkable for what the Federalist press had tried to do to him by the middle of his first term. Finding it hard to fault Jefferson's record as chief executive, the Federalists had worked overtime to discredit Jefferson personally. Their chief ally in this effort was James T. Callender, whom Jefferson had hired back in 1797 to write anti-Federalist propaganda. Callender's *History of the Year 1796*, published after Jefferson first contacted him, had been vigorous in charging Hamilton and other Federalists with an array of unsavory and unethical undertakings. Jefferson cultivated Callender, steered work his way, and funded at least some of his onrushing stream of anti-Federalist journalism. In 1799, the Federalists prosecuted Callender under the Sedition Act, and he served several months in prison. Jefferson pardoned Callender almost immediately after taking office in 1801.

As Callender saw it, the presidential pardon was hardly sufficient reward for all that he had done to raise the Democratic-Republicans to power. He bluntly asked the new president for the patronage position of postmaster of Richmond, at an annual salary of $1,500—a lordly sum in 1801. Jefferson resented Callender's imperious approach and responded to him by cutting him off, ignoring his further appeals. When the outraged office seeker threatened to release information damaging to Jefferson, the president froze him out even more resolutely. At this, Callender offered his services to the Federalists and began churning out anti-Jefferson articles for a Richmond Federalist newspaper.

By 1802, Callender was writing and printing stories about Jefferson's "Congo harem" at Monticello, and he pointed a finger at Jefferson's favorite mistress, "Dusky Sally" Hemings (Chapter 14, "The Lover"). Soon, Federalist papers across the nation picked up the stories.

As in the case of William Jefferson Clinton, the nation's forty-second president, a lurid sex scandal did surprisingly little to diminish the popularity of a chief executive most people believed had been good for the country. Even during the process of impeachment, President Clinton's approval rating remained high as that of his Republican prosecutors sank. In like manner, President Jefferson sailed into a second term. As for James T. Callender, a heavy drinker, he apparently fell into the James River one night and drowned, for that is where his body was found in 1803.

> In 1802, the Boston Gazette published "A Song, supposed to have been written by the Sage of Monticello." Sung to the tune of "Yankee Doodle," it went, in part:
>
>> Of all the damsels on the green
>> On mountain, or in valley,
>> A lass so luscious ne'er was seen
>> As Monticellian Sally.
>> Yankee doodle, who's the noodle?
>> What wife were half so handy?
>> To breed a flock, of slaves for stock,
>> A blackamoor's the dandy.

Did Jefferson feel any guilt about his relationship with Sally Hemings? (Assuming that we accept the DNA evidence discussed in Chapter 14 as conclusive proof of such a relationship.) We cannot know. What we do know is that Jefferson was grief-stricken at the outset of his second term and that he seems to have felt considerable guilt over the death of Polly because he had postponed visiting her while Congress was in session. When he finally came to her at Monticello, she was already at death's door.

As to the Hemings affair, Jefferson's second inaugural address bears closer inspection. After extolling the virtues of a free press— even one that sought to pillory him—Jefferson went on to remark that "no inference is here intended, that the laws, provided by the State against false and defamatory publications, should not be enforced; he who has time, renders a service to public morals and public tranquillity, in reforming these abuses by the salutary coercions of the law." It was, in effect, Jefferson's open invitation to his supporters to bring the hostile editors to account for libel, for making false statements to defame him.

For all his advocacy of lofty principle, Jefferson was human. Confident that no one could prove allegations concerning his "Congo harem" or "Dusky Sally," Jefferson appointed Pierpont

Edwards as judge of the federal district court in Federalist Connecticut in 1806. No sooner was he appointed than Edwards ordered indictments served on several prominent Connecticut publishers and editors for seditious libel against President Jefferson. Years later, Jefferson denied having authorized the indictments, but he certainly did nothing to discourage them. The president did call a halt to prosecutions when Judge Edwards subpoenaed prominent Virginians, including Gen. Henry Lee, to testify concerning another liaison Callender had written of and one that in 1805 was elaborated on in a letter sent by Thomas Turner, a prominent Virginian, to a Boston paper.

In 1768, Jack Walker, a friend and neighbor of Jefferson, had traveled to Fort Stanwyx, New York, as a member of Virginia's delegation to the negotiation of an important Indian treaty. Walker would be gone four months, and he entrusted Jefferson with the care of his young wife, Betsy, and their baby daughter. Walker trusted Jefferson so completely that, before setting off on his arduous mission to frontier New York, he named him chief executor of his will. In Walker's absence, Jefferson and Betsy Walker became intimate. When Pierpont Edwards's seditious libel prosecutions threatened to expose the truth of allegations about his affair with Betsy Walker some thirty-eight years earlier, Jefferson wrote to the Connecticut attorney general to stop the prosecution of the publishers of Callender's story and Turner's letter. The truth, after all, was a sound defense against prosecution for libel.

There would be no more prosecutions for seditious libel during Jefferson's second term. Amid the din of the scandal, the long-suffering John Walker demanded that the president apologize before the nation and the world. Jefferson demurred, but in 1806 he did send Walker an admission and apology in the form of a private letter. Walker contented himself with this.

Jefferson's second term, so promising at its outset, was, like the second terms of presidents Nixon, Reagan, and Clinton, clouded by scandal. In Jefferson's case, it was also shadowed by personal loss. First and foremost, there was the death of Polly. Then, in 1806, Jefferson's much-beloved mentor at law and surrogate father, George Wythe, died. He was eighty years old, but apparently he had succumbed to foul play and not his advanced years. Like his mistress, Lydia Broadmax, a slave he subsequently freed, and Michael Brown, the son he had by her, Wythe had been poisoned with arsenic. He and his son died; Broadmax recovered. Although he was never charged with murder, Wythe's grandnephew, tried and convicted of forgery, apparently had poisoned the three. With Broadmax and Michael Brown out of the way, all of Wythe's estate would go to the grandnephew—save Wythe's extensive law library, which had been left to Jefferson.

Three years later, in 1809, just after Jefferson left office, Meriwether Lewis was found dead, alone in room in a Tennessee tavern. Back in 1806, Jefferson had written Lewis a letter the instant he heard of his return from the great expedition. It expressed his joy at Lewis's safe homecoming as well as his "constant affection" for his fine young protégé. Now that bold and promising life was snuffed out: A desperate, debt-ridden alcoholic, Lewis had most probably committed suicide, although foul play has never been entirely ruled out.

If public scandal and personal loss proved debilitating, Jefferson also faced growing disappointment over the state of the nation as his second term unfolded. He and his fellow citizens looked across the Atlantic to behold all Europe engulfed in war, with England repeatedly victorious on the seas and Napoleonic France repeatedly triumphant on land. In the course of the French Revolutionary Wars, during Jefferson's first term, the United States had managed a profitable neutrality, trading with both England and France as well as the other nations of war-torn Europe. The Treaty of Amiens, which ended those wars in 1802, brought a sharp decline in U.S. exports, but as the Napoleonic Wars followed in 1803, America's role as a neutral vendor to all comers was responsible for a steady rise in exports. The diplomatic effect of the Louisiana Purchase played no small role in this prosperity, for the purchase significantly reduced Anglo-American tensions in North America.

But soon Jefferson's minister plenipotentiary to Great Britain, James Monroe, was reporting that, after Lord Nelson's decisive triumph over the French navy at the Battle of Trafalgar on October

21, 1805, the British government was preparing to take measures to curb American commerce with the French.

At the height of the French Revolutionary Wars, the British had begun intercepting American ships carrying French goods to French colonies. U.S. mariners soon discovered, however, that if they made a stopover in the United States before proceeding to the French colonial destination, British law reclassified the goods carried as American re-exports, which were not subject to interdiction. This dodge served American merchants and seamen well through 1805, when the High Court of Admiralty reversed its earlier position and ruled that merely touching an American port did not constitute importation of cargo into the United States. Backed by this new ruling, Royal Navy ships once again began intercepting and seizing American merchantmen.

At this time, the Royal Navy also began a program of impressment. A significant number of British sailors deserted the miserable, brutal, and often abbreviated life offered by the Royal Navy and took ship on American merchant vessels. British admiralty responded to epidemic desertions by ordering officers to intercept U.S. ships, board them, and "impress"—that is, abduct—any sailors the commander of the boarding crew judged to be deserters.

In 1806, in an effort to curb these abuses, Jefferson dispatched James Monroe and Charles Cotesworth Pinckney to England to negotiate a new Anglo-American treaty. The result was an agreement that reinstated noninterference with vessels carrying re-exported goods in exchange for an American pledge of neutrality. The treaty was silent on the subject of impressment, however. This silence, combined with a provision that the United States must refuse to honor any French blockade of Britain, persuaded Jefferson, perhaps rashly, to withhold the treaty from Senate ratification.

Jefferson's refusal to compromise with Great Britain, a nation he had always hated, brought on the rapid decay of Anglo-American relations. The result very nearly was war when, on June 22, 1807, HMS Leopard intercepted the U.S. Navy frigate Chesapeake in Hampton Roads, off the coast of Virginia. The captain of the Leopard ordered the Chesapeake to take on a boarding party in search of deserters. The *Chesapeake*'s captain refused, whereupon the *Leopard* opened fire, killing three U.S. sailors and wounding eighteen more. The outgunned *Chesapeake* admitted the British boarding party, which apprehended four suspected deserters. Amid a public outcry for a declaration of war against Britain, Jefferson responded with nothing stronger than an order that all British warships clear American waters and a demand for a British apology. The Royal Navy ships did clear out, but no apology was forthcoming.

Jefferson did not want to go to war against Britain, but he needed to find an effective reply to the repeated violations of American neutrality. At last, in December 1807, Jefferson proposed to his Cabinet an embargo on *all* European-bound goods. Jefferson believed that the deprivation that would be created by such an embargo would force European leaders, especially in Britain and France, to respect the rights of American neutrality. With the Cabinet's concurrence, Jefferson proceeded to sell the embargo idea to Congress, which passed an embargo bill on December 22 by a wide margin in both the Senate and the House.

Jefferson saw the embargo as serving three main purposes: It would force England and France to "return to some sense of moral duty," as Jefferson explained in a letter. It would also buy time, and "time may produce peace in Europe." Finally, "keeping at home our vessels, cargoes, and seamen saves us the necessity of making their capture the cause of immediate war."

The nation was willing to go along with the wisdom of the "Sage of Monticello" and accept the embargo—until people started feeling its devastating impact on the U.S. economy. Exports fell from a high of almost one hundred ten million dollars in 1807 to a mere twenty million dollars in 1808. Faced with staggering losses as goods rotted on wharves and in warehouses, American merchants quickly resorted to evading the embargo by smuggling via Canada and Spanish Florida. The smuggling became so pervasive that it rapidly undercut the effectiveness of the embargo.

In January 1808, in an effort to curb smuggling, the embargo was extended to inland waterways. In April, an Enforcement Act gave civil officers extraordinary authority to seize cargoes in the region of the New York–Canadian border. When stiff resistance was encountered, the region was declared to be in a state of insurrection. Enforcement was made even more stringent in January 1809, a move that nearly drove New England, from Maine to Massachusetts, to out-and-out rebellion. Once again, Jefferson found it almost impossible to maintain his own principles. The Democratic-Republican president who had dedicated his first term to reducing the coercive force of the American government now authorized federal coercion on an unprecedented scale.

In the meantime, England and France hung tough. The American embargo had no effect on bringing them to the peace table with one another or into negotiations with the United States. As his second term wound down, Jefferson recognized the failure of embargo. Thanks mainly to smuggling, exports were up from their 1808 low of twenty million dollars to about fifty million dollars by 1809 and were generally on the rise—but this was still far below the 1807 high of one hundred ten million dollars. The outgoing president had no desire to saddle his handpicked successor, James Madison, with a failed policy. A few days before he left office, Jefferson signed the Non-Intercourse Act, which reopened European trade to all nations except for Britain and France. In 1810, under Madison, this watered-down version of embargo would also end, to be replaced by Macon's Bill No. 2, which provided for trade with England and France unless one of these countries revoked its restrictions. In this case, the president could authorize an embargo on the country that had not also revoked its restrictions.

Deteriorating relations with England and France, culminating in the Embargo Act of 1807, monopolized much of Jefferson's time and attention during his second term, so much that he seems hardly to have taken note of an anonymous letter he received in December 1805. It warned of a plot hatched by Aaron Burr to create a separate nation in what was now the great American West and also to invade Mexico. Jefferson took no action on the letter. Shortly afterward, he received a report from the governor of the Louisiana Territory informing him that Burr had met in New Orleans with the former Spanish intendant (administrator) of Louisiana and with a group of disaffected westerners. Again, Jefferson took no action.

What finally got the president's attention was a letter from the U.S. district attorney of Kentucky, Joseph H. Daveiss, who wrote of Spanish plots and "traitors among us" who intended to bring about a "separation of the Union in favor of Spain." This time it wasn't Burr who figured prominently, but Gen. James Wilkinson, a highly respected military commander and aide to both Benedict Arnold and Horatio Gates during the revolution. Jefferson investigated further and learned that Burr had approached the sons of a trusted Jefferson friend in western Pennsylvania, attempting to entice them into joining a private military expedition. Then, in October 1806, a report came from Postmaster Gen. Gideon Grainger, revealing that Burr had offered Wilkinson command of an expedition intended to bring about the separation of the Louisiana Territory from the United States. After convening a Cabinet meeting, Jefferson ordered a federal agent to investigate Burr and, if he took any action on his treasonous plot, to arrest him immediately.

Then came the real bombshell. President Jefferson received a bundle of letters from James Wilkinson. The letters, written from Burr to Wilkinson in cipher (Wilkinson provided the key), detailed an extraordinary conspiracy. England would fund and provide ships for a ten-thousand-man invasion of Mexico via Vera Cruz. Conspirators situated from New York all the way to the Mississippi River were implicated. The plan was for Burr and a cadre of men to rendezvous with Wilkinson at Natchez, from which the invasion would be launched.

After his 1804 duel with Hamilton, Burr was a political pariah. Foiled in his attempts to rise to the top office of the United States and then of New York, Burr's thwarted ambition took him to the land of promise Jefferson had purchased from France. Apparently, he made overtures to Spain—or pretended to—but soon decided to turn against Spain, exploiting instead anti-Spanish feelings among American westerners to enlist their support in a scheme to invade, seize, and rule Spanish-held territory, including a large part of Mexico. Beyond this, Burr proposed that Wilkinson foment discontent in the Louisiana Territory by persuading the property holders there that their land titles would be challenged now that the territory was being incorporated into the United States. Burr wanted Wilkinson to stir the westerners to a revolution that would separate Louisiana from the United States. Thus Burr would come to rule at least part of Mexico and at least part of the vast Louisiana Territory.

Having reviewed the Wilkinson packet, Jefferson decided that he could not wait for a report from the agent he had sent to investigate Burr. On November 27, 1806, Jefferson issued a presidential proclamation warning all Americans against the plot and ordering Burr's arrest. In January, Jefferson revealed the plot in a special message to Congress. The president did not hesitate to prejudge a man he knew only too well. His guilt, he declared, "is placed beyond question."

In the meantime, Burr had moved with a small flotilla of ten boats and sixty men from Blennerhasset Island in the Ohio River toward the Mississippi. Once he reached Natchez, Burr learned of Wilkinson's defection. In a panic, he fled through the swampland of the lower Mississippi and decided to light out for Pensacola, Florida, where he would take refuge and presumably make an escape to Europe. Burr quickly realized that the escape attempt was hopeless, however, and he surrendered himself. He was arraigned before a grand jury in the Mississippi Territory, but that body of men decided that it had insufficient evidence to indict Burr, so he was ordered released. Military authorities instantly rearrested him, however, and he was taken to Richmond in March 1807 to stand trial for treason.

The presiding judge was none other than Chief Justice John Marshall. Caesar A. Rodney, U.S. attorney general, prosecuted Burr, who was defended by a team of lawyers that included Jefferson's cousin Edmund Randolph. The trial soon proved anticlimactic: Marshall quickly ruled that Burr may have contemplated treason, but he committed no treasonous act; therefore, he could not be convicted of treason. A man could not be punished for his thoughts. Marshall did agree to try Burr for instigating an expedition into Spanish territory, which, however, was a mere misdemeanor.

At Jefferson's insistence, the government continued to press for a treason trial. Although Wilkinson, who appeared before the Richmond grand jury on June 15, 1807, escaped indictment, Burr *was* indicted on charges of treason. However, once again, Marshall cut short the trial by ruling that unless witnesses could place Burr in person with the sixty-man force that had left Blennerhassett's Island, no other collateral evidence could be brought against him. Given this narrow ruling, the jury quickly voted to acquit Burr on the grounds of insufficient evidence. All Jefferson could do was sputter that the Richmond trial was equivalent to "a proclamation of impunity to every traitorous combination which may be formed to denounce the Union."

As for Burr, he cooled his heels for several years in Europe, mainly to evade his many creditors. While abroad, he sought support from Napoleon for a renewed expedition to the American West, but the emperor was not interested. Burr returned to the United States in 1812 and took up the practice of law in New York City until his death in 1836.

The failure of the Embargo Act was an economic disaster for the United States and only worsened Anglo-American relations, setting the stage for the War of 1812. The embargo also created a crisis of confidence for Jefferson, who became disillusioned about his fellow Americans. He had expected that they would be willing to make economic sacrifices to serve some of the ends of war without having to resort to war. Instead, the embargo had created a nation of lawbreakers, black marketeers, and smugglers.

Yet there was still reason for Jefferson to take heart in America and Americans. He had feared that the embargo disaster would kill the political party he had fought so hard to build. Incredibly, it did no such thing. The American people hated the embargo, but they still had faith in the party of Jefferson. In the general election of 1808, James Madison, the Democratic-Republican candidate for president, received 122 electoral votes to forty-seven for the Federalist Charles Cotesworth Pinckney. Madison's victory was Jefferson's vindication.

Part Six

Monticello Sunset

Chapter 22

Philosophy and Debt

The succession of his colleague, aide, and protégé, James Madison, to the presidency gave Jefferson a great measure of satisfaction and relief. In the short run, his second term had been disappointing at best and, at worst, very nearly disastrous—at least for the American economy. He had reason to believe not only that he had failed the American people, but that the American people had also failed him—or, rather, failed America. They had refused to make the kinds of sacrifices freely rendered by the generation of the great Revolution. By black marketeering and smuggling, they failed to give the embargo a chance to work. Yet Jefferson did not leave office in despair. These failures, after all, had occurred in the short run. As he saw it, Americans cast a vote of confidence in the future by bringing another Democratic-Republican into office. Hard times may have made his fellow citizens smugglers, but at least it hadn't made them Federalists.

Besides, even in the short run, Jefferson could be proud of at least one great second-term achievement. In 1807, he signed into law an act barring the further importation of slaves into the United States. Slavery continued, even on his own Monticello, but what was universally recognized as the cruelest aspect of slavery, the slave trade, was at an end. That bill had met with little opposition was additional cause for Jefferson to be heartened. The reason for its ready acceptance was even more encouraging; by 1807, every state except South Carolina, which still relied heavily on slave labor to cultivate lowland rice crops, had already banned the importation of slaves. Thus the federal law was not even coercive. The slave-importation ban was an example of states' rights and federal authority working toward a common moral good.

As he left office, Jefferson could envision the end of the slave trade as a prelude to the end of slavery altogether. After all, why had the states banned importation? Not alone to do the right thing, but because there was an overabundance of slaves. As the population of the republic grew and a larger class of yeoman farmers developed, the demand for slave labor was diminishing, even in the South. Or so it seemed.

Despite his customary technological savvy, Jefferson did not envision the effect of a machine invented in 1793 by a young Connecticut man named Eli Whitney. At the end of the eighteenth century and beginning of the nineteenth century, the big cash crops for the South were tobacco, rice, and indigo. Cotton was less important than these because the short-staple cotton raised in the lower South had seeds that were bound up with the fiber and required extensive handwork to remove. The process was so time-consuming that, even with slave labor, cotton profits were severely limited. Whitney's machine used a special toothed cylinder to separate the seed from the fiber so that each cotton gin (as the device was popularly called) could turn out fifty pounds of cleaned cotton each day—far more than manual labor could produce.

The use of the cotton gin made cotton so profitable that it rapidly displaced tobacco, rice, and indigo as the foundation of the Southern economy. With vastly increased cotton production came an increased demand for slave labor to pick the cotton and feed the gins. Having presided over the end of the slave trade, Jefferson would live to see slavery explode into an issue he thought might well dissolve the Union. In 1820, when the debate over whether to admit Missouri to the Union as a slave state or a free state threatened to bring immediate civil war, the seventy-seven-year-old Jefferson wrote that the dispute, "like a fire bell in the night, awakened and filled me with terror."

For now, though, Jefferson could also look back on his two presidential terms as a period of bloodless revolution in which the White House (the construction of which began in 1792 and was completed during Jefferson's first term) served not as some secretive executive headquarters, but as a center of official cordiality and genial intellectual ferment. John Adams, the first president to live in the unfinished executive mansion, gave formal state receptions in which, attired in formal black velvet breeches, he greeted his guests in the manner of royalty, elevated above them on a dais and deigning to acknowledge each guest with a stiffly formal bow.

Jefferson, in sharp contrast, abolished all state and diplomatic receptions. In their place, he held three dinner parties every week, each for a dozen guests. Invitations were formally printed, but instead of announcing "The President requests ..." they began simply: "Th. Jefferson requests ..." Jefferson made it a point to invite people of many interests and backgrounds, but his emphasis was on legislators, both Democratic-Republican and Federalist. To a skeptical congressman, Jefferson explained that the purpose of his dinners was to "cultivate personal intercourse with members of the legislature that we may know one another and have opportunities of little explanations of circumstances which, not understood, might produce jealousies or suspicions injurious to the public interest." Often Jefferson went beyond mere dinner conversation to deliver informal after-dinner talks on national and international affairs and, especially, on domestic economic, agricultural, and industrial developments.

Jefferson's two-term revolution was never covert. His White House was transparent, and Jefferson did much to endow it with the image it retains today: less an executive mansion than the people's house. Yet as much as the dinners did for the nation and for setting the tone of its government, they took a terrible toll on Jefferson's finances. For he did not believe it proper to pay for his entertainment from public funds. He reached into his own pocket, to the tune of some four thousand dollars each year for eight years.

Thomas Jefferson left office deeply in debt. He blamed it all on having turned the White House into a "tavern" for the benefit of all comers in Washington, D.C. To be sure, a significant part of his indebtedness was the result of those thrice-weekly dinner parties.

But he had lived above his means for most of his life. Like every other American, he was additionally suffering the results of a national economy that had been hobbled by embargo.

During Jefferson's troubled second term, Monticello must have beckoned him more invitingly than ever, promising a return to his own private Eden. But what he found when he journeyed home was a farm the worse for his long absence, groaning under economic depression and bearing the scars of depleted soil and several years of adverse weather. Whatever else his sunset years would be, they would be burdened by crushing debt.

Even before his retirement, Jefferson was popularly called the "Sage of Monticello," a title that conveys the reverential affection of the people but also implies that Jefferson became a hermit. Nothing could be further from the truth. By 1818, the ninth year of his retirement, Monticello was home to daughter Patsy and her husband, Thomas Mann Randolph Jr., and their eleven children, as well as to Francis Eppes, Polly's son. The loss of all but one of Jefferson's children was in great measure compensated by this plethora of grandchildren, whose love for their grandfather was extravagant. "I cannot describe the feelings of veneration, admiration, and love that existed in my heart towards him," one of the grandchildren recalled:

> When he walked in the garden, and would call the children to go with him, we raced after and before him ....
> He would gather fruit for us, seek out the ripest figs, or bring down the cherries from on high above our heads with a long stick, at the end of which was a hook and a little net bag ....

If Jefferson was embraced and crawled over by his adoring grandchildren, he was venerated with almost equal abandon by a continual stream of visitors, ranging from prominent lawyers, military men, members of the clergy, artists, scientists, and statesmen, to humble locals and distant tourists. They came to pay tribute to a man regarded as an oracle of democracy. Jefferson did nothing to encourage such veneration—like Washington, he distrusted the cult of personality—but he always welcomed his many visitors.

Unfortunately, his hospitality, in the form of generous lodging and unstinting refreshment, served to deepen his debt.

Jefferson's surviving child, Martha—Patsy—Jefferson Randolph, served as hostess and housekeeper of Monticello during Jefferson's long retirement.

(Collection: ArtToday)

As Jefferson seemed an oracle, so Monticello was universally regarded as a shrine. Over the years, its owner had crammed into it objects that had interested him throughout his life, including great American paintings, wondrous landscapes, portraits of Columbus and other New World explorers, the founding fathers—Franklin, Paine, Adams, and others—and historical canvases by John Trumbull. Visitors doubtless lingered in the great hall of the house, where marble busts perched on pedestals, including one of Jefferson and another, positioned just opposite, of Alexander Hamilton. Also decorating the house were the fixtures of the American West Jefferson had done so much to open: the trophy heads of elk and buffalo, as well as Indian artifacts brought to him by Lewis and Clark.

Patsy served as the de facto hostess of Monticello, sometimes entertaining upward of fifty guests in an evening. But when Jefferson truly craved some semblance of solitude, he traveled ninety miles to Poplar Forest, where he designed and built an octagon house, to which he repaired to "indulge myself in more favorite reading, in Tacitus and Horace and the writers of that philosophy which is the old man's consolation and preparation for what is to come." The man who gave to the world modern government and who championed the advancement of science and its application to technology reveled in the Trojan heroes and the wars of Pompey and Caesar. Had he not, in a somewhat more youthful time (or, at least, a time in which he had followed more youthful impulses), so severely injured his right wrist, surely he would have added his violin to the occupations of his old age. But while he continued to love music, his injury prevented his playing.

But his often painful wrist did not stop him from writing volumes of letters in response to the many philosophers, politicians, scientists, and just plain folk who wrote to him. Some wanted no more than a pleasant exchange of ideas, while others earnestly sought his advice on steering the nation through the hazardous times that followed his administration.

The gravest danger, of course, was the War of 1812, which was a direct outgrowth of the deterioration in Anglo-American relations created by the embargo. Jefferson expressed mixed opinions on the war. He hated war for its destructiveness and its sheer waste-fulness, an eater of money as well as of men. He saw the War of 1812 as the soiled hand of Europe yet again defiling the New World. Nevertheless, he also saw something positive driving the War of 1812: a desire to rid the United States once and for all of British tyranny, British principles, British manners, and even British goods. Jefferson might well have agreed with some later his-torians who liked to call the War of 1812 the "second war of American independence." Like many other Americans, Jefferson entertained an easy optimism about the war, declaring at its outset that "the acquisition of Canada this year ... will be a mere matter of marching." Spanish Florida would also become an American possession, he believed, and the War of 1812 would yield a verita-ble "empire of liberty," a shining example for all the world to see. The string of defeats beginning early in the conflict soon burst this democratic-imperial bubble.

Yet Jefferson could never be wholly pessimistic about anything, including the War of 1812. True, it had not produced an empire of liberty. True, it had created human misery, economic hardship, and—especially in New England—serious doubts about the con-tinued viability of the Union. But it also seemed to Jefferson to prove the usefulness of a militia rather than a standing army, and it produced a series of American heroes, including Oliver Hazard Perry and Andrew Jackson.

Of the many losses America suffered during the War of 1812, none hit Jefferson harder than the burning of Washington, D.C.—*his* capital—by the British under Maj. Gen. Robert Ross in 1814. For Jefferson, the worst of this destruction was the loss of the Capitol building itself, along with its modest congressional library. Jefferson offered to sell his entire personal library—now grown to sixty-five thousand volumes, plus rare early colonial manuscripts—to Congress as the nucleus of a new Library of Congress. Given Jefferson's intense love of books, the offer was a great patriotic sac-rifice, although, doubtless, Jefferson also saw an opportunity to make a dent in his formidable wall of debt. A neutral appraiser was appointed, who fixed a sale price of twenty-four thousand dollars on the collection. Even in early nineteenth-century dollars, it was a sum far below the true value of the books, but Jefferson did not quibble. His library could not go to a better place. Besides, selling his books gave him an excuse—despite his debts—to buy more. At the time of his death, eleven years after the sale, he had amassed about a thousand new volumes.

Try as he might, even during and after the War of 1812, Jefferson found that he could no longer hate the British so single-mindedly. Perhaps it was because he no longer had the ideology of a revolutionary France to oppose to England. Napoleon, ultimate product of the French Revolution, showed himself to be a tyrant, and Jefferson was relieved to see his downfall at last. Not that the fires of revolution were dead in the old man. He took great pleasure in the tide of revolution sweeping over the Spanish colonies of Latin America. He was proud that American independence, which he had done so much to shape, now served as the model for the people in the southern portion of the hemisphere, and he lived long enough to voice his approval in 1823 of President James Monroe's "doctrine" proclaiming the solidarity of the Americas and boldly warning Europe that the United States would consider an attack on any nation of the hemisphere an attack on the United States itself.

Nor did this chief architect of American independence cease to think about the nature of independence. Throughout his life, one of Jefferson's most cherished notions had been the creation of a nation of independent farmers, at once self-sufficient and mutually dependent. No other mode of living was more conducive to true democracy or to the health of the state and the individual than an existence based on the soil. Jefferson took every opportunity to contrast the virtues of rural life with the vices of the city, the pleasant advantages of farming versus the cruel hardships of manufacturing.

Now, in old age and retirement, he began to modify his agrarian romantic views. He advocated now an economy *balanced* among agriculture, commerce, and manufacturing. In a widely published letter of 1816, he declared to a Massachusetts correspondent that "we must now place the manufacturer by the side of the agriculturalist." In this way—and not as a latter-day Garden of Eden that was exclusively agricultural—could the United States achieve true, enduring economic independence and thereby defend liberty, if necessary, against the entire world.

> *On January 9, 1816, Jefferson replied to a letter from Benjamin Austin, a New Englander, to explain his revised thinking on manufacturing in America. The War of 1812, Jefferson, explained, taught him that ...*
>
> to be independent for the comforts of life we must fabricate them ourselves. We must now place the manufacturer by the side of the agriculturalist .... Shall we make our own comforts, or go without them, at the will of a foreign nation? He ... who is now against domestic manufacture, must be for reducing us either to dependence on that foreign nation, or to be clothed in skins, and to live like wild beasts in dens and caverns. I am not one of these; experience has taught me that manufactures are now as necessary to our independence as to our comfort.

Jefferson's retirement was crowded with the famous and the humble, with those who wished to pay homage, those who wished to partake of wisdom, and those who were merely curious. One class of visitor Jefferson always made ample time for: youths who sought him as a tutor. Some visited casually, seeking advice on what books to read. Others actually took up residence nearby and regarded Jefferson as a teacher in the fullest sense.

Jefferson not only loved to instruct and guide, but he never ceased to believe that education was the very foundation of democracy. To those who had argued for monarchy or at least some degree of aristocracy, Jefferson had always replied that, left to their own lights, the people generally choose their leaders wisely. Without his faith in education, however, this would have been a meaningless position. To choose wisely, the people required the blessings not just of liberty, but of a sound education. Soon Jefferson would "graduate" from instructing a handful of youths in Monticello to conceiving, planning, and even designing one of the world's great public universities. He would regard it as the great work of his sunset years.

Chapter 23

Virginia's University

Throughout much of his career in public office, Jefferson "confessed" to all who cared to listen his fondest ambition: to live the quiet life of a farmer at Monticello. Once he actually retired to his mountaintop house, however, Jefferson almost instantly wrote of wanting to act upon "two great measures at [my] heart, without which no republic can maintain itself in strength." These were, first, public provisions for "general education, to enable every man to judge for himself what will secure or endanger his freedom." Second was the division of "every county into hundreds [wards], of such size that all the children of each will be within reach of a central school in it."

Jefferson's plan for universal public education was eminently reasonable, with its logic neatly dovetailed into the structure he envisioned for democracy. The "hundreds" were to be both public school districts and units of local government so that *local* government would always be intimately bound up with *local* education. The hundreds would be the base of the government pyramid, with counties constituting the next layer, then on up through districts, states, and, at the apex, the federal government. A similar pyramid described the structure of public education, as Jefferson conceived it. The central schools in each hundred would administer elementary education, the foundation of the pyramid. Strategically placed throughout the state of Virginia would be "colleges" (which today we would call secondary schools or high schools), which would take selected students through roughly the equivalent of two years of modern college. Each college would be no more than a day's ride from the dwelling of any citizen of Virginia. At the apex of the pyramid would be a state university, which would offer roughly the equivalent of the last two years of a modern college education and even carry on into the postgraduate level.

As Jefferson saw it, elementary education was to be made available to all. Those who chose to pursue education no further would thus have a base of knowledge appropriate to the laboring classes of American society. General education, the level afforded by the colleges, was suited to the gentry of Virginia in the early nineteenth century, although the colleges would be available to any citizen who wanted to attend. Professional education, the province of the state's university, was reserved for those who wanted to be truly learned—lawyers, scientists, government leaders, professors, and the like. The university would be available to anyone who could pass an entrance examination.

Jefferson's ideas on education were by no means products of his old age. Back in 1778, one of the laws Jefferson proposed for revolutionary Virginia was a Bill for the More General Diffusion of Knowledge, which embodied many of the ideas he later proposed. Its defeat in the Assembly was a lifelong disappointment to its author. The next year, Jefferson unsuccessfully tried to reform and modernize the College of William and Mary, elevating what had become a backward and parochial academy into a genuine university. Again, he met with disappointment. Still committed to educational reform, he listened with great interest in 1794 to the proposal of François d'Ivernois, a Swiss expatriate living in America, who had a plan to transfer the entire College of Geneva to the United States. After the Virginia General Assembly declined to pursue d'Ivernois's proposal, Secretary of State Jefferson recommended it to President Washington as a way to establish the nucleus of a great national university. Washington, understandably enough, objected to erecting an American national university on the foundation of a foreign faculty that did not even conduct classes in English.

In 1800, Jefferson gave up attempting to reform an existing American institution or importing one wholesale from Europe. Instead, he wrote to the French philosopher Victor Dupont and the great British scientist-philosopher Joseph Priestley to solicit their thoughts on planning a fresh, new university for the United States. After studying their replies, Jefferson slowly moved in his own direction, producing in January 1805 a prospectus for a Virginia state university. Since by now Georgia, the Carolinas, and Tennessee had established state universities, Jefferson had reason to hope that the Virginia legislature would at last relent, if only from a sense of pride. In the prospectus he submitted, Jefferson took care to ensure that Virginia's university would offer something the others did not: a modern education. Jefferson's university would emphasize science, not classical education. Alas, the Virginia legislature once again failed to act on Jefferson's prospectus, and Jefferson once again appealed to Congress with the idea of establishing a national university. The proposal went nowhere.

Jefferson never gave up the fight, but it was 1814 before the first steps were made toward finally creating a University of Virginia. At the request of several Albemarle County worthies, Jefferson became a member of the board of a proposed private secondary school, to be called the Albemarle Academy. He used his position to transform the planned academy into a college. Jefferson drew up a bill to create Central College—a step he saw as intermediate toward creating a full-fledged university. The Virginia legislature at first voted this bill down but then passed it in February 1816. At that, Central College was incorporated as a private, nonsectarian institution that would enjoy no state funding but would be financed through the sale of certain lands, from contributions, and from a lottery. It was a modest beginning, but Jefferson had succeeded in planting in the state-sanctioned charter of Central College the seeds of growth. Virginia's governor named Jefferson, Madison, and Monroe to the college Board of Visitors. From this position, acting within the broad brief of the charter, Jefferson and his colleagues skipped over the founding of Central College and proceeded to design a university.

The curriculum Jefferson sketched out did not look like the work of a septuagenarian. Not only would science be emphasized, the university would focus on *state-of-the-art* science. In addition to the traditional liberal arts and more cutting-edge science offerings, the university was originally planned also to include a technical school, designed to train artisans, mechanics, and tradespeople of all kinds. Technical classes would be given at night, convenient to the needs of the working man. (This plan, unfortunately, never reached fruition.)

As Jefferson saw it, transforming the Central College involved more than just creating a university. He took the opportunity to draw up legislation to cover all three of the levels of education he had long contemplated. Funding for the elementary schools would come from property taxes, whereas funding for the colleges and for the university was to come chiefly from a "Literary Fund," a reserve of money already maintained by the legislature for the use of educating the poor.

In 1817, Jefferson submitted his proposed bill. It was overwhelmingly defeated, and legislation to fund charity schools was enacted in its place. All was not lost, however. Jefferson's friend and collaborator in the university campaign, Virginia legislator Joseph C. Cabell, succeeded in appending to the charity school bill a fifteen-thousand-dollar annuity from the Literary Fund to finance a state university. Miraculously, the amended bill passed. There would be a state university for Virginia, but the educational base that was to be provided by a system of elementary schools and colleges was not being funded. Jefferson was disappointed, but he was gratified to have received at least a half loaf.

The meager funding voted by the legislature would have to be supplemented by private contributions. Jefferson set to work on a fund-raising prospectus, which he published in the *Richmond Enquirer*. Eager to get a shovel into the ground and mortar between bricks, on October 6, 1817, Jefferson cheerfully attended the laying of a cornerstone on a two-hundred-acre tract he had personally chosen just west of Charlottesville.

To say that Jefferson had a lot riding on the university would be a profound understatement. The project engaged him on every intellectual and emotional level. The promise of public education that the university embodied was, for Jefferson, a pledge to democracy itself: Nothing was more important to a democratic government than education. As for the curriculum, Jefferson was the chief planner.

Because the general outline of the curriculum had to be approved by the legislature, he prepared a report for the assembly in 1818, explaining eloquently that education "engrafts a new man on the native stock, and improves what in his nature is vicious and perverse into qualities of virtue and social worth." Education, he declared, was essential to "the prosperity, the power, and happiness of a nation."

From these general statements, Jefferson went on to outline the design of a university curriculum divided into ten branches: ancient languages (Latin, Greek, Hebrew), modern languages, pure mathematics (plus military and naval architecture), physico-mathematics (mechanics, optics, astronomy, and geography), natural philosophy (physics, chemistry, and mineralogy), natural history, anatomy and medicine (a theoretical approach only; Jefferson did not propose including a medical school), government, law, and ideology (which included moral philosophy, literature, and fine arts). Each branch would be presided over by a professor qualified to teach the subjects in each area. In a spirit of academic freedom, the professors would be wholly responsible for the detailed formulation of the curriculum, together with the content of the courses themselves—with one exception: The content of the courses in the government branch was required to reflect the values of the American democracy. Jefferson himself recommended that the works of John Locke, as well as the Declaration of Independence, *The Federalist*, and Madison's "Virginia Report" on the Alien and Sedition Acts be included in the syllabus.

Academic freedom extended beyond the professors to the students. Jefferson wrote to his grandson Francis Eppes, "The fundamental law of our university [will be] to leave everyone free to attend whatever branches of instruction he wants, and to decline what he does not want." Thus the university would be an all-elective institution. Even more radical was Jefferson's insistence that study not be divided into classes—freshman, sophomore, junior, senior—but that all students should attend on an equal basis, proceeding through course work as their talents, interests, and abilities led them. As Jefferson trusted the students to guide themselves through the university's academic offerings, he trusted them to maintain their own discipline. In education, circa 1800, even at

the university level, corporal punishment and other harsh discipli-
nary practices were the norm. Jefferson believed that "hardening
[students] by disgrace, to corporal punishments, and servile humil-
iations cannot be the best process for producing erect character."
He recommended instead treating them with affection and allowing them to discipline themselves.

One course of study would not be available to University of
Virginia students. In contrast to virtually every other institution of
higher learning in the United States, Jefferson's university would
not offer religious instruction or maintain a chair in divinity.
Jefferson's hostility toward organized religion and theology made it
easy for him to omit this from the curriculum, but he based its
omission on something more important. As a state-sponsored,
state-supported institution, he held, the University of Virginia was
not free to offer courses in religion; the constitutional separation of
church and state barred this. In the *Report of the Commissioners for
the University of Virginia*, also called the "Rockfish Gap Report,"
after the place at which the commission met, Jefferson justified the
omission of sectarian religious instruction:

> *In conformity with the principles of our Constitution,
> which places all sects of religion on an equal footing, with
> the jealousies of the different sects in guarding that equal-
> ity from encroachment and surprise, and with the senti-
> ments of the Legislature in favor of freedom of religion,
> manifested on former occasions, we have proposed no
> professor of divinity; and the rather as the proofs of the
> being of a God, the creator, preserver, and supreme ruler
> of the universe, the author of all the relations of morality,
> and of the laws and obligations these infer, will be within
> the province of the professor of ethics to which adding the
> developments of these moral obligations, of those in which
> all sects agree, with a knowledge of the languages,
> Hebrew, Greek, and Latin, a basis will be formed com-
> mon to all sects. Proceeding thus far without offence to
> the Constitution, we have thought it proper at this point to
> leave every sect to provide, as they think fittest, the means
> of further instruction in their own peculiar tenets.*

As rector of the university, Jefferson not only outlined the overall curriculum, but drew up a catalogue of books to be purchased for the heart of the university, its library. At 6,860 volumes, the catalogue was extensive, and Jefferson arranged personally for their purchase. As if founding the university, formulating its philosophy, outlining its curriculum, and ordering its first consignment of books were not contribution enough, Jefferson was also instrumental in recruiting a faculty. He appointed a Virginia attorney, Francis Walker Gilmer, a longtime protégé, to travel to Europe to recruit professors to head each branch. By the 1820s, on the eve of the university's opening, the number of branches had been reduced from ten to eight; law and government were combined, and physico-mathematics was eliminated.

Jefferson, who loved all things American and had written *Notes on the State of Virginia* in part to defend American flora, fauna, and people against European charges of inferiority, nevertheless didn't believe that professors of sufficient caliber could be found in the United States. It is a pity, because Gilmer soon discovered that the best European professors were unwilling to teach in the wilds of Virginia and, in most cases, were even less willing to take a pay cut for the privilege. After much effort—and anxious despair on Jefferson's part—Gilmer did manage to recruit a presentable faculty, most of them Englishmen. Jefferson had insisted from the beginning that the professors of two branches, moral philosophy and the combined law and government branches, be chosen from among Americans, and so they were.

The University of Virginia owes its existence to Thomas Jefferson. More than any other man, he conceived it, shaped it, and injected it with his spirit. As he gave it intellectual and spiritual form, he also gave it physical form: Jefferson designed the buildings and the campus of the university. In doing so, he was animated by ideas he had expressed in a letter written back in 1810 to the founders of a new college in Tennessee. Rather than raise a single, massive building, he counseled the Tennesseans thus:

> *[It is] infinitely better to erect a small and separate building for each separate professorship, with only a hall below for his class, and two chambers above for himself; joining*

the lodges by barracks for a certain portion of students,
opening into a covered way to give a dry communication
between all the schools. The whole of these arranged
around an open square of grass and trees, would make it,
what it should be in fact, an academical village, instead of
a large and common den of noise, filth and fetid air.

An "academical village" is precisely what Jefferson set out to create in the University of Virginia. Working with the foremost architects of the early republic—the British-born Benjamin Latrobe, designer of many of the public buildings of Washington, D.C., and William Thornton, with whom Latrobe collaborated to design the original U.S. Capitol—Jefferson created a campus of uncommon order and beauty that still serves the university today. Its dominant building was (and remains) the grand Rotunda, outwardly a two-thirds-size version of the Pantheon in Rome, but modified inside to serve as a comfortable and capacious library.

The Lawn, Jefferson's great academical village at the University of Virginia. The photograph is from 1901.

Projecting from positions at either side of the Rotunda were two double-porticoed pavilions, housing the classrooms for each branch of learning, the professors' residences, dormitories ("barracks") for the students, and "hotels" for feeding them. The professors' residences had ample gardens—something Jefferson, who loved gardening more than anything except, perhaps, reading, believed his faculty members would appreciate.

The models for the buildings were all classical. The Rotunda was taken directly from classical Rome, whereas the pavilions were inspired by the work of Andrea Palladio (1508–80), who revived and reinterpreted classical Roman architecture for the Italian Renaissance. Yet the arrangement of the buildings and the manner in which they were adapted to an "academical village" were the unique products of Jefferson's mind and imagination. This was typical of his genius. So much of Jefferson's thought—on government, on ethics, and on education—was grounded in the classical world he loved and loved to read about, yet he always made this world his own, remodeling it to suit the demands of his age and his own radical approach to the problems and promise of that age.

Embodied in the brick, stone, and marble set among gracious lawns and tree-lined walks, Jefferson's neoclassical innovations made a profound impression on his contemporaries as well as on posterity. Boston-born George Ticknor, the first American scholar to achieve an international reputation, called Jefferson's university "more beautiful than anything architectural in New England, and more appropriate to a university than is to be found, perhaps, in the world." Today, visitors to the university continue to be drawn, first and foremost, to "The Lawn," as Jefferson's "academical village," the heart of the campus, is called. It remains an active and very attractive part of the university.

Classes commenced at the University of Virginia in January 1825, with about fifty students enrolled. The following year, the enrollment doubled. In 1826, the year of his death, Jefferson watched workmen install the marble capitals—newly arrived from Italy—on top of the Rotunda's columns. In April, just three months before he died, Jefferson completed the plan for a botanical garden to be laid out on campus.

Chapter 24

The Fourth of July

Benjamin Rush was a Pennsylvania-born signer of the Declaration of Independence, a political writer, and a scientist. Perhaps the foremost American physician of his time, he decided in 1810–11 to heal the breach between his two friends and colleagues in revolution, John Adams and Thomas Jefferson. He first approached Jefferson, who replied with an account of an exchange that had taken place in 1804. Abigail Adams had written him in condolence on the death of his daughter Polly. This prompted Jefferson to invite a reunion, which John Adams rebuffed. In view of this, Jefferson told Rush, he did not see how a reconciliation was possible. Undaunted, Rush turned the next year to Adams, writing to him, "I consider you and [Jefferson] as the North and South Poles of the American Revolution. Some talked, some wrote, and some fought to promote and establish it, but you and Mr. Jefferson thought for us all."

Although Rush's intervention did not produce immediate results, it opened the door. A few months after Rush approached Adams, Edward Coles, James Madison's private secretary, also visited with him. The conversation drifted to the subject of Jefferson. Adams protested the treatment to which Jefferson had subjected him. Coles replied that, despite their political differences, Jefferson felt great affection for Adams. Caught off-guard by this, the crusty old New Englander suddenly exclaimed: "I always loved Jefferson, and still love him."

Coles reported the conversation to Jefferson, who wrote to Rush that Adams's "statement of love is enough for me. I only needed this knowledge to revive towards him all the affections of the most cordial moment of our lives .... His opinions are as honestly formed as my own. Our different views of the same subject are the result of a difference in our organization and experience." Rush, in turn, conveyed these sentiments to Adams, who, on January 12, 1812, wrote Jefferson a letter. It was the beginning of a rich, lively, and often profound correspondence that would stretch over more than a decade. Adams would write a total of 109 letters to Jefferson, who, heavily occupied during this time with the creation of the University of Virginia, replied with a mere forty-nine. Their reconciliation in the autumn of their lives was a delight to both men, and their letters—graceful, clear, and elegant, with Adams's often colored by dry humor verging on sarcasm and Jefferson's carefully crafted into miniature essays—stand as important contributions to the history as well as the literature of the early republic.

In 1813, after Benjamin Rush died, Adams wrote to Jefferson, "You and I ought not to die before We have explained ourselves to each other." But they never really got around to doing that. Their letters say less about their politics than about the history of the Revolution, history in general, philosophy, literature, and, on a more personal note, the process of aging. Jefferson's favored topics were the classics, including Greek pronunciation, Indian religion and cultural practices, and various aspects of modern science. While the correspondents avoided unpleasant disputes, they remained competitive. Adams crowed about having read "forty-three volumes ... in one year, and twelve of them quartos!" Jefferson had to admit that he didn't quite measure up: "Dear Sir, how I envy you! Half a dozen 8 vos. in that space of time are as much as I am allowed."

Without the rancor of earlier days, many of the letters reflect the essential differences between the two men. Adams continued to justify the existence of an aristocracy, even in a democratic republic. Jefferson replied by formulating more succinctly than ever before his notion of a "natural" versus an "artificial" aristocracy. Whereas the artificial aristocrat is the product of wealth and birth, the natural aristocrat possesses natural gifts, virtues, and talents: "The natural aristocracy I consider as the most precious gift of nature, for the instruction, the trusts, and government of society." He observed that "that form of government is the best, which provides most effectually for a pure selection of these natural *aristoi* into the offices of government."

To Jefferson's assertion that the "artificial aristocracy is a mischievous ingredient in government, and provision should be made to prevent its ascendency," Adams suggested, only half playfully, that artificial aristocrats should be locked in a separate chamber of the legislature. Jefferson responded that "the best remedy is ... to leave to the citizens the free election and separation of the *aristoi* from the *pseudo-aristoi*, of the wheat from the chaff. In general they will elect the really good and wise." Adams did not directly dispute this opinion, but he did allude to the failure of the French Revolution as an example of the will of the people run amok. To Jefferson's undying optimism, his faith in the perfectibility of humankind, the incurably pessimistic Adams responded: "Let me ask you, very seriously my friend, Where are now in 1813, *the perfection and perfectability* of human nature? Where is now, the progress of the human mind? Where is the amelioration of society?"

> *Jefferson to Adams, October 28, 1813:*
>
> For I agree with you that there is a natural aristocracy among men. The grounds of this are virtue and talents. Formerly, bodily powers gave place among the aristoi. But since the invention of gunpowder has armed the weak as well as the strong with missile death, bodily strength, like beauty, good humor, politeness and other accomplishments, has become but an auxiliary ground of distinction. There is also an artificial aristocracy, founded on wealth and birth, without either virtue or talents; for with these it would belong to the first class .... May we not even say, that that form of government is the best, which provides most effectually for a pure selection of these natural aristoi into the offices of government?

That Jefferson remained an optimist to the end of his days is remarkable for many reasons—and not just because his correspondent John Adams so persuasively advocated the opposing point of view. Jefferson had lived through many disappointments, disasters, and heartbreaks. The French Revolution, in which Jefferson had invested considerable hope, had failed, degenerating first into the blood of the Terror and then into the bloody tyranny of Napoleon. The issue of slavery, as evidenced in the tortured Missouri Compromise of 1820, was clearly pulling the Union apart. Shortly after the compromise was enacted, Jefferson wrote, "I regret that I am now to die in the belief, that the ... sacrifice of themselves by the generation of 1776, to acquire self-government and happiness to their country, is to be thrown away by the unwise and unworthy passions of their sons, and that my only consolation is to be that I live not to weep over it."

In 1819, the nation was caught in the grip of a great financial panic, brought on by debts incurred in the War of 1812, by the recklessness of state banks, and by the mismanagement of the Second Bank of the United States. The Panic of 1819 reawakened hostilities between the North and South and between conservatives and liberals. It was particularly hard on agriculture because it brought a great depression in the price of most crops. Jefferson had lived to see his beloved Virginia, once the wealthiest, most populous, and most powerful American state, shrink into decay and become an economic backwater as the Northeast grew increasingly powerful in an Industrial Revolution that simply passed Virginia by.

As hard as the Panic of 1819 was on the nation and the state, it was particularly devastating for Jefferson. In the depressed economy, the produce of his plantations fetched less than ever, while the Second Bank of the United States suddenly tightened its credit policies. State banks followed suit.

"Never were such times seen as we have now here," Jefferson moaned. "Not a dollar is passing from one to another."

Just when it looked as if things could get no worse, Jefferson suddenly found himself liable for two loans he had cosigned on behalf of his friend Gov. Wilson Cary Nicholas, who, at the height of the 1819 panic, defaulted to the tune of twenty thousand dollars. Fearful that he, too, would go bankrupt and lose Monticello or, at least, be unable to bequeath it to Patsy, Jefferson had to scramble to borrow from one bank to pay off another, each time increasing his crushing interest burden.

The ultimate humiliation came in January 1826, when he hit upon the desperate scheme of appealing to the state legislature for permission to sell much of his property, save for Monticello, by lottery. In these depressed times, Jefferson found it virtually impossible to sell his land directly; instead, he would sell lottery tickets, with parcels of land going to the winners. After an uphill fight, the legislature approved the lottery in February 1826. By this time, Americans from all over the country had read in the newspapers of Jefferson's financial plight. Some bought into the lottery, but many more donated funds directly to Jefferson. The old man was heartened, believing that he had saved Monticello for Patsy.

The sad fact is that even the proceeds from the lottery and other donations proved insufficient to keep Monticello in the Jefferson and Randolph families. The estate was sold shortly after Jefferson died.

To compound Jefferson's fears for his nation and his despair over his own finances came a bout of illness in 1818, brought on when Jefferson took to the waters at Warm Springs hoping to relieve his advancing rheumatism. Instead, he contracted a serious case of dysentery that proved almost fatal and left him more or less unwell for the rest of his life. Four years later, in 1822, he fell and broke his left arm, the agony of which added to the constant pain in his right wrist, which never properly mended after he broke it in 1786.

Of course, Jefferson was all too accustomed to loss—of his wife and all but one of his children—yet he never yielded to despair and would not do so now. In November 1824, he showed himself capable of great joy when the Marquis de Lafayette, triumphantly touring the United States, called on him at Monticello. The pair attended a banquet given in the unfinished rotunda of the university, with Madison and Monroe in attendance. His voice too weak to deliver the address he had written in honor of the Frenchman, Jefferson handed the speech to another. The three-hour dinner would be his last public appearance.

Jefferson's final illness, judging from its symptoms, may well have been a compound of colon cancer, diabetes, and a severe urinary tract infection. The illness came in 1825 and was severe by February 1826. By March, Jefferson was well aware that he was dying. He drew up a will, only to discover how little he had left to give. To his grandson Francis Eppes he had already bequeathed his octagonal house at Poplar Forest. To James Madison he left his gold-headed walking stick—as well as the responsibility for husbanding the affairs of the University of Virginia. To each of his grandchildren he was able to leave a watch. His library, which had been reborn since the sale to Congress and contained about a thousand books, he gave to his beloved university. His papers, including correspondence spanning the creation and early history of the United States, some twenty-eight thousand letters, he entrusted to the care of his grandson Jeff Randolph.

Among whatever other heartbreaks Jefferson felt as he faced the end, he must have been especially pained by his powerlessness to free his slaves. In his will, George Washington had freed all of Mount Vernon's servants. However, Jefferson's slaves no longer belonged to his estate but to his creditors. He requested of these creditors freedom for five: his body servant, Burwell; John Hemings and two of his sons; and Joe Fosset, the blacksmith of Monticello. He asked further that houses be built for them all and that the University of Virginia employ them, except for Burwell, to whom he left three hundred dollars and a request that he remain at Monticello. Finally, he asked the Virginia legislature to exempt these men from the law requiring freed slaves to leave the state within a year of their emancipation. All of these deathbed requests were honored.

As for Jefferson's other slaves, he could only hope that their new owners would treat them well. Of Sally Hemings there is no mention during his final days.

On June 24, 1826, Jefferson summoned sufficient strength to write a reply to an invitation he had received to attend a celebration of the fiftieth anniversary of the signing of the Declaration of Independence. He expressed his thanks for having been invited to be present with the citizens of Washington "at their celebration," but illness forced him to decline:

> It adds sensibly to the sufferings of sickness, to be deprived
> by it of a personal participation in the rejoicings of the day.
> I should, indeed, with peculiar delight, have met and
> exchanged there congratulations personally with the small

band, the remnant of that host of worthies, who joined
with us on that day, in the bold and doubtful election we
were to make for our country, between submission or the
sword; and to have enjoyed with them the consolatory
fact, that our fellow citizens, after half a century of experience and prosperity, continue to approve the choice we
made. May it be to the world, what I believe it will be,
(to some parts sooner, to others later, but finally to all,)
the signal of arousing men to burst the chains under which
monkish ignorance and superstition had persuaded them to
bind themselves, and to assume the blessings and security
of self-government.

All eyes are opened, or opening, to the rights of man.
The general spread of the light of science has already laid
open to every view the palpable truth, that the mass of
mankind has not been born with saddles on their backs,
nor a favored few booted and spurred, ready to ride them
legitimately, by the grace of God. These are grounds of
hope for others. For ourselves, let the annual return of
this day forever refresh our recollection of these rights, and
an undiminished devotion to them ....

As the city of Washington prepared the celebration he could
not attend, Jefferson declined into coma alternating with wakeful-
ness through the evening of July 2. On July 3, the coma deepened,
but, at seven that evening, Jefferson stirred. He turned his head to
Dr. Robley Dunglison.

"Oh Doctor, are you still there?"

His voice, Dunglison recorded, was "husky and indistinct. He
then asked, 'Is it the Fourth?' to which I replied, 'It soon will be.'
These were the last words I heard him utter."

As the people of Washington celebrated the Fourth of July,
Thomas Jefferson died at about one in the afternoon. John Adams,
too, lay dying in Quincy, Massachusetts. His final words, on that
Fourth of July in 1826, were, "Thomas Jefferson still survives."

Chapter 25

Tombstone

The introduction to this book began by looking at the obelisk Thomas Jefferson designed to mark his grave, which bears the epitaph he wrote for himself:

Here was buried
Thomas Jefferson
*Author of the Declaration of American Independence
of the Statute of Virginia for religious freedom
and Father of the University of Virginia*

In that introduction, we pondered less what Jefferson chose to include among his achievements than what he had left out. The introduction briefly catalogued those many omissions, so we need not review them here, but let us linger a moment on what Jefferson did choose to include.

Three items are listed. Their diversity—a great political declaration, a law guaranteeing freedom of religion, and the foundation of an educational institution—is obvious. But they have two qualities in common. First, they concern individual liberty. Second, they all look toward the future rather than the past.

The first two achievements, authorship of the Declaration of Independence and creation of Virginia's Statute of Religious Freedom, gave legal substance and sanction to concepts of liberty— to liberty in its most profound and universal form: in the Declaration, to liberty as a birthright and a natural inheritance; in the Statute of Religious Freedom, to liberty of thought, of belief, and of soul.

The obelisk that marks Jefferson's grave at Monticello. This is a
late nineteenth-century reproduction of the original that Jefferson
designed, which bears the epitaph he wrote for himself.

(Collection: ArtToday)

The creation of the University of Virginia was no less a contribution to individual liberty. Jefferson believed in an aristocracy of
nature, the perfectibility of humankind, and the ability of all people to govern themselves—in short, he believed in the individual
capacity for freedom within society. All of this came by way of a

universal birthright, but that birthright, as century upon century of global tyranny attested, was not realized naturally. It required the nurture of education. In an American republic in which government would no longer be the province of an artificial aristocracy endowed only by the accident of "noble" birth and a certain degree of wealth, the people had to be the government. To create a good, great, and enduring government that fostered rather than suppressed liberty, the people had to be educated to what was theirs by natural right. Jefferson's university, like the Declaration of Independence and the Statute of Religious Freedom, was, therefore, an instrument of liberty.

Consider now the first line of the epitaph: "Here was buried ...." Thomas Jefferson was a brilliant, eloquent, careful writer. He loved language, and he weighed his words. He chose the past-tense, *was*, to announce to the world the identity of the body beneath the obelisk. The message is clear: The body of Thomas Jefferson *was* buried, but the substance of the man could never be—for that is the stuff of the future. He wrote the Declaration of Independence in 1776 and the Statute of Religious Freedom in 1777; the University of Virginia was officially chartered in 1819. These dates mean little because, like the vines Jefferson lovingly cultivated in his Monticello vineyard, such works are planted at a particular moment, but they bear fruit perennially. Like Monticello itself, for Jefferson a lifelong work-in-progress, the works of individual liberty are never finished but are always becoming, evolving into an ever-expanding future.

Thomas Jefferson not only composed his own epitaph, but he designed the obelisk on which the epitaph appears. To think about the life of Jefferson is to be dazzled by the breadth and variety of the man's interests and attainments: philosopher, architect, inventor, lawyer, writer of law, author, naturalist, scientist, political leader, radical, public servant, scholar, educator, and educational theorist. For all their variety, these pursuits as Jefferson practiced them share a common quality. They all concern *design*: whether for a university curriculum or campus, for a new kind of plow or a machine to make multiple copies of written documents, for a revolution or a government, for a body of law or a way to upend and revise a body of law, for a new nation or a nation whose natural rightness will create a new world.

Jefferson reveled in his imagination and in communicating the products of his imagination to his fellow citizens and even to all humankind. He created the pattern to guide the others who did the building. As Benjamin Rush wrote to John Adams, "Some talked, some wrote, and some fought to promote and establish [the American Revolution], but you and Mr. Jefferson thought for us all."

Jefferson was always far less interested in the building than in the planning. Build something and it is over and done; its tense is past. Create an idea, however, and it is always *becoming*. What frightened people like John Adams and Alexander Hamilton was Jefferson's blithe willingness to take down whatever was built and rebuild it so that it better fulfilled the original plan. The Federalists had built a government and then moved heaven and earth to preserve it, even at the cost of compromising the ideals of liberty that lay behind it. Jefferson was willing to tear down that government again and again, if need be, to make it a fuller expression of those ideals. If a building no longer served its purpose, tear it down and rebuild it! If a government proved inadequate, do the same! Hence the "second revolution" of Jefferson's Democratic-Republican presidency.

Jefferson built his own house facing the future. The front door of Monticello looks to the west. Jefferson moved Virginia's capital out of the crusty old Tidewater town of Williamsburg and inland to rising Richmond. When the opportunity came to acquire the vast land west of the Mississippi, Jefferson did not hesitate to make the Louisiana Purchase. Even his headstone moved west. The obelisk that now marks Jefferson's grave at Monticello was erected in the 1880s. The original monument was presented by the heirs of Jefferson to the University of Missouri on July 4, 1883, because that institution was the first to be founded in the Louisiana Purchase while Jefferson was president.

Would Jefferson have been upset by the uprooting of his obelisk and its transfer west of the Mississippi? Almost certainly not. He believed in the permanence of ideas and ideals, not in the permanence of things and institutions. People who crave such permanence—an unchanging façade and the frozen expression of an idea—are hard-pressed to identify the legacy of Thomas Jefferson in today's America.

This book has drawn on several extensive biographies of Jefferson, all of which are informed by their authors' obvious admiration of their subject. However, one book among these sources takes an acutely critical approach to Jefferson. In *American Sphinx: The Character of Thomas Jefferson*, Joseph J. Ellis dares to ask *"What is still living" in the Jefferson legacy?* His answer is unblinkingly frank: "[S]ubstantial portions of Jefferson's legacy are no longer alive; they have died a natural death somewhere between 1826 and now."

Ellis describes aspects of this dead legacy as a "series of sand castles on a beach, located different distances from the shoreline but all vulnerable to the tide of time." That tide has brought wave upon wave of change. The aftermath of the Civil War, Ellis argues, destroyed the Jeffersonian doctrine of states as "sovereign agents in the federal compact." That was the first wave. The second, striking between 1890 and 1920, was the transition of the United States from a rural nation to a predominantly urban one, populated by immigrants from many countries. These "demographic changes," Ellis observes, "transformed Jefferson's agrarian vision into a nostalgic memory." Wave number three "arrived in the 1930s with the New Deal." Franklin D. Roosevelt, under whose administration Thomas Jefferson was honored by the serenely domed memorial on the banks of the Potomac, expanded the federal government drastically during the Great Depression so that it reached, with benevolent intent, more deeply than ever into the lives of every American citizen. Finally, the Cold War in the 1950s brought a fourth wave to assault yet another Jeffersonian sand castle, as the United States created what Dwight Eisenhower called a "military-industrial complex" of unprecedented magnitude. It was a standing army far greater than anything Britain's George III could have imagined.

Does this mean that the legacy of Jefferson is, after all, just a ghost?

Not even the highly critical Professor Ellis suggests this. The illusion, he points out, is in trying to pin the institutions of today's America literally and permanently on this or that aspect of the

Jefferson legacy. One after the other, the sand castles may have washed away, but the design of those castles remains, and Americans (as well as many others throughout the world) remain passionately attached to those designs. As Professor Ellis observes, even as the American federal government has assumed gargantuan proportions, the American people entertain more strongly than ever the Jeffersonian "antigovernment ethos."

That, of course, is a great American contradiction: a huge central government built and supported by a people who inherently distrust big central governments. And we don't have to think very hard to come up with more American contradictions: a massive military-industrial war machine raised in the name of peace ("Peace is our profession" goes the motto of the U.S. Air Force Strategic Air Command, the people who wield our nation's nukes); in the 1950s, the followers of Senator Joseph McCarthy willing to sacrifice American liberty in order to preserve it; and, fifty years later, the defenders of freedom of religion rushing to embrace federal subsidy of sectarian private schools.

The list could go on and on because America, after all, is very much about contradictions, some destructive, some constructive, and most at least lively. The philosopher we hold up to the world as most typically American, Ralph Waldo Emerson, declared a "foolish consistency [to be] the hobgoblin of little minds" and said that he would inscribe but one motto on the lintel of his doorway: "Whim." Walt Whitman, whom we esteem as our most American poet, asked in his *Song of Myself*, "Do I contradict myself?" and blithely confessed:

> Very well then I contradict myself,
> (I am large, I contain multitudes.)

Likewise for Jefferson. No one could ever accuse him of harboring any "foolish consistency." Many of his contemporary critics thought him whimsical, and, certainly, this man who contained multitudes was full of self-contradiction: a lawyer who distrusted law, a man of peaceful rationality who relished revolution, a lover of scholarly solitude who enacted his thoughts upon a nation and broadcast his philosophy to the world, a hater of slavery who kept slaves, a lover of ageless liberty who never quite saw beyond the racism of his time and place, a radical modernist who was most comfortable among the heroes and architecture of ancient Greece and Rome, and an advocate of a presidency subordinated to the legislature who nevertheless assumed executive powers that even his high-handed Federalist predecessors shied away from.

The point is this: Perhaps Jefferson's very contradictions make him most American, a figure whose relevance today seems undiminished despite the ruin of all his sand castles. Even more important, perhaps his ability to flourish by these contradictions, to work not just in spite of them but *with* them, perpetuates his presence not as a long-dead "founding father" but as a source of political leadership and ethical inspiration more alive than most of our living leaders. Certainly, the elements of these contradictions, the greatness and nobility of most and the gaping deficiency of a few, make Thomas Jefferson enduringly human for us today.

"Here *was* buried Thomas Jefferson," his self-composed epitaph begins. For our evolving political, intellectual, and spiritual lives, the present tense of John Adams's deathbed declaration is far more telling: "Thomas Jefferson survives."

The Jefferson Memorial, Washington, D.C.

(Collection of the author)

Appendix A

Visiting the Jefferson Legacy

Colonial Williamsburg This elaborate outdoor museum recreates life in Virginia's first capital, the town in which Jefferson studied and practiced law and in which he began his political career. Phone 1-800-HISTORY (1-800-447-8679) or visit www.history.org on the Web.

Independence National Historical Park Located in the "Old City" neighborhood of Philadelphia, the park consists of Independence Hall and related buildings. It was in Independence Hall (then called Carpenters' Hall) that the Continental Congress met in 1776 and drafted Thomas Jefferson to write the Declaration of Independence, which was subsequently debated and signed in the hall. Independence Hall and most of the buildings are open daily, year-round. Visit www.nps.gov/inde/exindex.htm on the Web.

Jefferson National Expansion Memorial The great "Gateway Arch" architect Eero Saarinen conceived for the city of St. Louis is part of a national monument to the spirit of the western pioneers and to St. Louis as the portal to the territory that Jefferson opened by the Louisiana Purchase and the Lewis and Clark expedition. In addition to the arch itself, the memorial includes the Museum of Westward Expansion, containing an extensive collection of artifacts, mounted animal specimens, an authentic American Indian tipi, and an overview of the Lewis and Clark expedition. Phone 314-655-1700 or visit www.nps.gov/jeff/main.htm on the Web.

Monticello   The preeminent destination for anyone interested in Thomas Jefferson is, of course, his magnificent home, Monticello. Located in the Virginia Piedmont, Monticello is about two miles southeast of Charlottesville and approximately 125 miles from Washington, D.C.; 110 miles from Williamsburg; and seventy miles from Richmond. It is open every day of the year, except Christmas. Phone 804-984-9822 or visit www.monticello.org on the Web. Visitors may tour the mansion, the grounds, the gardens, and the plantation. Jefferson's grave site is located here as well.

Mount Rushmore National Memorial   This epic sculptural group features the faces of Thomas Jefferson and three other American presidents, George Washington, Theodore Roosevelt, and Abraham Lincoln, carved into a mountain among South Dakota's Black Hills. The sixty-foot high faces are five hundred feet up. Mount Rushmore National Memorial lies within Black Hills National Forest and is twenty-five miles southwest of Rapid City, South Dakota, via U.S. 16; and three miles from Keystone via U.S. 16A and SD 244. Visit www.travelsd.com/parks/rushmore/index.htm on the Web.

Natural Bridge   Jefferson was so awed by this wonder of nature that he purchased the site, obtaining a patent from King George III in 1774. He considered his stewardship of the bridge a public trust, and he wrote eloquently of the site in his *Notes on the State of Virginia*. Natural Bridge is located on Route 11 between exits 175 and 180 from Interstate 81. Phone 1-800-533-1410 or visit www.naturalbridgeva.com on the Web.

Poplar Forest   Jefferson designed and built a beautiful octagonal house on this forty-eight-hundred-acre plantation near Lynchburg, Virginia. He used it as a secluded retreat from Monticello, which, as his principal residence, was open to a continuous stream of visitors. Poplar Forest, a National Historic Landmark, is located off Route 661, southwest of Lynchburg, in Bedford County. Phone 804-525-1806 or visit www.poplarforest.org on the Web.

Thomas Jefferson Memorial   Dedicated in 1943, the graceful memorial is located on the National Mall in Washington, D.C., and is open daily, year-round. Phone 202-426-6841 or visit www.nps.gov/ thje on the Web.

University of Virginia Visit "the Lawn," the original campus of the university, which Jefferson designed as an "academical village." The entire university, from its founding and construction to its educational philosophy and curriculum, was Jefferson's brainchild, and the institution offers many resources for those interested in Jefferson. The university is located in Charlottesville. Phone 804-924-0311 for general information, or visit www.virginia.edu on the Web.

White House The White House, 1600 Pennsylvania Avenue, Washington, D.C., was begun in 1792 and was completed during President Jefferson's first term. For tour information, call 202-456-7041.

Appendix B

Suggestions for Further Reading

Ambrose, Stephen. *Undaunted Courage: Meriwether Lewis, Thomas Jefferson, and the Opening of the American West.* New York: Simon & Schuster, 1996.

Banning, Lance. *The Jeffersonian Persuasion: Evolution of a Party Ideology.* Ithaca, NY: Cornell University Press, 1978.

Bear, James. *Jefferson at Monticello: Recollections of a Monticello Slave and a Monticello Overseer.* Charlottesville, VA: University Press of Virginia, 1967.

Becker, Carl L. *The Declaration of Independence: A Study in the History of Political Ideas.* New York: Random House, 1958.

Boorstin, Daniel. *The Lost World of Thomas Jefferson.* Chicago: University of Chicago Press, 1948.

Brodie, Fawn M. *Thomas Jefferson: An Intimate History.* New York: W. W. Norton, 1974.

Brown, David S. *Thomas Jefferson: A Biographical Companion.* Santa Barbara, CA: ABC-CLIO, 1998.

Burstein, Andrew. *The Inner Jefferson: Portrait of a Grieving Optimist.* Charlottesville, VA: University Press of Virginia, 1995.

Chinard, Gilbert. *The Commonplace Book of Thomas Jefferson: A Repertory of His Ideas on Government.* Baltimore: Johns Hopkins Press, 1926.

Cruise, Conor. *The Long Affair: Thomas Jefferson and the French Revolution*. Chicago: University of Chicago Press, 1996.

Crupe, Helen. *Thomas Jefferson and Music*. Charlottesville, VA: University Press of Virginia, 1974.

Cunningham, Noble. *The Jeffersonian Republicans in Power: Party Operations, 1801–1809*. Chapel Hill: University of North Carolina Press, 1963.

Dabney, Virginius. *The Jefferson Scandals*. New York: Madison Books, 1981.

Davis, Richard Belae. *Intellectual Life in Jefferson's Virginia, 1790–1830*. Chapel Hill: University of North Carolina Press, 1964.

Dumbauld, Edward. *Thomas Jefferson and the Law*. Norman, OK: University of Oklahoma Press, 1978.

Ellis, Joseph J., *American Sphinx: The Character of Thomas Jefferson*. New York: Oxford University Press, 1997.

Gordon-Reed, Annette. *Thomas Jefferson and Sally Hemings: An American Controversy*. Charlottesville, VA: University Press of Virginia, 1997; reprint ed., 1998.

Jefferson, Thomas. *Notes on the State of Virginia*. New York: W. W. Norton, 1972.

———. *The Papers of Thomas Jefferson*. Princeton, NJ: Princeton University Press, 1950.

———. *The Portable Thomas Jefferson*, Merrill D. Peterson, ed. New York: Viking Penguin, 1975.

———. *The Works of Thomas Jefferson*. New York: Knickerbocker Press, 1904.

———. *The Writings of Thomas Jefferson*. Washington, D.C.: Thomas Jefferson Memorial Association, 1903–04.

Koch, Adrian. *The Philosophy of Thomas Jefferson*. Chicago: Quadrangle Books, 1964.

Lewis, Jan Ellen, and Peter S. Onuf. *Sally Hemings and Thomas Jefferson: History, Memory, and Civic Culture.* Charlottesville, VA: University Press of Virginia, 1999.

Malone, Dumas. *Jefferson and His Time,* six vols. Boston: Little, Brown, 1948–81.

Mayo, Bernard, ed. *Jefferson Himself: The Personal Narrative of a Many-Sided American.* Charlottesville, VA: University Press of Virginia, 1968.

McDonald, Forrest. *The Presidency of Thomas Jefferson.* Lawrence, KS: University Press of Kansas, 1976.

Miller, John Chester. *The Wolf by the Ears: Thomas Jefferson and Slavery.* Charlottesville, VA: University Press of Virginia, 1977.

Onuf, Peter, ed. *Jeffersonian Legacies.* Charlottesville, VA: University Press of Virginia, 1993.

Peterson, Merrill. *Adams and Jefferson: A Revolutionary Dialogue.* Athens, GA: University of Georgia Press, 1976.

———. *The Jefferson Image in the American Mind.* New York: Oxford University Press, 1960.

———. *Thomas Jefferson and the New Nation.* New York: Oxford University Press, 1970.

Randall, Willard Sterne. *Thomas Jefferson: A Life.* New York: Henry Holt, 1993.

Index